IN HIP HOP TIME

In Hip Hop Time

MUSIC, MEMORY, AND SOCIAL CHANGE IN URBAN SENEGAL

Catherine M. Appert

OXFORD
UNIVERSITY PRESS

Oxford University Press is a department of the University of Oxford. It furthers
the University's objective of excellence in research, scholarship, and education
by publishing worldwide. Oxford is a registered trade mark of Oxford University
Press in the UK and certain other countries.

Published in the United States of America by Oxford University Press
198 Madison Avenue, New York, NY 10016, United States of America.

Library of Congress Cataloging-in-Publication Data
Names: Appert, Catherine M., 1983– author.
Title: In hip hop time : Music, memory, and social change in urban senegal
in urban Senegal Catherine M. Appert.
Description: New York, NY : Oxford University Press, 2018. | Includes bibliographical
references and index.
Identifiers: LCCN 2018011266 (print) | LCCN 2018011322 (ebook) |
ISBN 9780190913502 (Updf) | ISBN 9780190913519 (Epub) |
ISBN 9780190913489 (cloth) | ISBN 9780190913496 (pbk.) |
ISBN 9780190913526 (companion website)
Subjects: LCSH: Popular music—Social aspects—Senegal. | Rap music—Social aspects—Senegal. |
Social change—Senegal. | Senegal—Social life and customs—21st century.
Classification: LCC ML3917.S46 (ebook) | LCC ML3917.S46 A66 2018 (print) |
DDC 782.42164909663—dc23
LC record available at https://lccn.loc.gov/2018011266

For Modou, who helped me begin, and for Moustapha, who saw me through

Contents

Acknowledgments

ASSALAAMAALEKUM; A BIG shout out to waa Rap Galsen, especially Bourba Djolof (RIP), Lamine Ndao, Books, Almamy Bathily, Amadou Fall Ba, Falsower, Musa Gambien, Coumbis Sorra, Simon, Mame Xa, Djily Bagdad, Baye Njagne, Lady Sinay, Kalif, Kronic, Hawa, Profete, Madou and Alou (KTD Crew), N-Jah, Gaston, Y.Dee, Bakhaw and Djiby (Da Brains), Baïdy (Bideew bou Bess), Toussa, Sister Dia, Sista Anta, waa Niamu Mbaam, DJ Flex, waa FuknKuk, Thiat and Kilifeu (Keur Gui), Xuman, DJ Awadi, Ndongo and Faada Freddy (Daara J Family), Gnagna Gnagne, Assane Masson, Keyti, Big Fa, Drygun, Don Zap, Mollah Morgan, Nix, waa Zair ak Batine, the staff at Africulturban, and last but never least, ResKp. Thank you for your music, your wisdom, and your generosity. Thank you for sharing your time and your stories, and for waiting all this time for me to share them too. Je vous remercie pour votre sagesse, votre générosité, vos histoires, et votre patience. Jaajëf waay.

This project came to life during my time as a graduate student in Los Angeles. Shout out to Sandstorm Ja and Smoka Seezy, who introduced me to Senegalese hip hop through their own music and the generous loan of their prized cassette tapes; to Esther Baker-Tarpaga, who opened the door to the Dakar hip hop scene with a single phone number; and to Pape Diouf and his family, who taught me to play sabar.

Shout out to the former members of UCLA's Working Group in Hip Hop Cultural Studies, whose energy and enthusiasm ignited my own back in the day: H. Samy Alim, Christina Zanfagna, Jooyoung Lee, Brenna Reinhart Byrd, and Lauren Mason Carris. To my advisors, Andrew Apter, Chris Waterman, and Tony Seeger, who pushed me to ask different questions and to question differently. And to Tim Taylor, who has been a selfless and dedicated mentor from the day I walked into his office thirteen years ago with a piano performance degree in hand and very little idea of what it meant to be an ethnomusicologist, although I suspected it involved drums.

This book took on its final form in the years since I moved to Ithaca; shout out to my colleagues at Cornell, especially Judith Peraino and Alejandro Madrid, and my ladies Ariana Kim, Nandi Cohen-Aponte, Jamila Michener, and Shorna Allred. Adi Grabiner-Keinan and Jenny Stoever grounded me, as Arlyn Burgess and Bonnie Gordon did before them in Charlottesville. The graduate students in my Writing Musical Ethnography seminar challenged me to reconsider the choices I made in writing these chapters. The undergraduates in my Performing Hip Hop and Global Hip Hop courses inspired me to rethink how we tell hip hop stories, and to try to write something they would want to read. Maxwell Williams provided a fresh take on intellectual conversations that I had nearly written off and an ongoing dialogue on hip hop musicality and diaspora; I am beholden to him for his formative feedback on Chapter 1, and for taking on the index.

Shout out to the colleagues who have critiqued and bettered my work through blind peer review and open dialogue. Certain passages, versions of various bits and pieces, and early renderings of some of the arguments in this book appear in "On Hybridity in African Popular Music: The Case of Senegalese Hip Hop," *Ethnomusicology* 60, no. 2 (2016): 279–299; "Locating Hip Hop Origins: Popular Music and Tradition in Senegal," *Africa* 86, no. 2 (2016): 237–262; and "To Make Song without Singing: Hip Hop and Popular Music in Senegal" *New Literary History* 46, no. 4 (2015): 759–774. Colleagues in the Society for Ethnomusicology, the African Studies Association, the American Anthropological Association, and the International Association for the Study of Popular Music gave me feedback over years of presentations and on nascent elements of the book. Adriana Helbig challenged me to start the manuscript over in a different voice, and an anonymous second reader's critical insights helped me sharpen and redirect my questions.

Shout out to Griff Rollefson and Kendra Salois, my own hip hop cypher, who stepped up on the book's most important chapters. To Liza Flood, for her thoughtful response to Chapter 5. To Michelle Kisliuk, who pushed me to write differently, and who read and commented on the introduction. To Sidra Lawrence, who always assumed I would write *my* book. To Michael Silvers, who read every word that follows, over and over again and then just once more, and whose friendship has been a rock for what is beginning to feel like a very long time indeed; and to Saxon Burns, who fielded my fussiest questions about grammar. Many other ethnomusicologists have lent eyes and ears and shoulders; special shout out to Liz Macy, my rid or die, and to Lei Ouyang Bryant and Marië Abe.

Shout out to the organizations who got me to Senegal, and to the people who kept me going once I was there. I carried out my research with generous funding from the UCLA International Institute, the Fulbright-Hays program, the American Council of Learned Societies, the Mellon Foundation, and the Cornell Humanities Council. In Dakar, the West African Research Center (WARC) supported me during many research trips over the years. Sidy Gueye helped me to communicate, first in French and then in Wolof, and became my friend in the process. Cait, Karima, and Kerry were a trifold (if alliterative) pillar of sanity in our shared apartment in Dakar in 2011. The Konaté family gave me a home in Dakar, and I thank them, especially sama yaye Dieynaba.

Shout out to my family, who have tolerated my prolonged absences over the years. My parents, Tom and Nancy Appert, proudly stood by me as I followed an unpredicted and unpredictable path. Since 2013, Cheikh Fall and Meissa Mane have welcomed my comings and blessed my goings.

My final and loudest shout out goes, again, to Moustapha Fall, for all these years of stalwart support, and for his reluctant finessing of translations on demand. *Yalla na la Yalla fey*.

IN HIP HOP TIME

1

SAMPLING MYTH

I COULDN'T SAY, then or now, where the street ended and hip hop began.

We had walked here, brothers Books and Bourba and I, moving slowly but purposefully through Medina's grid of streets, their precise layout tracing a hundred years of colonial and national memory. The night air weighed on us with the promise of a rain that had been absent for days, until the heat and smog threatened to smother the city. We didn't use the sidewalks, with their unpredictable dips, the abrupt peaks where roots have surfaced after decades of struggle, the protruding legs of tables set on their sides until commerce begins again in the morning.

At this hour, the street is empty of cars but not truly quiet. Bits of light and noise leak from the houses closed against the night despite the heat. Every block or so, small shops spill a line of brightness and music and chatter across our path. The mosques are silent.

Assalaamaalekum, they said, every time we passed a knot of people seated in a doorway or crowding the entryway to a shop. Assalaamaalekum, I murmured in turn. Books swung off to the side and rejoined us with two cups of spiced coffee. I took mine and continued following them, soon losing myself in the web of streets. We heard our destination before we saw it, encroaching on the not-quite-quiet of the surrounding blocks.

A stage, set up in the middle of the road, flanked by stacks of speakers, open to the heavy sky that threatens to end the show before it's begun. We converge with other rappers from the Jolof4Life label, their oversized T-shirts in red, green, and yellow paired with baggy jeans and chunky sneakers. Young people gather, mostly men and a few women, slipping away from the closed houses and humming streets to fill this space with their energy and noise. Books and Bourba take the stage as rap duo Sen Kumpë, and I'm left alone to watch them perform (Fig. 1.1).

"Medina in the house!" they shout as they spring into movement, the other rappers circling behind them in a kaleidoscope of matching shirts, the platform bouncing up and down under their shifting weight. The audience clustered in front of the stage cheers affirmation. It's hard to understand their words, their voices distorted over the speakers; one of the mics is cutting in and out, so they pass the other back and forth. And yet there is something and everything familiar in their performance. In the instrumental beat, its constant looping and layering of repeating, synthesized snippets of melody, its heavy drums, its global ubiquity tempered only by the locality of the voice. In the words, whose meaning I don't understand but whose rhythms articulate against the beat to pull me in, their syncopation etching the aural contours of a uniquely *Dakarois* mixing of Wolof and French, enveloping English words in a linguistic rootedness that is, in itself, global. They reach the hook, its lighthearted words jarring against the heavy minor

FIGURE 1.1 Bourba Djolof (right) and Books (left) perform in Medina in 2008.

beat, Books's trilingual declaration, "Kumpë Sen is back, Kumpë Sen is back, Get up, Stand up, *allez allez*," trading off with Bourba's, "La-di da-di relax your body, *yëngal* Senegal, New York, *ba biir Paris*." Smiling at the Slick Rick reference, I watch and listen as their words, cadence, gestures, and music project through the streets of Dakar, layering aural memories of hip hop's diasporic movements between Senegal, the United States, and France.

AN ORIGIN MYTH

Long before France put down roots in Senegal, which would become the administrative center of its African colonial project, the transatlantic slave trade uprooted millions of people. In the centuries that followed, and against all odds, the seeds of culture that survived this violent transplantation flourished, as enslaved Africans and their descendants in the United States revisioned their musical heritages into field hollers and shouts and spirituals. In the Reconstruction and post-Reconstruction South, new liberties with instruments and time coupled with these slave songs to produce the blues, a music that alternately led or followed newly free Black Americans as they migrated en masse away from the nouveau-slavery of the sharecropping South and toward the burgeoning industrial cities of the North. The blues spread to a scattered audience through the nascent music industry of the early twentieth century, even as they made their first troubled forays into the Black Church. White performers repackaged urban Black musicians' rhythm and blues as rock 'n' roll. In the 1960s, gospel and soul led Black music away from the static catharsis of the blues, moving on up with the growing civil rights movement and the recognition that a change was gonna come. When the 1970s saw that promise go unfulfilled, funk diverted the movement's soul toward a more strident Black nationalism, while disco danced its way into the mainstream.

Enter hip hop. Disillusioned minority youth in the burned-out neighborhoods of the postindustrial South Bronx of the 1970s take these musics and fixate on the break, that moment where melody and voice fall away, and all that's left is a percussive, low-end groove to be endlessly looped and manipulated, never changing, never quite the same. They repurpose turntables as musical instruments, street corners as stages, and flattened cardboard boxes as dance floors. West Indians plug into a heritage of massive sound systems. At rent parties and nightclubs, emcees join the new deejays to urge on the crowd in a role that soon takes on a life of its own. Hip hop emerges, as the saying goes, by making something out of nothing.

Born from the musical remnants of the civil rights struggle, hip hop can't stay so party-oriented for long. Youth with stolen cans of spray paint (re)claim public spaces, and hip hop's young godfather, Afrika Bambaataa, christens graffiti into the family fold of the new musical culture. At the dawn of the 1980s, Melle Mel's incisive lyrics over the stripped-down instrumentals of "The Message" provide a stark soundtrack to the burned-out city's even starker reality. The decade turns again, as Public Enemy raps an antiauthoritarian Black nationalism, while on the opposite coast, gangsta rappers declare: "Fuck tha Police." Hip hop you don't stop gives way to a new political consciousness inextricably tied to these new ways of producing sound and movement and images. The 1990s usher in the jazz-based, socially conscious music of the Native Tongues Posse, whose Queen Latifah sings of "U.N.I.T.Y." in her pro-women anthems. The Wu-Tang Clan encodes Black Muslim ideology in their lyrics. Tupac and Biggie rise and fall as hip hop martyrs.

By now, this is all a memory. When Nas proclaimed that *Hip Hop Is Dead* on the cover of his 2006 album, he merely amplified widespread whispers: that the rap music flooding the US airwaves, with its interchangeable instrumentals and unabashed celebrations of consumption, is not hip hop at all, but an imposter. Others say that real hip hop isn't dead but in hiding, *underground*, where embattled emcees keep its flame of knowledge alive.

This is hip hop's story. Or at least, it is *a* story about hip hop. As its tellings and retellings circulate between the United States and the global hip hop nation of which it is part, hip hoppers and scholars alike recite its mythical litany. Hip hop has four elements: rapping, writing, breaking, and scratching. It was born in the South Bronx. It is political. It is resistant. It is Black. Or it was—political, resistant, Black, *conscious*—back in the day when it was young.

Senegal's own story of hip hop is bound up with this origin myth even as it exceeds it. Beginning in the early 1980s, hip hop transcended language to captivate youth around the world with its rhythms and rhymes, movements, fashion, and graphics. As hip hop matured into a global musical and cultural force, its aesthetic practices served as conduits for its histories, real and imagined. Irrevocably encoded in hip hop's sonic substance, these histories were quickly taken up and adapted in service of diverse realities. Yet even as hip hop gained global force as a social mobilizer, it never left behind the fundamental beats and rhythms that first drove its worldwide expansion.

This book zooms in from this bird's-eye view of hip hop globalization to consider how and why hip hop continued to mean *musically* in a particular postcolonial African city—Dakar, Senegal—even as it was at times instrumentalized as resistance. It does so through two interconnected claims. First, the stories that people tell about music, across generations and on both sides of the Atlantic, actively inscribe meaningful links between Africa, past and present, and its diaspora. As practices of remembering, these stories trace multiple pathways of connection to produce a place in the world that is always already global. Second, these diasporic connections are strategically reimagined through practices of musical genre, in which narrative, memory, and myth imbue hip hop's multivalent layering of texts and sounds with meaning that is at once locally specific, historically shifting, and globally implicated. Focusing on hip hop as musical practice and on musical genre as social practice, this book shows that hip hop's significance in Dakar is as indebted to Senegalese musical history as to hip hop's own origin myths.

The primary stories about hip hop in Senegal—what practitioners, in a slang inversion of Sene-gal, call *Rap Galsen*—rework two origin myths told by practitioners and scholars around the globe.[1] One concerns hip hop's origins in the inner-city struggles of Black youth in the South Bronx. The other links hip hop to indigenous orality, often located in the practices of hereditary West African bards called *griots*. In exploring how Senegalese hip hop practitioners make sense of, negotiate, and reimagine their place in the world through the stories they tell about and through musical performance, this book locates Rap Galsen at the shifting intersection of these two myths—one about urban marginalization and resistance, the other about African aesthetics and tradition. These myths are not immutable; like nesting dolls, they open to reveal other myths: of the ghetto, of resistance, of voice, of commercialism, of *Africa*; like woven cloth, they pull apart, yielding threads of history and memory to be spliced back together in any number of combinations.

At particular moments in recent Senegalese history, hip hoppers have mobilized these same myths, guided by their positioning vis-à-vis local and international audiences and in conversation with a range of musical practices that preceded and coexist with their own. They have, at times, placed particular importance on the spatial dimensions of hip hop history—that is, its debated geographic origins and the directionality of its movement. For many, resonances between hip hop–mediated images of the postindustrial South Bronx and the lived experience of the postcolonial African city articulate through hip hop practice to bring historic diasporic connections into conversation with contemporary understandings of race in a globalized world.[2] At the same time, the Bronx myth, when distilled into a generalizable marginality, allows for alternative stories of origins whose assertions of hip hop indigeneity disrupt the unidirectionality of hip hop globalization and its links with cultural imperialism and capitalism (Alim et al. 2009).[3]

In representing African hip hop as an engagement with the familiar, however, we miss that the rappers who tell these stories are cosmopolitan subjects who consciously engage, and at times subvert, global narratives. And that these stories vary, not only from place to place, but within locales, over time and contemporaneously. To recount origin myths, then, need not mean to explain hip hop origins, but rather, to "take modes of self-fashioning seriously, and allow competing voices that claim Hip Hop as part of their history into the discussion" (Pennycook and Mitchell 2009, 40).

To call these narratives *myths* is to acknowledge how people understand them as relating to formative or transformative events or periods; to emphasize the weight that certain stories carry for different individuals and communities, at different times and in different ways; and to explore how myth is consciously constructed in practices of memory that sometimes contradict the official memory of the historical record, itself a highly constructed and negotiated collection of presences and absences.[4] Origin myths *diasporically* remember both the griot and hip hop, (re)tracing connections across time and space; they partially efface historical memory, overlaying it with new memories that work in the service of the present (Assmann 1997, 14). Diaspora, as produced through the palimpsestic memory of origin myths, cannot be reduced to either a generalized marginalization or a specific historical forced migration originating in Africa; it both evokes and surpasses these.[5]

The following chapters trace diasporic memory through the conjunction of musical aesthetics, verbal narrative, and social action that I call the practice of hip hop genre.[6] Positioning sound and musical gesture as social actions, I ask how local and global histories are remembered both in discourse about musical form and through musical practice itself. I argue that diaspora emerges as a conscious strategy of globally local emplacement, enacted through music making and the stories people tell about it and sounding at the crossroads of western[7] imaginings of Africa and African imaginings of African America. Histories of music and musical myths, layered together in the cyclical ebb and flow of hip hop time.

What, then, is hip hop time? It is a memory of hip hop, and a collective remembering through hip hop, that (re)imagines the dynamic between locality and globality as one that is diasporic. It is a particular way of negotiating generational difference and social change; it is an epoch brimming with possibility and shadowed by disappointment. It is a retemporalization of diaspora, a postcolonial remapping of urban space as diasporic space. It is a refiguring of the past in the service of the present, but also a reconfiguration of the present through collective mythmaking. It is, and is produced through, hip hop form, defined by constructions of meter and practices of layering—the former inscribing distance from indigenous performance even as the latter permits new musical engagements with tradition that bridge the past and the present.[8] Ultimately, *hip hop time* refers to how all these things—memory, age, social change, tradition, modernity, past(s), and present(s)—are translated into hip hop flows and beats, in a practice of genre that opens an analytical path through (but not around) lyrical texts and toward an understanding of how music means, in, through, and as "time."

ARRIVALS, FAREWELLS, AND OTHER ETHNOGRAPHIC MYTHS

In the summer of 2008, about a month before the concert in Medina, I waited for a rapper named Modou at Just4U, a restaurant and live music venue across the street from Cheikh Anta Diop University in Dakar.

I had picked a table in the middle of the restaurant, uncertain, thrown by its emptiness and the measured yet directionless movements of the few staff there so early in the day; I'd yet to learn to move with their deliberate slowness in the pressing heat. Fans whirl lazily under the thatched roof. My Coke sweats through the napkin below it as I steal glances around the room, noting the small stage nestled in one corner, the bright mural on the wall behind it. Steeped in the lethargy of the scene, I'm startled when he enters, announcing, I am looking for Catty! as though the lone white[9] girl sitting in the center of the space was not a dead giveaway.

He had come with his manager, Lamine Ndao. They gave me Sen Kumpë's press book, told me about the group's history. I was taken by his confidence that was not bravado, his extroversion that was not brash. He was amused by my diffidence, my insecurity, but most of all, I sensed, by the occasional sparks of personality that passed through the anonymizing wall of French between us (Fig. 1.2).

He was tall—at least head and shoulders taller than me—and already slim by the time I knew him. His short dreadlocks hadn't grown to his shoulders yet, and

FIGURE 1.2 Bourba Djolof with the author at Just4U.

they bounced around as he spoke, giving a sense of perpetual motion to a body that was often still.

Modou was an oasis of calm in a city that left me high-strung and jumpy with its ceaseless noise—from vehicles, animals, mosques, people—and its constant verbalized attention to my whiteness. He sensed and buffered my shyness. He was kind. Even in pain. He whisked me around Dakar, handing me off to his brother and musical partner, Books, or to Lamine Ndao when the exertion was too much (Fig. 1.3).

Through him, I met rapper Simon, owner of Jolof4Life Records, and the other groups on the label at that time: 5kiem Underground, Tigrim Bi, Zair ak Batine. We moved as a group, Books, Modou, Lamine, and I. They took me to meet Keur Gui, back when the group still had three members (in 2017, I will encounter Mollah Morgun again, and we will remember, together, the day Modou brought me to meet him and his former partners). We ate rice together in his room, and his sisters smiled at me, babies on their backs. We met their neighbor Almamy (stage name Nigga Mee) and his partner Falsower, who formed the duo 23.3 Wisdom Connection.[10] We surely met more, but I couldn't keep track. Everywhere we went, Books bought me spiced coffee until I felt what I imagined were the stirrings of an ulcer and begged him to stop. I met Lady Sinay; she frequented Modou's house, where we three would stand on the roof in the evenings looking down into the street as tree roots and table legs became indistinguishable in the fading light. I traveled with her to Kaolack one day to meet the men for a concert.

FIGURE 1.3 (l–r) Lamine Ndao, Books, and Bourba, 2008.

Before I returned to the United States, Modou grasped my left hand on a busy street corner, in a gesture of hope that we would meet again. *Ba beneen yoon*, he said. Until next time.

Over the years that have passed since our leave-taking, I confronted ethnographic myths—of holistic field sites, of participant observation, of narrative authority, of gender neutrality—that themselves intersected with local myths about music making. I came to find that my research was delimited and defined through the same conditions that have spurred a hip hop practice of diaspora in Senegal: the fragmentation of traditional structures in an urban context, the broadening of social relations across space, the limitations on expression and mobility associated with certain identities, the particular nexus of economic and political power that aligned with race, nationality, and language, but was complicated by gender and age. Setting up, analyzing, and at times knocking down the myths that alternately guided and impeded my project shed light on the ways in which myth functions in Rap Galsen.

The following chapters pull at these myths of hip hop and ethnography. Each addresses a particular facet of hip hop mythology, teasing out hip hop's twists and turns through memory and musical history; as a whole, they trace the challenges of working in urban and popular music field sites, the dynamic between oral history and memory as accessed through ethnographic interviews, the inescapable influence of gender dynamics as they intersect with geopolitical privilege, and the ways in which ethnography might work as a mode of musical analysis.

Chapter 2, "Globalizing the Underground," reads global hip hop myth through the specificity of the postcolonial city to reconstruct Rap Galsen's origins and show how the "underground" has been causally linked to social and artistic visibility. (Re)tracing the city through its musical histories, Chapter 3, "Remembering the Griot," considers how claims to (and rebuttals of) hip hop's African origins intersect with contemporary African oralities, which are coopted in commercial music genres and by the postcolonial state. Chapter 4, "Voicing Galsen," implicates these musical histories of orality in Rap Galsen's invocations of voice, contesting the naturalization of agency and resistance in hip hop. Chapter 5, "Gendering Voice," reveals how hip hop voice is itself predicated on mobilizations of tradition that actively gender urban space and musical and speech genres. Chapter 6, "Producing Diaspora," shows how hip hop's musical form layers origin myths to produce globally articulating palimpsests of sound and memory. A final remix, "Consuming Resistance," critically reflects on the resonances between scholarly projects, global hip hop narratives, and State interventions in Rap Galsen.

But first, we cycle back to a beginning.

URBANITY, YOUTH, AND HIP HOP CONNECTIONS

I remember how terribly hot it was, the day I found myself in Kaolack (a small city four hours southeast of Dakar) with Sen Kumpë in 2008. We hadn't planned for an overnight stay, but the concert's outdoor venue meant that we waited there almost two days for the rain to stop, crammed into a large room whose floor was covered in mattresses for us to sit and eventually sleep on.

In the heat of the afternoon, I pause in the doorway; my gaze pans the room, full of the dozen or so men whom I've met briefly in the last few weeks as Sen Kumpë and I made the rounds for interviews. Modou, standing by one of only two windows, sees me hesitate and beckons. Turned toward each other, inner elbows resting on the windowsill, we watch the motionless, sandy street as we talk about this and that. I call him by his given name, but I'm curious to know about his emcee pseudonym, Bourba Djolof. He tells me that Jolof is Senegal Senegal is Jolof. There was a great empire that was called Jolof. And Bourba means "king" in Wolof. His narrative of naming followed collective memory back through centuries, tracing a history of translocal exchange. Before Europeans ever came to the continent, diverse ethnolinguistic groups populated what is now Senegal, exerting differing levels of influence over the region as empires rose and fell. The latest of these, the Wolof-dominated Jolof Empire, collapsed around the mid-sixteenth century.

And yet, this distant history was far from anyone's mind that evening in Kaolack. Tired and miserable, without a change of clothes or contact lenses, I'd huddled restlessly in a corner of the room while the rappers of the Jolof4Life label unintelligibly debated local and international politics for most of the night. The only word I picked out easily was *toubab*, the term for "white person/foreigner" liberally peppering the animated Wolof speech patterns that sounded angry to my unaccustomed ear. I grew increasingly uncomfortable, shrinking in on myself as my eyes followed the conversation, until Simon stopped suddenly, looked at me, and laughed something to his friends. Another rapper sat down next to me and gently explained, in slow French, their discussion about France's interference in African governance. The conversation weighed on me, as I thought about my own name and its histories; although my ethnic background is best described as assorted Western European, the vagaries of patrilines, coupled with a Catholic heritage, have landed me with a name as French as Senegal's colonial past.

I didn't know, when I started spending so much time there, how the Medina neighborhood—home to Sen Kumpë and many of the other Jolof4Life rappers—was itself a vestige of this colonial history.

Another day, Bourba and I again stand looking out a window, this time in his family home. We're silent for a moment, waiting for the call to prayer from the nearby mosque to fade before resuming conversation. The contrast with Kaolack's calm, sandy streets is pronounced. Butting up against the prime area of land known as Plateau—home to the city's downtown, major port, and municipal buildings—Medina's organized grid of paved streets is full of children playing, dodging the cars, taxis, mopeds, and horse-drawn carts that swerve from one side of the road to the other to avoid potholes. Women do laundry on the sidewalk, and storefronts open onto the street, luring customers inside with displays ranging from makeup and skin-bleaching creams, to handcrafted leather shoes, to intricately embroidered costumes waiting to be picked up from the tailor. Two blocks over, we hear the constant honking and yelling of *cars rapides*, small public buses rendered from old Renault vans and painted bright colors with "alhamdulilaay [Praise be to God]" across the hoods; slightly farther away, a muezzin gives the call to prayer through the loudspeaker in a mosque. These days, the power is out more than it is on, and in the next week or so, when the rains begin in earnest, the streets will be flooded so badly that this scene will change completely, as certain blocks become impassable, the stench penetrates the surrounding homes, and hordes of malarial mosquitoes take up residence.

Yet it was under the pretext of sanitary concerns that, in the early twentieth century, the French forcibly moved the indigenous population to this poorly structured "Native Quarter" and away from the coveted land on the coastal plateau that would become downtown Dakar (Bigon 2009). In the second half of the twentieth century, as more and more rural Senegalese and other West Africans migrated to the city, new working-class neighborhoods, called *banlieues,* arose on its outskirts. As the formal sector failed to keep up with rapid urban growth, soaring unemployment contributed to the rise of slums and the predominance of informal sector labor (Sommers 2010).

From the mid-twentieth century onward, urbanization went hand in hand with a woloficization that quickly outpaced colonial cultural influence, until there was nothing unusual in a Bambara man with family from Mali calling himself Bourba Djolof. Dakar residents from widely varying ethnic backgrounds communicate primarily in Wolof, some without speaking the languages of their grandparents or even French, despite its status as the official national language.[11] The Wolof spoken in Dakar borrows heavily from French vocabulary while retaining Wolof syntax and grammar (McLaughlin 2009; Swigart 1994).

The city's ethnic diversity notwithstanding, Wolof musical practices have likewise dominated its soundscapes, from *sabar* drumming traditions to indigenized popular musics. In the mid-twentieth century, urban dance bands that originally developed to play for French and elite African audiences in the city's nightclubs increasingly drew on Wolof rhythms, singing styles, and speech genres, syncretizing them with Afro-Cuban son and jazz to create *mbalax*, the most popular music in Senegal to this day.

These linguistic and musical processes point to how, for both new residents and established migrants, the city in some ways represents a break with traditional lifeways, until, for many, rural Africa comes to represent the "real" Africa, where people speak "deep" Wolof or other indigenous language unmarred by French, and where non-Wolof cultural practices abound.[12] As ties of kinship and lineage-based occupation loosen in the urban context, alternative trajectories open to youth, whose "transversal" ways of navigating the city create broader and further reaching relationships (Simone 2005, 517; see also Sommers 2010). Nevertheless, traditional concepts of age and gender—and the postcolonial state's investment in these— continue to limit youth's agency in relation to their elders and the public sphere, and to complicate women's movements through public space. At the same time, the very category of "youth" has come unmoored from chronological age, as people unable, for primarily economic reasons, to fulfill the rites of marriage and procreation that would render them adults are trapped in a state of permanent nonadulthood (Durham 2000; Honwana 2012; Matlon 2015; Simone 2005, Sommers 2010).

When hip hop arrived in Africa in the 1980s, its origin myths resonated with these continental continuities of urban experience and spoke to youth as a marginalized social class.[13] Senegal was no exception. Since at least the early 1990s, youth throughout Dakar and its banlieues have mobilized hip hop to describe the city's ghettoized spaces and to connect them through musical collaborations and networks.

Medina was one such space. The very street corner where I said goodbye to Bourba, the only place I could reliably find my way to in Dakar back then, was, as I would come to find, at the center—or at least, *a* center—of hip hop's story in Senegal.

When I left Dakar in 2008, Bourba grasped my left hand tightly on a street corner in Medina and said, Until next time.

I would never see him again.

VOICE, GENDER, AND SOCIAL CONSCIOUSNESS

January 2011. Outside the Jolof4Life studio on a rooftop in Medina, a host of rappers wait their turn to memorialize Bourba Djolof, a year after his passing. As Lamine Ndao takes pictures with my camera, I hesitantly reintroduce myself to those gathered. I've only just arrived back in Dakar, adrift despite a wealth of contacts from my previous trip and some Wolof classes under my belt, aimlessly taking French lessons, waiting weeks before I finally call Lamine and tell him that I'm here. I take a taxi to our corner in Medina, only to lose myself as I walk past the house, whose façade has changed, the window I looked out of with Bourba gone, his room converted into a tailor's atelier facing out onto the street. I ask some boys, seated on a bench outside a shop, where Sen Kumpë lives, and they direct me back the way I've come. Lamine finds me there and we walk to the studio together. The session goes on all day, as the men file in and out recording their two bars, hanging out in the studio or in the sun on the rooftop when they aren't in the booth. Two women come and sing on the track and then leave; two others stop by, flirt for a bit with the rappers, then disappear.

The track is quickly mixed and mastered, to be released with a simple video clip three days later, on the anniversary of Bourba's death. I hear its composite parts as a whole for the first time in the living room of Sen Kumpë's home in Medina, watching television with the women gathered there for prayers and offerings on that day.

Singer Njaaya opens the song, positioned in front of a condenser mic, her raw, strident voice falling from the top of its register, layering on itself, then ceding to a sparse, unchanging hip hop beat whose *kora* riffs rise and fall endlessly. Her image gives way to a stream of individual rappers; they take her place behind the mic to exchange two-bar phrases, rhythms and flows running into each other, sometimes clashing, held together only by the beat looping beneath them and the thematic thread of saying goodbye to someone we loved. At the end of the video, the camera zooms in on the same microphone that has been centered the entire clip, now unmanned. Watching, the women and I audibly inhale together as Bourba's disembodied voice, hoarse and gravelly from the illness that took his life, fills the empty studio and spills over into the room where we sit, transfixed:

> Lu mënta ñak faut mu am [What can't be avoided must come to pass]
> Life bi nii la [This is how life is]
> Gëm sa bop la rek [It's just believing in yourself]
> Bourba, bu demb ak bu tey [Bourba—then, now]
> Xolam, jëfam du mësa fey [His actions will never fade][14]

The song fades out, but Bourba's words are etched in time, rendered as action through hip hop, in the voice recorded and disseminated.

Nearly a month later, I'm summoned with my camera to Bourba's memorial concert at Blaise Senghor Cultural Center, nestled between Fass, Colobane, and Grand Dakar. In a room to the left of the main entrance, streetwear and graffiti art are displayed for sale. A table centered on the wall immediately across from the door offers T-shirts with Bourba's face, name, and signature imprinted on the front. Other than the two young women there as part of the television crew, the space is filled with men. Around three o'clock, they screen Ben Herson's *Democracy in Dakar*, which chronicles rappers' roles in the 2007 presidential elections. There is a constant chatter during the film; in the room are many of its stars, one of whose conspicuous absence we are memorializing today.

That afternoon, I never imagined that within a few months, the political action featured in the film would repeat on a massive scale in the wake of the Arab Spring and the anticipation of a contested Senegalese presidential election the following year. And yet, perhaps I should have imagined exactly that. I knew already that youth in Senegal have historically harnessed the potential of hip hop's mass mediation to political and social ends. In 2011, as then-president Abdoulaye Wade attempted to push through legislation that would ensure him an unconstitutional third term and set up his own son as vice president and his likely successor, and as the population grappled with pervasive power outages, water shortages, flooding, unemployment, and teachers' and students' strikes, the country was primed for political unrest. Journalists and rappers—notably Thiat and Kilifeu of Keur Gui, many of the Jolof4Life rappers, and many rappers based in the banlieues—organized under the banner of *Y'en a Marre* (Enough is Enough) a movement catapulted into precocious adulthood in the demonstrations and riots that took place on June 23, 2011. During the rest of my time in Dakar, many rappers I knew participated in Y'en a Marre's efforts to effect change, holding meetings and demonstrations and canvassing for voter registration.

Hip hop's broad and timely dissemination (consider that "R.I.P. Bourba Djolof" aired instantly on national television) creates a unique opportunity for far-reaching youth expression and, coupled with a history of social change movements, leads almost naturally into assumptions about voice and agency in Rap Galsen. Yet to consider hip hop primarily as a globalized genre that is localized through its characteristic expressions of marginality suggests that hip hop has pretty much the same meaning everywhere, simply tweaked to suit local realities. What if, instead of—*Why hip hop?*—a question easily answered through tropes of resistance, we were to ask—*Why not something else?*—taking into account not only diverse socio-political contexts, but also local musical histories?[15]

Well before hip hop made its way there in the 1980s, music in Senegal mediated complex relationships between local tradition, colonial legacies, rapid urbanization, and religious hierarchies implicated in postcolonial governance. Whether through traditional griot verbal and musical practices, or in their popular offspring, mbalax, indigenous performance, namely, praisesinging, has bolstered

religious and political hierarchies, at once bridging and sustaining a distance between griots' performative speech and the political and social action of those in
power. Against the sound and materiality of oral tradition, Rap Galsen asserts a
referential, agential voice that speaks its claims to modernity over and through
globally intelligible hip hop beats and flows.[16]

And yet, situating hip hop within this particular musical history complicates
its association with social change. In this book, I nuance, and at times disrupt,
this common pairing, neither reducing hip hop to a musically-inflected political
resistance, nor eliding how hip hop consciousness can further marginalize those
on the periphery of already marginalized groups (Helbig 2014). For example,
while critiquing social and political structures as agents of underdevelopment,
male rappers have largely failed to challenge those structures' dependence on the
gendering of domestic and public space, of familial and political hierarchy, and of
economic and educational opportunities. The consequently gendered dimensions
of hip hop voice expose its limitations, and suggest that to focus on men, regardless of their dominance in the local scene or their work as political activists, sets
up a binary of resistance and nonresistance that is disrupted when we consider
women's participation through local systems of meaning.

When evening falls at Blaise Senghor, the whole scene has changed, with security at the gate and throngs of people outside. Inside the center, a deejay spins
records as young hip hop heads bounce around or listen quietly, while on the
outdoor stage, some rather artsy pop-locking is followed by a breakdance rou-
tine. The actual concert doesn't even begin until almost midnight. As countless
opening groups—all men—perform, I step outside for some space and air, only to
be accosted by a film producer who speaks to me in an exaggerated Parisian French
that I struggle to understand. A rapper I recognize, but don't know, approaches
to introduce himself in English. The two begin arguing, the francophone con-
tender angrily asserting first dibs, the anglophone smugly continuing to speak
to me in English and delighting in his opponent's frustration. As I stand frozen
in embarrassment, rapper and graffiti artist Docta approaches, taking me gently
by the elbow. Lady—he says politely in Wolof. Let's go inside; I don't remember
if I understood his words, after "lady," or just the gestures. I follow him gratefully
back into the concert. Hours in, still no women have performed, and very few
women are in the audience. I wander through the crowd until I find Bourba's sisters standing about halfway back. They see me before I do them, calling out my
name. Grateful for a familiar face, I stand with them until Books finally comes
on stage.

Although hip hop is often described as a youth culture, in a country where
young women slightly outnumber young men, I rarely encountered women at

concerts or in studios, spaces where negotiating gendered interactions often took center stage over the work I had come to do. The little time I did spend with women rappers helped put these challenges in perspective; it discouraged my tendency to imagine my experiences as exceptional, despite my frustrations moving around the city as a highly visible, clearly foreign woman, and highlighted the extent to which my racial and national privilege were directly to thank for my relatively uninhibited mobility in Dakar and my access to hip hop practitioners and spaces (Appert 2017).

The hip hop masculinity that complicated my and other women's movements through the hip hop scene only partially drew on hip hop's generic self-fashioning and marketing in the United States. It emerged primarily from the local systems of gender, class, and caste that have unevenly accommodated the economic shifts of the mid- to late-twentieth century *and* from particular social histories of music making in Dakar that led male rappers to associate indigenous music making with women even as they positioned it as a foil to hip hop voice. Both hip hop narratives about voice and hip hop's ability to voice youth experience therefore rely on gendered understandings of how speech and music are interwoven in indigenous music and in hip hop.

In the pulling apart and recombining of verbal and musical performance, origin myths reimagine popular genres in ways that emphasize memory, temporality, and generational difference. Hip hop voice, then, speaks not only through lyrical representation and indexicality but also, crucially, in sound and form.

FORM, GENRE, AND MUSICAL MEANING

February, 2011. Back inside the large courtyard at Blaise Senghor Cultural Center, I stand with Bourba's sisters as Books finally appears onstage to the opening sounds of "Fly On," a tribute to his brother. I first heard the song weeks earlier, sitting in the courtyard in Medina, when he took out his earbuds and passed me his simple Nokia cell phone to listen. Then, the Wolof lyrics thwarted my conversational ability; perhaps what touched me were the English words mixed into the refrain—Fly on, so long—or the familiar harmonic progression. Or the increasingly tense quality of Books's voice and its release into melody toward the end of the track.

Home that night, I listened to the song on repeat and mourned.

The producer had remixed the international version of Idrissa Diop's song "Fly On," which replaces the kora of the original with a simpler guitar. The hip hop beat reworks the guitar into a five-pitch melody that repeats without any respite, high in the mix. During Books's verses, Diop's hoarse vocals remain in the background, merging into the dense musical texture to reemerge as speech in a refrain that changes slightly each time. The bird is beautiful when he is in flight. On the ground, it seems that he is no longer beautiful. The crowd moves in unity, waving lighters and cell phones in the air; standing flanked by his sisters, I embrace a fleeting illusion of anonymity in the sea of lights. As Books stands onstage, head bowed, the microphone dangling from his hand, Diop's voice returns for the last time:

Bourba Djolof said he is that bird. The bird when he is in flight . . .

In Books's poetic memorial to his brother, layered over recreations of local musical sounds, lyrical and musical meaning intertwine. Hip hop's effectiveness as a representational speech genre—that is, one that communicates experience—has contributed to its widespread adoption around the world for addressing social ills. Nevertheless, in the history of global hip hop writ large, people have engaged with its sounded, visual, and embodied practices before its lyrical content. In Senegal, as elsewhere in the world, audiences were drawn to the movements of breakdancing, the sounds of hip hop music (rapping and deejaying), and the images of graffiti. They engaged hip hop first as dancers and in their style of dress, then mimicked English-language lyrics, then wrote original lyrics over US beats, and finally, once resources allowed, they made original musical tracks. It is in this moment, where original lyrics sounded over original beats, that Senegalese hip hop practitioners narrate the emergence of what would be called Rap Galsen.

This book considers hip hop primarily as a musical genre, not as an aesthetic vehicle for protest, nor as a sonic force of resistance or identity construction—although it can be and has been all these things— but as a conscious musical practice guided by formal conventions that are increasingly shared throughout the world and that articulate with diverse musical histories.[17] In doing so, it comes up against perennial concerns that to focus on hip hop as music reduces it to text, privileging product over process and musical structure over social meaning. However, I consider verbal and musical texts as emerging from the purposeful weaving together of utterances into recognizable forms that both comment on and dialogically produce social realities (Barber 2007; Bakhtin 1986).[18] In this sense, to consider music as text is not to hold it apart from (or even position it within) ethnographically (re)constructed social contexts, but rather, to approach musical form itself ethnographically.[19]

As an ethnography of musical genre, this book foregrounds local understandings of the sonic elements of hip hop and demonstrates how these are produced in ways that cannot be disentangled from lyrical content or various rememberings of history and myth.[20] Musical sounds and gestures are imbued with meaning through discourse and human intention, until the ways in which sound is formed into music communicate social facts, shape human interactions, and evoke affective and embodied responses without verbal exegesis. Music's representational potential opens a path past lyrical and extramusical resistance when considering hip hop's relationship to social realities.[21] In the case of Rap Galsen, the representational quality of musical sound drove the development of a hardcore musical aesthetic modeled after Public Enemy in the 1990s, and it also has informed rappers' varying attitudes toward the use of indigenous instruments in hip hop over the last several decades. And yet, writing about African praise poetry, Karin Barber suggests that it is through form—rather than representational content—that texts reveal things about social experience and produce social realities (2007, 106). If we were to focus on hip hop's musical *form*, while distinguishing it (if only for a moment) from its representational content, whether lyrical or musical, what spaces of meaning open up?

Hip hop form emerged from the recontextualizing of earlier pieces of music, first through deejays' break beats and later through digital sampling. The same sample can be used in myriad ways, carrying distinct meanings for those who produced it and for its differently positioned listeners. At times, these recycled bits of musical material are stripped of historical meaning to fill a purely aesthetic function; in other words, samples convey meaning in different ways, and sometimes they don't mean at all, at least not symbolically (see Williams 2013). Contemporary hip hop beats (instrumental tracks) comprising completely new material are still structured through layering and repetition, a compositional model that grew out of these earlier practices.[22] Sometimes new beats are constructed to give a sonic impression of historical sampling that masks their actual novelty.

This book asserts that, regardless of whether the components of a musical track are intentionally referential, the musical structure that emerges from sampling takes on meaning as a conscious social practice in Dakar. And so, although I discuss the representational content of lyrics and instrumental tracks, I remain most interested in the practices and narratives of genre through which that material *becomes* hip hop. While interpretations of hip hop's layered form have emphasized the Afro-diasporic roots of repetition and layering, or invoked models of bricolage and pastiche to describe hip hop's postmodernist aesthetic,[23] I read hip hop's characteristic layering as a practice of aural palimpsest memory (Shaw 2002, 8).[24] There is an erasure implied in palimpsest that makes space for something new, even as there is a conscious or unconscious guarding of things past. To describe hip hop as palimpsest is to emphasize how musical form is tied to collective memory, which also erases or strategically forgets in order to make space for new ways of knowing. It is also, however, to allow for multiple memories and diverse constructions of diaspora to coexist. The palimpsests I examine in this book layer discourse, story, memory, and sound; for me, palimpsest is a way of getting at how people understand and mobilize musical form, rather than a metaphor for that form itself.[25]

The idea of hip hop as aural palimpsest emerged from a musically informed participant observation (Appert 2017) that centered on conversations about hip hop aesthetics, social impact, and musical meaning. And yet, the primary voices in this book are those of rappers, not beat makers, because I am concerned with how those practitioners who are most often (self)positioned as the voice of the people hear music and music's intersections with speech. Rappers constantly listen to and comment on hip hop from Senegal and the United States (and less commonly, France); listening with them, I eventually began to recognize the narratives they traced in sound and form.[26] To mark how musical meaning is situational and learned, throughout the book I describe music as I hear it, rather as it "is," and note how this changes over time.

Finally, to consider hip hop as a practice of genre that works through palimpsestic processes of layering breaks open binaries—between commercialism and resistance, globalization and localization—that often guide conversations about hip hop. For if Rap Galsen's claims to hip hop are claims to diaspora, to globally emplaced locality, they are also claims—not alternatives, nor resistance—to modernity, and thus to power (Weidman 2006, 9). These claims are inseparable from unbalanced global flows of commerce and ideology (Maira 2008, 338). To position hip hop circulation as a counternarrative to globalization obscures what Anna Tsing has described as the struggles over the terrain of circulation, the social conditions that allow flow, and the privileging of certain players; in other words, the role of cultural legacies and power inequalities in creating the institutional arenas and assumptions through which circulation takes place (2000, 337). African cities like Dakar emerge from profoundly unequal interactions with these global movements (Fredericks and Diouf 2014, 10). When we consider the violent ways in which Africa has been incorporated into global capitalism and recognize that hip hop is inherently tied to global technological and economic forces (Saucier 2014, 199; Zeleza 2013b, 5, 18), we might hesitate to look at global hip hop through rose-colored glasses of resistance, even as we recognize hip hop's "hypercommodification as a global cultural form" as a primary force behind the diverse engagements with diasporic Blackness that emerge within global hip hop scenes (Perry 2008, 639).[27] In how it allows for a layering of globality and locality, of commercial concerns and social action, hip hop palimpsest opens a path past resistance to consider hip hop genre as a practice of aesthetic, narrative, and social articulation that *produces* diaspora, both as an alternative to exploitative global flows and as a claim to a modernity firmly situated within them.

PASTS, PRESENTS, AND REMEMBERING RAP GALSEN

> To listen carefully to stories is to take local subjectivity seriously; to repeat them shifts focus to remembering, to how musical experience becomes meaningful by being vocally emplaced.
>
> STEVEN FELD (2012, 8)

The following pages fall impossibly short of a comprehensive history of Rap Galsen.[28] Instead, they present the perspectives of a relatively small sampling of hip hoppers, as narrated to me in 2011–2012, although subsequent developments are addressed throughout the text as needed.[29] I interpret these narratives through nearly ten years of intermittent engagement with Rap Galsen and its broader ethnographic site: a Wolof-centric, primarily Muslim, urban Senegalese society differentiated by class, age, caste, and gender, and violently, partially incorporated into global neoliberalism.

From my early and sustained relationship with Sen Kumpë, I followed webs of hip hop connection that branched throughout the city. Close friendships within the hip hop scene emerged naturally through proximity to my friendships in Medina, while other relationships comprised a single interview and a handful of surface encounters in hip hop spaces. I worked with a range of artists, including internationally-renowned ones, underground legends, and teenagers just cutting their teeth on hip hop. Rappers across these strata of fame and generation themselves interact, often moving in the same spaces. Their stories overlap and echo each other's in ways that are made, from my perspective, more compelling for their shifting concord and discord across levels of celebrity, market success, age, and musical talent.

At the same time, this uneven engagement was compounded by my shifting language abilities and initially naïve cultural consciousness. The often-fraught gender dynamics of working in male-dominated hip hop spaces closed off certain kinds of ethnographic immersion that I had hope for and expected, so that I often found myself keeping my space even as I longed to spend more time with the men I interviewed, to do "better" research.[30] The result is an ethnography that is at times notably thin in its treatment of individual artists as positioned social actors.[31] To accept, and at times highlight, that thinness, as I do in this book, critically acknowledges the limitations of ethnographic methods while exploring how history and memory thicken ethnographic description.

In particular, grappling with ethnographic thinness has meant questioning the central role of interviews. One the one hand, to rely on interviews risks privileging narratives that affirm our own, or that come from more vocal informants (in the case of Rap Galsen, those internationally recognized artists who speak French,

English, or both) (Gubrium and Holstein 1998, 570–571). The interviews that I quote or summarize in this book, however, represent perspectives that were repeated to me over a wide sampling of responses, and I have indicated when these traced fault lines in the broader hip hop scene. Still, participants can only narrate what they know (or believe) and are willing to share in the context of the interview's unequal power dynamics (Briggs 1988, 3).

On the other hand, Senegalese rappers' tendency to conflate journalists and researchers, and to provide both with the same codified narratives, highlights the performativity of interviews and the often conscious storytelling they entail.[32] In interviews, rappers shifted between responses that were markedly performed (for me and for a broader imagined public) and a conversational flow. In representing their words here, I have differentiated between conversational and oratory delivery, transcribing the former in block text and the latter with line breaks that follow speech patterns, sometimes shifting between the two, just as their responses did. Line breaks also draw attention to how repetition works within and across interviews, underscoring not only certain stories, but certain ways of marking speech as true or hedging it as conditional. I have used quotation marks to signal speech taken from transcribed interviews, while leaving remembered speech (as recorded in my field notes) without quotation marks to signal its inexactitude. I often mark the linguistic practices of particular participants, because the choice between French and Wolof—which is not always really a choice—as well as the occasional use of English, highlights how my identity as a researcher is tied to Senegal's history of colonialism and contemporary encounters with neoliberalism, while illustrating how gender, age, and geography are often directly implicated in linguistic practices in Dakar.[33]

My interviews with rappers were guided by a shared awareness that their responses would shape my writing and a constant negotiation—on both sides—of the possible (mis)interpretations of our words (Bauman 2004, 161). And so, although I privilege these narratives, I also recognize that they are interpretations of experiences, conarrated between us, and that they produce realities as much as they comment on them (Briggs 1988, 3; Bruner 1997, 270; Ebron 2002, 26).[34] I therefore engage interviews as I would song texts or instrumental tracks, layering them with other narratives, following when they spark analysis that exceeds them, and allowing them to set new stories in motion.

In fact, it is precisely this conarration that interests me—how global narratives (re)emerge in or are even (re)created through ethnographic encounters. "Leaving traces" (Abu-Lughod 1993, 29) of my presence throughout the book, I mark this coproduction (between me and my interlocutors, and at the global intersections of hip hop myths) without pretending to give voice to my informants simply by including their words.[35] The stories here emerge from this confluence of narratives, the points of connection between them.[36] If there are topics that receive little attention (a few that come immediately to mind are the history and contemporary practice of Islam, transnational migrant networks, and undocumented immigration, but there are countless others) their absence indicates only my focus on other questions. Ultimately, the memories and stories recorded here create an only partial narrative.

In highlighting rather than eliding these contradictions, and in approaching all knowledge production as narrative that often achieves the status of myth, I hope to avoid privileging certain types of narratives—the academic, the written, the western, over others—the local, the oral, the musical, while destabilizing the binary implied in this very process.[37] The dismissal or endorsement of certain myths can in many instances be read as a struggle for or assertion of power over representation, especially if we view myths as collective narratives of memory and self (Assmann 1997, 15). Veit Erlmann has argued that, in our efforts to understand how situated actors make sense of their lived experiences of modernity, we should seek not to distinguish fact from fiction, but to "examine the kinds of truths that are produced in colonial and postcolonial contexts" (1999, 5). This book locates those truths in the gaps between what is said and done; in the fissures and points of connection between the oral histories that emerged in interviews, the officially documented history of the region, and national and diasporic collective memories; in the complex call and response of memory and myth that is reproduced in hip hop practice.

It does so through a hip hop sampling of popular, scholarly, and practitioner stories: stories told about hip hop and other musical practices, and the stories of urbanization, colonization, diaspora, modernity, memory, and tradition that are told and negotiated through hip hop. Throughout its chapters, I have interwoven historical and ethnographic accounts with scholarly and musical analysis in ways that are not always chronological or seamless, precisely because I am interested in how social actors remember histories differently, situationally, and toward divergent and sometimes contradictory ends. In telling these stories, I vacillate between the past and the present to reflect how memory and narrative fluctuate, so that sometimes I remember, placing myself in that moment to describe it in the now, and sometimes I tell a story, in the past; sometimes story transitions fluidly into memory and vice versa.

For if hip hop instrumentals work as palimpsests, so do memory and myth. What does it tell us about experience—and about ethnography—that my remembering of the 2008 Medina where I said a final goodbye to a dearly missed friend is refracted through today's Medina, that in fact, I'm not sure

I can differentiate them at all? Or that, in January, 2018, nearly seven years to the day after the marathon recording session where I reencountered so many of the rappers that I had first met through Bourba, I ran into Lamine Ndao, Sen Kumpë's manager, in the street in Medina, and we again walked together to that studio, through roads busy with traffic at that time of day, picking our way carefully around potholes and the jagged places where roots had broken through the sidewalks. Up on the roof, we stepped inside, and it was as though the updated technology and the large image of Bourba's face on the wall were superimposed on the humbler studio I had encountered back then. I was shaken by the coincidence, by the similarity and the discord between this present and that memory, by the feeling of cycling back through hip hop time only to repeat it with a difference.

Ethnography necessarily recalls and narrates the past.[38] But it is also mediated through the multiple presents that elapse between the time we do fieldwork and the time we write about it. As I finalize this book in early 2018, I inevitably recollect the narratives, music, and events of 2011–2012 through the layers of experience since. In this way, my own memories, and my own writing, are themselves a palimpsest; I cannot remember, nor can I write, in a way that doesn't dredge memory through the time elapsed between that past and this present, losing detail while accumulating new meaning along the way.

2

GLOBALIZING THE UNDERGROUND

MOVING INLAND FROM downtown Dakar on the tip of the cape, past the bustling Medina and its neighboring *quartiers populaires*, but long before you reach the crowded *banlieues*, just on the fringes of Dakar proper lay the neighborhoods of the Société Immobilière du Cap-Vert (SICAP); spacious and relatively calm, founded in the 1950s to accommodate a growing population of civil servants, and still largely inhabited by upper-class families whose children speak elegant French and travel abroad (Diouf 2008, 349). On a quiet side street in one of these neighborhoods, SICAP Amitié II, sits Studio Sankara. Inside, a secretary disappears into the back and returns with DJ Awadi (Fig. 2.1), who greets me warmly, moving us briskly back to the main studio space, squeezing me into a busy day. As he leans back on the red sofa, comfortably at home, I rush to begin. One of *les anciens* of Senegalese hip hop (many would say *the* elder), he describes his first encounters with the music.

The first time was a really long time ago, it was—
The first time was "Rapper's Delight."
That's what it was, and well, I was really young, I was on vacation in Benin and this was something that arrived from Nigeria, and then later I saw "Rapper's Delight" again on shows that we had here . . .

FIGURE 2.1 DJ Awadi at Studio Sankara in SICAP Amitié II.

and so, there was "Rapper's Delight" live—

"I say the hip, hop, a hippy"—

He channels the familiar performance, rapping a global origin story in which hip hop spreads to the masses via the Sugarhill Gang's 1979 recording, wrapping his own story within it,

—and so, I really liked it, I didn't know it was called rap, it was just cool,

and then after, during breakdance and smurf, there was Grandmaster Flash, "The Message," and then after there was *Beat Street*, and so that started to educate everyone a bit.

Another day, another studio, another SICAP neighborhood a bit farther from the city's center. In Studio Boite Sacré, Daara J's two remaining members, Faada Freddy and Ndongo, finish mixing a recording, and we move to the rehearsal room, where they've had me set up my camera to center them in front of a large abstract painting (Fig. 2.2). Their answers are short and precise, honed through years of interviews. Faada Freddy takes up Awadi's narrative as though he's heard him across the residential neighborhoods that lie between them.

So, in Senegal, hip hop arrived with the breakdance movement. It was with films like *Beat Street*, '84, with the music videos that we received from groups like Public Enemy, Afrika Bambaataa, all of these waves influenced us to

FIGURE 2.2 Ndongo (left) and Faada Freddy (right) at Studio Boit Sacré.

enter into the hip hop movement. I think that that was the first skill in the '90s. So, we entered via dance, then added poetry . . .

Hip hop arrived in Dakar through global media channels directly from the United States, by way of a localized hip hop scene in France, and via remitted recordings and videos that came through networks of migrants moving between Africa, Europe, and North America. Engrossed by these films and music videos, most, if not all, of Senegal's "old-school" rappers were first dancers, only transitioning to rapping in the 1990s as frontmen for their dance crews.

This is Rap Galsen's story—one honed through years of repetition, the bumps smoothed out, the tellings polished and concise, its skilled narrators carefully framing interviews and camera shots in a familiar exchange.

Late one afternoon, a taxi leaves me by a mosque on yet another SICAP street. Standing exposed in the middle of the road, engulfed in stillness, I recognize Xuman's dreadlocked silhouette as he emerges from a gated house at the end of the block; his long gait brings him to my side in a matter of seconds. He chooses the courtyard for our interview, noting the position of the sun and the fading light, sending his teenage daughter to buy beignets for us as I set up my camera (Fig. 2.3). Another of *les grands*, Xuman picks up the thread, recounting the same beginnings, the same early encounters with hip hop.

I think that above all, hip hop here—

first, before all else, there was a history of—

FIGURE 2.3 Xuman at his home.

that started with dance, here. That started with dance.

So, there was a year where there were many more dancers here than hip hoppers, than rappers in fact. So that started with dance, and then after a while rap became involved. So, there are groups, as I was, for example, my group was first a dance group and later became a rap group. My group was Pee Froiss. And first we danced, and then transformed little by little into rappers. But even so, there were dancers and rappers in the group. I had the mic and I was behind and I rapped, and the dancer was in front. So, before, the two went together, because the dancers were much more successful in Senegal than rappers; rappers came way after.

In many ways, these stories could stand in for the story of hip hop globalization writ large: early encounters with films like *Beat Street* and *Wild Style*, artists like MC Hammer inspiring youth to try their hand at hip hop dance and visual culture regardless of linguistic barriers; English-language mimicry of American artists; exposure to Public Enemy and a dawning recognition of hip hop's potential as a form of social commentary; the move toward original lyrics in local languages corresponding to the taking-up of hip hop's Bronx origin myth; local stories of marginalization framed through global imaginings of Blackness, newly couched in mother tongues; democratizing technological developments creating space for equally local musical tracks.

But Rap Galsen's story is also its own: of colonial and postcolonial power traced through the avenues of irregular urban growth; of indigenous music and popular genres, transformed in the city's nightclubs and echoing through its neighborhoods in naming ceremonies and weddings; of increasingly rooted engagements with Islam, inscribed in murals and sounded through amplified chants on city streets—streets that have been witness to and conduits of social agitation and political activism for decades.

At the heart of Rap Galsen's origin myth are some of its earliest groups: Positive Black Soul (PBS), Daara J, and Pee Froiss, whose music reached international and local audiences simultaneously in the mid-1990s. This was the Senegalese hip hop that I could track down and purchase online before I went to Senegal for the first time in 2007, although it wasn't the first that I heard; in 2006, a Senegalese friend in Los Angeles had lent me a cherished cassette of Da Brains, worn from repeated listening. Soon after came the "hardcore" underground rappers—groups like Rap'Adio, Yatfu, and Waa BMG 44—who emerged from the city's working-class neighborhoods around the same time, but, lacking resources, recorded and self-released their albums slightly later. I would have had to know exactly what I was looking for to find their music, which didn't even show up on YouTube until a decade after its initial release in 1998.[1]

On the surface, it is easy to categorize this latter group within a "global underground" of marginalized youth who take up hip hop to contest local inequities while refusing to participate in the global capitalist consumption of mainstream US hip hop (Osumare 2007, 58). This binary schema of underground and commercial music has been broadly, if often uncritically, cited in popular and scholarly discourse, even as it has clearly informed practitioner engagements with hip hop within and outside the United States.[2]

Note, however, the specificity of global connections, how they follow the paths worn by colonial movements of extraction and subjugation, so that early Senegalese encounters with hip hop were partially mediated through France, where youth mobilized tropes of the hardcore, the street, and the ghetto to express their own experiences of urban marginality on the periphery of the city.

Note that, nevertheless, urban marginalization is not globally homogenous, that neither the US inner city nor the French city's periphery can stand in for Senegalese urbanity without eliding important material differences. As they connect the distinct spaces of the city across time and space, hip hop networks in Dakar navigate the expectations of older generations, the possibilities of a present moment of increased translocal and global mobility and interconnection, and the limitations of an underdevelopment historically grounded in colonialism and exacerbated by postcolonial institutions and global neoliberalism. In a sense, it is not Senegalese hip hop but Senegalese youth themselves who are underground; underground status is imposed by institutions and structures of power even as it is also reclaimed by rappers as a badge of hip hop authenticity.

Note that to emphasize "socially conscious" lyrical meaning over musical or aesthetic practices flattens the complexity of local engagements with global hip hop narratives. From an outsider's perspective, it's hard to argue that early mainstream rappers' largely Afrocentric critiques were not socially engaged. Nevertheless, hardcore rappers in the 1990s critiqued that music as apolitical, rejecting as frivolous what international publics celebrated as conscious. They distinguished their music from "commercial" hip hop (as they designated PBS and other groups) in terms of beats, flow, and language use as much as through topical content.

And note, finally, that to consider publics and reception muddies, perhaps contradictorily, the distinction between mainstream and underground hip hop. Rap Galsen's underground persona was first a foil to social acceptance, as rappers' rough language, disrespect for their elders (including government officials), physical posturing, and abrasive instrumentals discouraged mainstream media from disseminating their music. Ironically, however, underground ideals have ultimately led to increased social integration, and the more Rap Galsen plays into global imaginings of hip hop resistance, the more visible it becomes on a global scale.

Note all this, and then loop back to where it all began.

BEGINNINGS

Listening to Positive Black Soul's *Salaam* album again all these years later, the background chatter and noises of my first listening (Los Angeles 2007) morph into intelligibility. I recognize the sounds of young men sitting around, chatting and making tea, and I struggle to remember a time when this banal ritual was unfamiliar; the sound of liquid poured from one cup to another and back again, producing a layer of foam in each tiny glass; the contrapuntal complaints that the tea is taking too long. Memory—mine, theirs—suddenly transitions into a hip hop beat, as Duggy-T's nasal voice extends an invitation in Wolof, "Come on, let's drink tea." The beat loudens, a hint of new jack swing in its crisp snare; Duggy-T and DJ Awadi trade four-bar phrases, their French peppered with Wolof words. The song cycles through the traditional three rounds of tea, from the first bitter cup to the last cloying one, interrupted by a bridge that I described long ago as "incorporating a *balafon* and traditional singing," but whose layered wooden xylophone ostinato and male voices, still the same after all these years, now offer something more over the continuing hip hop beat: a circumcision song from southern Senegal. As we fade into the next track, a spoken exchange gives way to a call and response between kora and flute, before Duggy-T begins to sing in English.

While Senegalese hip hoppers generally credit Mbacke Dioum and MC Lida with recording the first original Senegalese rap songs, PBS is widely considered the first group to establish Senegalese hip hop as more than a novelty. As DJ Awadi tells it, when he met Duggy-T, who would become his partner in the renowned hip hop duo, the two were in competing dance squads in high school in Sacré Couer, where Duggy-T had recently moved after a childhood spent in France. After meeting at Awadi's birthday party and freestyling together, they combined their groups into one: Positive Black Soul.

Years before Awadi built the SICAP studio where we met, he and Duggy-T produced their first songs, rapping over the B side of US hip hop records, capturing both the instrumental and their own lyrics on cassette recorders. This all changed in 1992, when Senegalese-French rapper MC Solaar came to Senegal to play at the French Cultural Center in downtown Dakar and asked PBS to open for him. The following year, he invited them to France. Sprawled across from me in his red plush chair, Awadi reminisced in flawless French, "He had talked a lot about us and there was a buzz. For us it was a dream, signing with Island Mango, the label of Bob Marley. When we went to sign our contract, they put us on Air France, first class. Imagine: two little rappers from the neighborhood."

Salaam's layering of hip hop beats, R&B vocals, traditional instruments, indigenous and colonial languages, and Afrocentric imagery sound the convergence of multidirectional global movements that marked a turning point in Senegalese hip hop. Back in the courtyard of his house, Xuman's faultless French matched Awadi's as he said, "The first rap album was in 1990, there were only two. Afterward PBS came with a compilation released in Europe, and from that moment it permitted people to pay more attention to rap."

Following close on PBS's heels—and working with them—Xuman's group, Pee Froiss, released their own international album. Daara J was not far behind. International connections opened local doors for these early groups to record new instrumental tracks in professional Dakar studios. This music, the earliest mainstream hip hop in Senegal, was a hybrid of globalized diasporic genres that blended rapping with reggae–dance hall and R&B, in the singer-rapper-toaster format that would become a defining feature of the era. Cosmopolitan Senegalese audiences, I'm told, appreciated this hip hop that was filtered through familiar musical styles, from indigenous sounds to the imported reggae and R&B they'd been listening to for decades. I imagine that international audiences heard a music just foreign enough, in keeping with the world music craze of the time, to neutralize hip hop's subversive potential. Senegalese hip hop was coming into its own on a local and global stage.

Perhaps the most thorough retelling of this history came from television and radio personality Y.Dee, an avid follower of US hip hop and a fount of knowledge about the local scene. On the street outside his family home in Sipres, his coordinated, crisp white bucket hat and Jordans were like a beacon, drawing me to him even before he waved (Fig. 2.4). I'd come to expect that Y.Dee speak not a word of French or Wolof with me. Years at the British Institute may be responsible for his fluent English, but his inflections and word choices, his careful subversions of Standard English grammar, perform a version of American Blackness indirectly accessed through hip hop artifacts. He tells me his own story: his years at the same high school in downtown Dakar as many of the Medina rappers, his role as the founder of Senegal's Tupac Fan Club in the 1990s. He is assertively friendly, pleased to be conversing with an American about his greatest passion. I shift the conversation, and he obliges, recounting a now-familiar history,

> I can't tell you early, in the beginning, but what I know is the first rapper in Senegal, who first came out with a record on TV and on the radio, was Mbacke Dioum. Mbacke Dioum was the first one to come out with a record. And after that we had uhhhhhm, Positive Black Soul . . .
>
> That was the late '80s, early '90s. After that we had MC Lida, and after MC Lida we had Daara J, and from then, you know, some other crews start coming out like Daara J, like Pee Froiss, what else, VIB, they used to live in Reubeuss, Ruebeuss is the neighborhood where I used to live before we come here [*he gestures to the apartment*] you know, VIB . . .

FIGURE 2.4 Y.Dee on the balcony of his family home.

His voice trails off and he murmurs, "I miss my niggas, I haven't talked to them for a while . . . " and then he continues,

> And who else, who else, who else—we had Boul N'Baï, we had Da Brains.
> And at that time, the suburbs, actually, they only had BMG forty four.

He translates this back into French, quickly, like an aside to himself, "BMG quarante-quartre."

> That was the only hardcore crew coming out of the suburb. But all the rest of the crew in Senegal, they was coming from this side. When I say this side, I mean like CAP-SI [SICAP] Medina, Grand Dakar, Plateau, Sacré Couer or whatever, you know. But today we got more rappers coming from the suburb than this side. And they think hip hop's—they own hip hop. They own Senegalese hip hop. Because they repping it. They are repping hip hop like no one else. That's what they think. And they don't understand one thing. Like—

He pauses to gather his thoughts.

> They have the voice today to do what they doing from the elders. And who are the elders?
> Positive Black Soul.
> Daara J.
> Pee Froiss.
> Yatfu.
> Crews like Rap'Adio.

A few weeks later, I found myself on what was beginning to feel like a wild goose chase for one of those elders: Drygun, of Yatfu. It wasn't easy to find his store, Galsen Shop, the only one-stop destination for local and imported streetwear in Dakar; the taxi circled the neighborhood a few times before I recognized the boutique's signature graffiti from across a divided street (Fig. 2.5). He greets me on the sidewalk with a smile and handshake, offering and preparing instant coffee before we settle in for our interview, carefully framed in front of an array of merchandise (Fig. 2.6). T-shirts from local hip hop clothing lines cover the walls: Banc Lieux Arts, Trust Yourself, Mbeddu Djolof. Assorted Nikes are prominently displayed in front of the door.

FIGURE 2.5 Galsen Shop.

FIGURE 2.6 Drygun at Galsen Shop.

Drygun begins, in effortless French,

Yeah. Um, we'll start off first of all by saying, "hello Catty," ok?

And I think that hip hop, I heard it when I was really, really little, because to begin with, I grew up in a musical family, we love music and everything.

So, the first time I listened to hip hop I was really young, I was really young, and we won't hide that it was always due to an influence from the United States that we listened to certain songs, that we listened to certain movements, certain rhythms, and later there were hits, and all, and we discovered that this was hip hop.

It was when I was really little, because I started with dance.

I clarify that he was dancing to American rap, and he continues, "yes there was Public Enemy, there was Afrika Bambaataa, *voila* it was good, there was Kool Herc." "Old school!" I interject, and he agrees,

You see it was really the old school. The old school, and—

He cuts himself off, starts over,

To back up a little bit, I want to say hello, Catty, and what's more I'd like to introduce myself first!

Because I didn't do it.

So, this is Drygun, from the group Yatfu, made up of Gofu and Jojo, we are three in the group, which has existed since 1995, and we put out our first album in '98, and at that time I was a dancer with two other groups, there was Jojo, Gofu, and Big D.

Drygun reminisces about when Big D left the group in 2000 and Drygun took his place, a natural choice considering his passion for writing lyrics after his heyday as a breakdancer in the early 1990s. He brings us back,

So, to return to your question, so the old school is the reason, because we are part of the old-school groups in the Senegalese hip hop movement.

So when they say PBS, Daara J, they say Pee Froiss, there is always Yatfu, there is Rap'Adio.

Voila, we will say that those are the five old-school groups who are here, who put in their time, and there is also BMG 44, an old-school group who put in their time.

And we are part of the big names, because we've put out three albums and we're about to put out the fourth.

OK?

So that's why I talked to you about Kool Herc, Kool Moe D, Afrika Bambaataa, Public Enemy, all that.

Because, quite simply, I was in the hip hop movement very early, and I was accompanied by—it's true that I'm not very old, it's true that I'm still young, but early on I hung around guys who were older than me who immersed me in hip hop.

As Drygun outlines hip hop's trajectory, intently focused on the camera, he offers a corrective, inserting the hardcore into the old school. His telling implicitly aggregates early hip hop groups into two categories: PBS, Daara J, and Pee Froiss on the one side, and Rap'Adio, Yatfu, and Waa BMG 44 on the other. Even as the former were bringing hip hop to Senegalese audiences for the first time in the early 1990s, the latter drove a musical subcurrent through the working-class neighborhoods on the fringes of downtown and at the outskirts of the city—one that would swell to bursting in 1998 when these three groups released their first albums. In Medina, the overpopulated, colonially designated "native quarter," rappers Keyti, Iba, and Bibson (formerly of Pee Froiss), under the moniker Rap'Adio, wrote music inspired by the politicized hip hop of US groups like Public Enemy. As Keyti told it,

> For years we were so frustrated, because all of the people we started with, like PBS, Pee Froiss, Sunu Flavor, they had all released albums, people knew about them, they became superstars, they were organizing big concerts while we were still in the underground.
>
> We had that frustration but we were like, we're not changing what we're doing. Our time will come.

Rap'Adio's album, *Ku Weet Xam SA Bop* [One Knows Oneself in Solitude] favored Wolof over French and emphatic rapping over the melodic refrains, singing, and toasting of earlier hip hop records. Yatfu and Waa BMG 44 released albums with similar aesthetics the same year, generating a new, hardcore hip hop identity. Keyti continued,

> I started the group with Iba in '92 and we released our album in '98, that was six years while the others were known, touring, going to Europe, and we were still in the underground. We released that album in '98 and a lot of things had changed. Because when Kocc 6 left, he went to Pee Froiss with Xuman and

Bibson, and then after Pee Froiss separated and Bibson came to Rap'Adio, it was like we were exchanging elements. Time proved us right, because when we released that first album in '98 it changed the whole rap scene.

As Keyti says, membership in these early groups shifted frequently, as rappers matured and diverged in their musical styles. Women were a part of this first wave, often in association with particular groups or collectives—Fatim with Waa BMG 44, Lady Sinay and the other women of Jafaroy within Rap'Adio's collective Cartel Underground; but unlike their contemporaries, women's stints as rappers were fairly short, often due to social pressure to marry and have children.

By the time I got to Senegal in 2007, these hardcore groups had mentored a new generation of rappers who, while noting the influence of PBS, Daara J, and Pee Froiss, as well as exposure to foreign hip hop, all described 1998 as a pivotal moment in Rap Galsen. In the Medina blocks between the noisy markets of Colobane and Tilene, young men growing up near Rap'Adio in the mid-1990s coalesced into Cartel Underground, a collective of emerging rappers that included, among others, Bis bi Clan, Sen Kumpë, 5kiem Underground, and Lady Sinay.

THE STREET

On a sunny afternoon during Ramadan in 2011, I meet Djily Bagdad in the street about a block from his family home in Medina (Fig. 2.7). We exchange familiar greetings, he asking after my parents, I after his 5kiem Underground partner, Baye Njagne. We set up on the sidewalk, trading the heat and dimness inside the house for a sonic backdrop of horns, engines, and buggy wheels from Avenue Blaise Diagne, which travels southeast, toward downtown, and northwest, toward the university and eventually the SICAP neighborhoods. As we talk, small children cluster behind him, some staring into the camera, others carefully positioning themselves in its range while pretending not to see it. He shoos them away; in a few minutes, others take their place.

Like Y.Dee, he speaks fluent English that incorporates elements of African American Vernacular English, but here the cadence is more natural, less self-aware, signaling the several years he spent studying in Atlanta as a youth. That was before the 1994 devaluation of the West African franc that left many Senegalese students abroad unable to finish their studies, and before the rigorous visa restrictions imposed after September 11, 2001. Here in Medina, armed with my own ideas about ghettoized urban space, I ask him about the importance of neighborhoods in Rap Galsen; there's a moment of confusion, as I can't for the life of me think of the English word for *quartiers*, and I finally ask the question in French. He says

FIGURE 2.7 Djily Bagdad in front of his home in Medina.

that it's very important, that a rapper's reputation can depend on where he's from, which block, which part of town. He says that "Medina is known to be, like, a big, like, big project type."

Global hip hop myth filters understandings of local urban experience. The US music videos and films that circulated to Dakar in the 1980s and 1990s foregrounded the often harsh realities of the US inner city, with an increasing emphasis on ghetto imagery that would render the street a "symbolic and mythical construct" as much as a literal origin for hip hop culture (Forman 2002, 84).[3] As the ghetto became synonymous with hip hop authenticity, US rappers reclaimed urban space and counteracted the stigma of a very real lived poverty, even as they played into dominant constructions of Black youth as dangerous and violent (Forman 2002; Rose 1992).[4] Around the world, hip hoppers have adopted the discourse of the mythical ghetto while adjusting it to local realities;[5] hearing how Rap Galsen's early vocabulary echoes that of early French hip hop, for example (e.g., calling dance *smurf,* an emphasis on the hardcore), it seems likely that ideas of the ghetto came from both the United States and France (see Prévos 2001, 903). Hip hop, then, does not just describe the ghetto; rather, as specific experiences of urban marginalization are read and made sense of through hip hop texts from the United States, the very word *ghetto* takes on meaning through hip hop genre (Bakhtin 1986; Bauman 2004).

Djily Bagdad hesitates, lands on his comparison between Medina and a housing project, and continues.

So, when you come from Medina, people be like, "oh people out there are grimy people, they too shady in Medina, there's a lot of bad people, there's a lot of drugs, lot of violence," that's what they say, that Medina is like that.

And it's very popular, like, a lot of people, you know?

Lot of kids and everything.

So when you come from this type of block or this type of area, before even saying anything you have a little respect, they respect you because you come from this side of town.

Djily's designation of his neighborhood as "popular" is an English-language rendering of *quartiers populaires,* as present-day Medina and its surrounding neighborhoods—Fass, Colobane, and Grand Dakar—are called, in reference to their working-class populations and sheer volume of inhabitants.[6] In the early twentieth century, the French displaced large numbers of indigenous people to Medina from their former homes on the Plateau, the prime area of land that would become the city's downtown.[7] They never properly developed the new quarter, which was constructed on poor land and prone to flooding (Bett 1971, 152; Antoine et al. 1995, cited in Morales-Libove 2005). Compounding this physical segregation, the French categorized European zones as "urban" zones and African zones as "non-urban," discursively excluding the indigenous population from modernization by characterizing them as rural, no matter their location (Bigon 2009, 226). By mid-century, however, Medina and its surrounding neighborhoods were home to multiple generations of city-dwellers who occupied a somewhat privileged social standing vis-à-vis new rural migrants, as Dakar's population continued to swell in the postwar period. In 1950, nearly half a century after France moved its center of colonial operations from the northern city of Saint-Louis to Dakar, the SICAP was formed in response to a shortage of housing for French administrative and military personnel, as well as elite Africans in those roles (Ndiaye 2011, 57).

The spatial marginality of Medina, constructed on the periphery of the colonial city, echoed thirty years later in the construction of Dakar's banlieues, underserviced and underdeveloped neighborhoods on the margins of the city. As urban migration increased in the interwar and then post-World War II periods, Medina was bursting at the seams, as was the more recently constructed Grand Dakar, yet a step farther out from Plateau. In response, the banlieue of Pikine was constructed twenty kilometers from Plateau, and parcels of land were granted to those urban residents (not rural migrants) willing to move farther from the city center and build homes (Verniere 1973, 217). The banlieues have since expanded to include Parcelles Assainies, Guédiawaye, and Thiaroye. Like Y.Dee, hip hoppers who spoke English used the word *suburb* to refer to the banlieues, urban neighborhoods that more closely resemble the US inner city than its suburbs; an inner city on the outskirts of the metropolis.[8] The quality of life in the banlieues and quartiers populaires declined further in the wake of the structural adjustment programs of the 1980s, which led to rising rates of unemployment and reduced funding for social services, negatively affecting education, healthcare, basic sanitation, and average income (Morales-Libove 2005, 48).

Held up to these histories like a dull mirror, hip hop depictions of the US ghetto cast back identifiable shapes whose details are blurred. These reflections of marginalization bolster local claims to hip hop realness. Djily says,

> Like, where rich people are, like in Almadies, Fann Residence, and stuff like that, when somebody comes from out there saying he's an MC people are like "please, man, you're living a very good life, you have no problems, why you wanna rap, whatchu gonna rap about," you know?
>
> And then, they be like [*his voice changes, pitched up, as he impersonates these anonymous rappers*], "man we're gonna rap about our good life, about just, our partying, and bling bling, nice cars, stuff like that."
>
> But people usually don't appreciate that.
>
> They want to listen to people who come, like, from the hood, from the ghetto, the dungeon and stuff like that.
>
> They appreciate emcees coming from like the popular areas of the city better than people coming from the nice and rich area.

Months later, Djily's words echoed in my mind as I spoke with Kalif, of Undershifaay, one of the first rap groups from the Guédiawaye banlieue, who said,

> Hip hop, no matter what we say, is a music of the street.
>
> It's a music of the street.
>
> So the quartiers where the street doesn't live, hip hop doesn't live; this is logical.

(I recall the places where the street doesn't live, the quiet sidewalks of SICAP Amitié II, the road that runs by the mosque in Liberté VI with not a person in sight.)

> So, I, I don't know, I would say that I had the luck to grow up in Guédiawaye, [*he laughs*] you see, a quartier where in fact, you have Senegalese reality, you have everything in this quartier . . .

And we don't regret this, because what I lived is what forged us, it gave us this experience.

For example, when people respect my group in terms of its culture, its verbs, and all that, it's thanks to Guédiawaye, because everything we recount, in fact it's this quartier that forged us, that gave us things to live and things to feel and things to truly convey, you see.

Also, it's because Dakar is a big banlieue.

Dakar is a big banlieue.

When people say "banlieue," that doesn't only mean Parcelles, no; even downtown it's the banlieue!

That's the banlieue, that's a banlieue, you see, we have almost the same lives, you see, a young person from Guédiawaye or a young person from Fass or Colobane it's practically the same, we have the same reality . . .

so when I say Guédiawaye, it's really the street of Dakar.

The quartiers populaires and the banlieues: the street of Dakar, Rap Galsen's reflection and re-sounding of the hip hop ghetto, a complex of specific spatial relationships of local and global domination set in motion by colonialism and continuing into the present. "Just as urban space and its infrastructures were produced unevenly in the colonial period in an effort to control populations," write Rosalind Fredericks and Mamadou Diouf, "so do infrastructures in the postcolonial city manifest governmental prerogatives and unequal citizenship across the urban landscape" (2014, 7). Mapping the specificity of urban experience is an important corrective to hip hop's global ghetto, not least because, as the history of Dakar demonstrates, spatial relationships are also relationships of power (Forman 2002, 6, 42).

The staggered hardcore wave of Senegalese rappers from the mid-1990s onward invoked their neighborhoods of origin as the hip hop underground, claiming a hip hop realness defined through experiences of the street that they felt earlier groups like PBS could not claim. If most youth were socially underground vis-à-vis elders (including the state), those growing up in the quartiers populaires and the banlieues were doubly marginalized. The street came to stand for this marginalization within marginalization, the basis of a new hip hop authenticity sounded through hardcore aesthetics.

SOUNDING THE UNDERGROUND

I'm more than a decade late to Rap'Adio's first album, *Ku Weet Xam SA Bop*; I didn't know to go looking for it until rapper after rapper flagged it for me in interviews and conversations. By the time I listen to one of its oft-cited tracks, "Xabaaru 1-2-Ground [News of the *un-deux*-ground/un-da-ground/Underground]," the ambiguity that marked my early encounters with Positive Black Soul has dissipated. The song opens with men's and women's voices playfully exchanging the group's name, yelling it, spelling it out, quietly chirping it, chanting it in call and response. Bibson places us in time—"ci atu un-neuf-neuf-huite [in the year 1998]"—his voice slightly anticipating the track's fall into a simple beat; based primarily on a drum kit sample, punctuated with horn and flute riffs, it never emerges from behind the vocals. Keyti takes over, launching into the first verse. He crams words into bars, swift, overwhelming percussive wordplay, vulgar language: clashing other rappers, likening himself to folk hero Lat Dior's struggle against the French in the nineteenth century, moving quickly to denouncing the poor quality of life in the quartiers populaires, so quickly that, like time travelers, we hear the link between anticolonial struggle and contemporary urban marginalization in Dakar, where Rap'Adio is "exploding like a nuclear bomb," like a bird whose wings have been freed, escaping its cage. His rapid battery of Wolof continues, "Do re mi fa sol la, emcees yu bëri fong ne mbir mi fo la [a lot of emcees think this thing is a game]" but it's not—not a joke, not a game, not something that's in the clothes you wear—and just like that, he returns to clashing hip hop crews who are playing around. He rattles off a mocking medley of familiar sources, quoting Daara J, "lekketi loxo yi si kow [put your hands in the air]," rapping against a second voice's exaggerated, nasal rendition of Duggy-T's melodic hook on PBS's song "Daw Thiow," throwing a jab at Sunu Flavor. I laugh aloud at the level of shade, trying to imagine my elders, *les grands* of the underground, grown collaborators and friends, as beefing teenage emcees.

A chorus of voices joins in on the chanted hook, conjugating the English "get down" into Wolof grammar:

> Ñoo ngiy ñëw di get down, ñoo ngiy ñëw di get down [We're coming and getting down, we're coming and getting down]
>
> Xabaaru 1-2 Ground yes yes ya'll [News of the underground, yes yes ya'll]
>
> Medina Big Town, Fass Big Town, Medina Big Town

It's Bibson's turn. He dedicates his verse to eviscerating other hip hop groups, likening Jant Bi to a yowling cat and singing a snippet of one of their tracks before shifting his attack to love songs. He sings a couple of bars of Daara J's music in a now-familiar nasal timbre, "lay lay lay lay lay beggel and loving," and then jumps to criticizing rappers for failing to address political corruption. He leads us back into the refrain with "we're making real hip hop." In the final verse, Iba continues clashing other artists, scolding emcees to either make real rap or join a circle of women performing praise poetry, or *taasu*. I wince in appreciation even as I perk up at the reference. If only I'd understood Wolof all those years ago, or known to look for these recordings . . . Beneath it all, the beat cycles back predictably, over and over again, withholding even the suggestion of a melodic respite from the tireless barrage of words.

Gaston, formerly of Sen Kumpë and one of the voices that I heard on the hook to "Xabaaru 1-2-Ground," was one of many rappers mentored by Rap'Adio in their early days. As we set up for an interview on the roof of his studio in Parcelles Assainies in 2011, he breaks the silence to ask, with exaggerated concern, if he isn't too ugly to film. I turn the screen of the camera toward him and he playfully fixes his dreadlocks before okaying the image (Fig. 2.8). We've hardly begun before he interrupts himself to greet me formally and thank me for the interview. Then we're back to talking about his first encounters with hip hop as a child in France, listening to French rappers. It was when he returned to Dakar in 1994 and began to spend time with Rap'Adio's Iba, who introduced him to groups like Das EFX, the Wu-Tang Clan, and others, that he really got into hip hop. I ask him to tell me about how hip hop started in Senegal, and he responds,

There are people like Keyti, Iba, Kocc 6, Mbacke Dioum who were the first rappers to rap here—they can really respond to that question.

But I can only say that I started to get into rap in '94, and at that time PBS had just—

FIGURE 2.8 Gaston on the roof of Def Dara Studio in Parcelles Assainies.

that's to say, that in terms of big groups, we can't talk about African rap in general without citing PBS, because they were the big names, so, *voila.*

And then I frequented Rap'Adio because they were also the elders, so they just taught me, that is to say, the evolution of hip hop a bit.

He traces some of the complicated trading of members between Pee Froiss and Rap'Adio, back in the day, and then continues,

So what I can say, and all I can say about this, is that the history of rap, it was born, that's to say, the first groups who did rap were the ones I just told you about, Mbacke Dioum, MC Lida, and then PBS, Daara J—

but when we talk about real rap, not real rap but underground rap, it was through Rap'Adio that there was a real change.

In the beginning, it was rap that was rather, [*he breathes out in hesitation*] it wasn't engaged, engaged, engaged—

(*Engagé, engagé, engagé;* in Gaston's characteristic quirk of repeating words to communicate the extent to which they signal—or don't—what they are meant to, I hear the refrain of repetitions of this word, *engagé,* a thread that runs through the underground, a declaration of social implication, a local rendering of global hip hop myths of social consciousness.)

—it was not very social.

Rap'Adio brought this social side, this engaged side, this side of research into writing.

So Rap'Adio brought this wave.

But before, we knew Daara J, we knew Pee Froiss, and that wasn't really the rap that we took.

When I finally meet Keyti of Rap'Adio fame, he is taking time out from a rehearsal with his new band to talk with me. Despite his open welcome, I'm a little in awe, and I nervously set up my camera and recorder under an awning in the courtyard outside the house where they are working. He sits across from me, leaning forward in his chair, hands clasped in front of him as he looks intently into the camera (Fig. 2.9). In nearly perfect English, he tells me about how he came to hip hop; that as a teenager in the mid-1990s, he hid his texts, feeling ashamed of what he wrote. But, he says,

FIGURE 2.9 Keyti, taking a break from rehearsal to talk.

The first time, really the first time some people saw what I was writing, they couldn't believe that I wrote it, it was in *Wolof,* 'cause contrary to a lot of people here, most of the rappers here, like, people like Awadi, Duggy-T, Xuman, all of those people who started hip hop here, they started rapping in English.

I never started rapping in English, I started directly writing in Wolof.

A few weeks earlier, as the light began to fade in the courtyard of Xuman's home, he himself had marked this linguistic shift as a turning point in Senegalese hip hop, saying,

And also, before, we rapped in French and in English.

And as we were rapping in French, and in English, it was not clear—

the audience—

most people didn't necessarily understand.

They thought we were copying Americans, they thought that we were doing the same thing as Americans.

So, it took time for us to start speaking Wolof, for us to start rapping in Wolof, so that the audience could understand what we were saying.

So, Wolof-language rap began to be used in Senegal, that's when the public began to listen, and when the public began to listen we began to talk about things that were much more interesting; we began to speak about politics, we began to speak of struggle, we began to speak of things that, *voila*, things that belong to Senegal, you see?

On Pee Froiss' 1997 track "Lara Biranane," Xuman raps in Wolof about the *taalibe*, young boys who, orphaned or given up by their families, beg in the streets to finance their lodging and Qu'ranic education. Kocc 6 sings the plaintive Wolof-language refrain over an R&B beat full of arpeggiated guitar phrases. And yet, despite its local relevance and linguistic intelligibility, at the time such music was criticized as commercial and inauthentic by rappers setting themselves up as the underground, in a dynamic that would become central to Rap Galsen's origin myth.

In the middle of the summer in 2011, I again take a taxi to Medina, this time to meet Baye Njagne, of 5kiem Underground. I remember where to get out from when I visited Djily Bagdad's home; when I call to tell Baye Njagne I'm on his street, he comes out to find me where I'm standing in the sweltering heat. His broad smile belies a slight shyness, despite the years we've known each other. We walk slowly until we reach the welcome shelter of his home, where he sits in the open doorway of his small bedroom, leaving the mattress to me (Fig. 2.10). His discomfort with our French conversation dissipates with the clumsy tone of my questions and my own grateful resort to Wolof words from time to time. He recalls growing up in Medina, coming under the wing of Rap'Adio as part of their collective, Cartel Underground; he remembers going around with Gaston and Bourba. He tells me

FIGURE 2.10 Baye Njagne in his room in Medina.

that the collective was powerful, that it "wreaked havoc" at shows, that people noticed and would say, "They don't do soul, they don't do reggae, but they are rappers, guys who do rap."

A few months later, Keyti described his first connection with Rap'Adio co-founder Iba as someone who was "doing hardcore rap like mine, no melodies, much more focused on saying what we want to say, saying the truth as it is and as we feel it . . . me and Iba were always like, we got to talk about politics. It's the Public Enemy influence."

The Public Enemy influence went beyond lyrics. Public Enemy's beats were not just a medium for radical lyrical content; they signaled a break from earlier, party-oriented traditions of hip hop at a time—the late 1980s—when the post–civil rights rhetoric of racial equality was fundamentally mismatched with the lived realities of racial minorities in the United States (Kajikawa 2015, 51). In turn, Rap'Adio and other hardcore groups offered aggressively rapped hooks in place of mainstream groups' local musical references, reggae-inspired toasting, and R&B-inspired melodic refrains; their instrumental tracks were virtually indistinguishable from those being produced in the United States in the mid-1990s. And so, this real hip hop, this music of the street, was not a music that was audibly, musically local. In fact, it was deliberately *not* local. This hardcore musical style, coupled with Wolof-language critiques of political and social structures and physical posturing, produced a music that was as unappetizing to international audiences as it was locally subversive.

Lyrical representations of the street merged with and emerged from aural ones; hip hop texts and beats locked in symbiosis to sound the underground.

MAPPING THE UNDERGROUND

I remember that concert in Kaolack, in 2008. An hour before the show would finally begin, baseball caps and carefully folded fresh T-shirts appear as though from nowhere around the room. Rappers exchange their sandals for Nike and Adidas sneakers. Lady Sinay appears in a fresh pink top, with matching laces in her black high-tops. I grimace at my own rumpled T-shirt and jeans, stretched from having been slept in, and regret not having washed my hair before leaving Dakar. With the Jolof4Life rappers—Simon, 5kiem Underground, Sen Kumpë, Tigrim Bi, and Zair ak Batine—we finally head to the venue. Looking a mess, camera in hand, I watch with Bourba and Books backstage as Sinay struts out to begin her first performance in several years (Fig. 2.11).

After her short set, I am escorted—I can't remember by whom, it must have been Lamine Ndao—to a prime seat in front of the stage; this will become a

FIGURE 2.11 Lady Sinay waits to perform in Kaolack, 2008.

familiar sequence, as artists choose the vantage point for my photos and videos. Sen Kumpë appears, the two brothers rousing the crowd as they shout, "Medina in the house!" The groups support each other just as they had the previous week, in the middle of the night on a poorly lit stage set up in the middle of a Medina street, wearing matching Jolof4Life T-shirts in various colors, weaving in and out of each other's performances, hyping up the crowd (Fig. 2.12).

A week or so after the concert in Kaolack, the sun is going down as I leave Djily Bagdad's home, where both he and Baye Njagne, who were still 5kiem Underground back then, have given me interviews for my project. They leave us at the corner. Bourba, Books, Lamine Ndao, and I continue walking slowly through the streets, fairly calm and cool at this hour, cutting across the brief bustle of Avenue Blaise Diagne and past Marché Tilene before turning into the quieter blocks before Rue 22 and home. Medina's even grid of streets always gives me a feeling of relief in a city as apparently disorganized as Dakar. Yet, even in its orderly sprawl, this ten-minute walk is long enough that these two groups of men might easily never have met if not for the hip hop events that they all frequented at the neighborhood's Miami Club in the mid-1990s.

The hardcore elements of Rap Galsen's old school ignited a musical movement in Dakar's quartiers populaires and banlieues. Hip hop took on a life and identity

FIGURE 2.12 Jolof4Life groups Zair ak Batine and Sen Kumpë on stage in Kaolack, 2008.

of its own, in and of the street, where it renewed neighborhood ties even as it facilitated cross-neighborhood connections. "The street" became more than a reference to urbanity; it connected youth who, despite the kilometers between them, shared a feeling of social invisibility. These connections would become vitally important as youth at the turn of the century rode hip hop into the political spotlight and eventually a begrudging mainstream acceptance.

As hip hop radiated outward from its multiple centers, the studio and the stage mediated these new social relationships. Themed compilations, hip hop collectives, and guest featuring—when one rapper records a verse on another's song—spun immediate neighborhood ties into a web connecting the quartiers populaires to the banlieues. When Bis bi Clan's Simon returned from France in 2000, determined to start his own Senegalese branch of the French 99-Records label, his first recruits were his friends from Medina and former Rap'Adio protégées: Sen Kumpë, 5kiem Underground, and Zair ak Batine, whose members had been part of Bis bi Clan with Simon. The label's fourth group was Tigrim Bi, from Pikine.

By the time I met Sen Kumpë in 2008, its founding members, Baye Sene (aka Gaston) and Bourba Djolof, who had started rapping together in 1996 with Cartel Underground, had long gone their separate ways, and Bourba had been joined by younger brother Books to reconstitute the group, with their neighbor Lamine Ndao as manager. After Bourba passed away in 2010, Books continued performing solo under the name Sen Kumpë. For a while, his friend Madou from the neighboring area, Colobane, provided backup for him at concerts while also forming his own rap duo, KTD Crew, with another lifelong friend and neighbor, Alou. In the meantime, Gaston, the second founding member of Sen Kumpë, established Def Dara recording studio in the Parcelles Assainies banlieue. Almamy, Sen Kumpë's neighbor in Medina, nephew of Rap'Adio's Iba, and Books's former musical partner, eventually paired with rapper Falsower, who hails not from Medina but from Grand Yoff, to form the duo 23.3 Wisdom Connection.

The first wave of hardcore rappers had changed the landscape of hip hop in Dakar, ushering in a new identity for the genre and fostering hip hop connections throughout the city. They had transformed their imposed locality into a badge of honor, and rendered it audible through language, lyrics, and musical aesthetics. Ironically, however, the performance of hardcore identities ultimately drove the growing hip hop movement of the mid- to late-1990s truly underground.

In his family apartment in Sipres, as Y.Dee continued recounting Senegalese hip hop's history, his narrative soured,

Yo, they came out with some hardcore albums. Because before Rap'Adio came out, they used to say that Senegalese hip hop, you know, it was all about fun, they not doing what they supposed to do; "how you gonna come out with some hip hop record and you got girls dancing to it," that's what they used to say, like, you know. To *them*, that wasn't hip hop. "A true hip hop record, a girl doesn't have to shake her ass to it." You know. I was like, I'm sorry, but at that time we was a little young, and we didn't understand too much stuff, but now that, you know, we're getting older, we're starting to understand many things. But, Rap'Adio, when they album came out, it did a lot of good for Senegalese hip hop. But also a lot of bad things for hip hop, for Senegalese hip hop.

I ask what he means, and he responds,

Um, because if you don't curse or if you don't diss a rapper or if you don't diss the government or if you don't talk about what the society is living—

I mean, even before that, some other rappers like Xuman, like Pee Froiss, like Positive Black Soul, Daara J, they was all talking about a lot of negativity that used to, you know, that the country used to live, the community used to live, you know what I'm saying.

But not the way Rap'Adio came out with it, Rap'Adio came out with it, aggressively.

You know what I'm saying?

Rap'Adio, they came out aggressively.

Like, "yo, don't talk, if you really wanna talk about that shit, talk about it straight up, don't be nice with it," you know what I mean, 'cause that was they mentality, you know what I mean.

Since they came out, a lot of rappers today they don't have the nerve to come out with some love song, you thinking people not gonna love it or if I do it they gonna diss me or somebody gonna, you know what I mean, talk bad about me or whatever.

And that was a shame, because before Rap'Adio came out, every other artist that used to put out an album, albums used to sell like hell, because at that time everybody, old, young, boys and girls, everybody was listening to hip hop.

When I say listening, I mean they was *listening* to it, you know what I mean, from all angles, you know, to the radio, to TV, and every time there was a show, people were buying tickets to go to see the show.

Shows were *packed* back then. But now, to have a full show, to pack a concert, it has to be a free show.

As hip hop became more hardcore, its performances were largely relegated to open-air spaces, with obvious complications arising during the rainy season.[9] When I lived in Dakar in 2011–2012, a lack of quality materials led most rappers to perform *playback* (rapping into an open mic over the instrumental and vocal tracks), despite a preference for live performance. The often-massive number of groups desiring to perform at any given concert created a situation in which rappers were limited to performing one or two songs, and their performances were often cut even shorter due to "technical difficulties," where, at the prompting of concert organizers, CDs mysteriously stopped playing or microphones were inexplicably shut off.

As hip hop concerts became notorious for violence and harassment, and hip hop songs grew increasingly unpalatable to the wider Senegalese public, who were accustomed to the melodies of mbalax music and international hip hop, Rap Galsen became increasingly inhospitable to young women. While girls did continue to listen to hip hop, the shift towards open-air shows drastically reduced their presence in hip hop spaces, because, as Sen Kumpë's manager Lamine Ndao told me, "it doesn't seem safe, or because they are harassed and when they resist being hit on, people are vulgar towards them." I asked rapper Almamy about women's seeming absence from the hip hop scene, one day as we sat together in his room, just around the corner from Sen Kumpë in Medina, and maybe a ten-minute walk from the family homes of 5kiem Underground's members. He gestured toward a photograph, pinned to the wall, of his uncle Iba, formerly of Rap'Adio.

In the beginning, long before Rap'Adio, there were so many girls at concerts.

But now, you see [*as he continues, his smile sweetens the timbre of his voice*] when the Rap'Adio movement came, they were too engaged; they came, they used swear words, and they put—

there was a bit of violence, because Rap'Adio's fans were brutal and would even attack other groups—

they imposed their rap and they imposed their audience.

And during this period, there were many people, fathers, who refused to let their daughters go to concerts, because, they said, "rap is a violent music! If you go there you risk being attacked, you risk being hurt,"

and so after that, girls told themselves, "ah, since this music is a violent music"—

which is false, rap is not a violent music, but since they had an idea of rap, that's how many girls judged it to be—

but even now there are certain girls who stayed and who still come to concerts.

You can't go to a rap concert and not find girls.

If hardcore aesthetics and posturing had driven hip hop underground, however, its underground ideals and self-implication in simmering political change brought it at least partially back into the national spotlight. But Rap Galsen has had a varied and uneven relationship to the state. Sitting in the doorway of his bedroom in Medina, Baye Njagne's seeming shyness finally dissipated, his words quickening with confidence as he told me,

Rap in this moment is recognized on a political level.

We sense that the young rappers are here.

In 2000 it was the PDS [Parti Démocratique Sénégalais] regime that was here.

It was in 2000 that the PDS came and ravaged—and took the election.

But in that moment we wanted change.

That's what Abdoulaye Wade had promised, change—*sopi sopi* means change—and what we, the youth, also wanted: a change.

They coincided, you see.

We were there with hard words, you see, rap music was really serious in that moment, people said things that really, if you said that when the PS [Parti Socialiste] was still in power, rappers would be dead or in prison because rappers said things.

They denounced.

They bothered.

But while respecting the rules and saying that truth is true.

So we came, the PS fell, the PDS came.

Like that, Mr. Abdoulaye Wade, when he held his rallies he had rappers there, he knew that we could do major work when it came to this.

Baye Njagne described a pivotal moment in Senegalese political history. Since its independence from France in 1960, the country had known only two presidents, from a single party (the Socialist Party). Leading up to the 2000 elections, presidential candidate Abdoulaye Wade gathered support for his Senegalese Democratic Party under the banner of "Change" (*Sopi* in Wolof). At that time, many rappers—not only those who considered themselves to be underground—were part of *Bul Faale*, a movement centered on ideas of youth self-determination.[10] However, the movement's figurehead, wrestler Tyson, endorsed the incumbent Abdou Diouf in the 2000 presidential elections; once politicians had compromised the movement, rappers quickly turned away from it (Havard 2009; Mbaye 2011). Independent of any formal movement, rappers performed songs criticizing Diouf's regime and encouraging youth to vote for change, often facing government retaliation.

When Wade won the election, hip hoppers were largely credited with stimulating the youth vote that had enabled his ascent to power. Hip hop enjoyed somewhat greater mainstream acceptance and an increasingly formalized social presence in the years that followed. Hip hop cultural centers emerged in the banlieues, funded by local and foreign governments, and major communications companies, like Orange, featured rappers in their promotional concerts. Nevertheless, hip hop's material marginality remained largely unchanged through the first decade of the twenty-first century.

In early 2011, Wade's controversial announcement that he would run for an unconstitutional third term was closely followed by his proposal of a bill that would enable a presidential candidate to win in the first round of elections with only 25 percent of the vote, rather than the constitutionally mandated 50 percent. As the incumbent against a fractured, multicandidate opposition, Wade could be confident of his 25 percent, and the bill was sure to pass in the parliament, dominated by his own political party. When Parliament met on June 23 to vote on the bill, youth poured into the streets in protest. From the kindling of the newly conceived Y'en a Marre movement, the M23 (*Mouvement du 23 Juin*) was born.[11]

After a turbulent year of demonstrations and widespread youth mobilization, Wade was ousted in the second round of the 2012 elections, and his former cabinet member Macky Sall was elected president. During the lead-up to the elections, Y'en a Marre made international news, particularly following on the heels of the Arab Spring and its highly audible hip hop voices. Y'en a Marre's sustained global resonance as a "hip hop movement," however, belied its quickly dwindling local relevance. And although some of its leaders were rappers, and many rappers were involved, the movement itself had little to do with hip hop as an *aural* and *musical* negotiation of the street.

REWRITING RAP GALSEN

When I asked aspiring rapper Don Zap to tell me the history of Rap Galsen, he responded that he was currently promoting a new single that gave an analysis of Senegalese hip hop, because, he said,

I realized that things have not been clear.

There's not even a definition of Senegalese hip hop.

I wanted to give the youth a history of the beginning of Senegalese hip hop until today.

So, I realized that there was a certain period of marvelous things that happened in Senegalese music, in Senegalese hip hop.

At that time, there were roughly, in each group, two guys who rapped and someone who sang. So it was roughly the same physiognomy that we encountered in each group: two guys who rap, and one who sings; and with this high voice, this beautiful voice doing the refrains, you see—at any rate, humming, in the different groups, which is what brought a large following to people who did rap.

And so, at that time, rap was listened to.

It was listened to and it was liked; the proof is that the concerts were packed, there was a great crowd beyond the speakers.

You see what I'm saying?

So, man, woman, young, old, showed up to see this new thing that was happening in Senegal. The youth were eager to follow this new thing in Senegal.

It was in '98 that we witnessed a certain rupture, when Rap'Adio said "this isn't it.

We shouldn't be talking about soft stuff every time, about love, that people dress in a very luxurious manner, because there are wrongs in society.

So it's the hardcore now.

It's the hardcore."

So it was in this moment that there was a great division between what they were doing back then, and this new wave that came, calling itself hardcore and bringing a new color to Senegalese hip hop. . . .

And so it was that truly conscious rap was born in '98.

Don Zap recites the standard origin myth for Rap Galsen—one that is as much tied to locally specific experiences of urbanization as it is to a broader global spread of a Black American musical genre. But stories come into being through their telling, and this particular story has been tweaked and adjusted to fit a strategic script. As Rap Galsen's texts, beats, and narratives of the street dialogued with globally circulating ideas of the underground, hardcore rappers self-consciously aligned their hip hop practice with dominant accounts of hip hop origins in ways that at times involved significant reimaginings of recent history.

Sitting with Keyti that day in the courtyard, I asked him the same question that I opened every interview with. "Do you remember the first time you heard rap music?" He answered, "I do very well." And then he chuckled. "Yeah."

He looks at me expectantly and drops, "Milli Vanilli." *Really?* I gasp. Pleased, he continues,

Yeah, so it's like, that's always funny to people when I say that, 'cause Milli Vanilli's not really a rap group, you know, but that's the truth.

Yeah but, the thing is at the time I really didn't know what it was but it was just cool, it was like, it was not, it was not sing—

They were not singing, but I didn't know what it was, but it was cool.

I think when I really realized that this is called rapping was when I first heard Rob Bass, it was the song, "It takes two to make a thing go right blah blah blah."

And then it went really fast; Public Enemy, Chubb Rock, people like KRS-One, 'cause that was the end of the '80s actually, end of the '80s, and there was the first FM radio in Senegal, and actually that was the only radio where you would hear, like, shows with modern music, I mean electronic music.

It was a mix of dance, techno, hip hop, you know, and that's actually, with that show there, with one guy called Aziz Coulibaly that we all discovered this new genre of music, this urban music.

But really that's where I first heard about hip hop.

I first heard some people rapping, Milli Vanilli, um, Rob Bass, and with Public Enemy, *then*, it was—

I mean usually I'm telling people, [*he lowers his voice, changes his inflection, pulls me into a conspiracy I don't yet understand, tilting his head to the side*] "yeah, I started with Public Enemy."

I stare at him, incredulous. "Because it sounds cooler?" I croak. "Yeah," he laughs, and I can't help but to laugh with him. "Yeah, it sounds cool." He sobers. "But I think the main influences I had, they came from Public Enemy."

Keyti's was my last interview in 2011, after months of meeting with rappers representing various waves and generations of Rap Galsen, carefully piecing together this narrative of its beginnings and evolution, the clash of international and hardcore rappers, and hip hop's spread throughout the city and increasing attachment to globally circulating ideas about social consciousness and the underground. It felt, at the time, like a moment of culmination, with Y'en a Marre filling the streets and the news, a testament to the underground's vitality.

It was only through my earlier contacts with younger rappers that I knew who Keyti was, enough to be nervous about meeting him, cautious about my questions, even as I was pleased to be placing the last piece in my puzzle of the story of Rap Galsen. Little matter that my painstakingly constructed story so closely matched an origin myth long recycled between rappers and western investigators, often garnered from decontextualized and formulaic interviews that are more predictable the more established the artist and the more contact they've had with journalists, filmmakers, and scholars over the years.

And then Keyti's playful commentary on these processes of mythmaking pulled a thread that threatened to unravel the whole thing.

How does Rap Galsen's myth align with its realities? Begin at the beginning, like Alice through the looking glass. Mine, like many retellings of Rap Galsen, jumps from Mbacke Dioum and MC Lida directly to PBS, Daara J, and Pee Froiss, although these were far from the only early hip hop groups popular in Senegal. There were many others, including Black Mboolo, Jant Bi, and Sunu Flavor, all now defunct. But Daara J and PBS remain the most visible, particularly to outside observers, most likely because they (or their members, in new configurations), are still making music. They are easy to locate for research and journalistic projects. They are skilled interviewees.

And what of the street? I can paint a picture of Rap Galsen organized by the structural binaries of myth: underground and commercial; affluent SICAP neighborhoods and the ghetto of the quartiers populaires and the banlieues; French/English and Wolof; superficial lyrics and social consciousness; musical hybridity and pure hip hop instrumentals. And yet things are rarely this clear cut, and despite some youthful beefing back in the day, that first generation of international and hardcore artists generally get along and collaborate as adults.

And what of hip hop resistance, of the underground as a site and agent of social change? Hip hop forays into political action did not draw on some resistant capacity inherent in the genre itself. Rather, they activated a hip hop collectivity that had historically brought youth together across the disjointed spaces of the city. The question remains, however, whether ultimately Rap Galsen's underground has in any way remedied the social invisibility that it originally mediated.

One Sunday in the middle of June, 2011, Books's sisters and I sit around a bowl of rice in the courtyard in Medina day. The men and children have eaten their fill, and now we pick away at the vegetables and burnt rice left in the bottom of the bowl while idly gossiping. When we finish, it's time to watch television and drink tea in the coolness of the darkened living room, but before we've made it to the second of three pots, Books reappears and invites me to come along to the studio. We crowd into a car with Simon and his wife, stopping to pick up brothers Bakhaw and Djiby of Da Brains in Sacré Couer. The studio is a two-room affair in someone's house, with brightly striped fabric covering the soundproofed walls and a large, wood-lined recording booth. Just as they go into the booth to record, the power goes out, and we file outside to wait for it to return.

The men start arguing about politics and why people don't vote. Djiby offers that Senegal is too divided. Thies votes for Thies, Kaolack for Kaolack, etc. Old people also tend to vote for their candidates regardless. Books quips that people vote based on photos—that he knows someone personally who votes for the most handsome candidate. Sitting there, taking notes on my cheap Nokia phone under the pretense of texting, I look up and laugh aloud at this, and the conversation derails for a minute as everyone turns their heads in surprise; Books asks—Catty, you understood that? The conversation shifts, and now they are talking about hip hop again. Simon asks why there is no government ministry for hip hop, when every rapper is making topical music, about AIDS, about hunger, about poverty. No one pays! Djiby interjects. There isn't even a night presence for hip hop on the radio or television—only during the day. The radio can't play an hour of hip hop— after only four songs, they've had enough, and it's back to mbalax. The power comes back on, and we return to the studio.

In 2011, hip hoppers estimated themselves to number around five thousand groups, an estimate that had jumped drastically from the three thousand I heard about when I first traveled to Dakar in 2007. The task of enumerating Senegalese rappers is a daunting one, and to my knowledge not one that anyone has actually undertaken. Instead, rappers' climbing self-estimations are best interpreted as a commentary on the very real swell in hip hop participation over the last decade, as hip hop has become more visible and production more democratized. Although, as an American, I found hip hop to be almost strangely well represented on local TV stations, hip hoppers resented what they saw as a discrepancy between their social presence and their media one, and they complained often that their music remained marginalized in Senegalese media and performance venues.

It's certainly true that, despite marked improvements in the quality of and access to video and audio production, releasing albums and music videos remains challenging for financial reasons. Albums don't sell, thanks to advances in home reproduction technologies—first ripping CDs and then passing MP3 files via Bluetooth or flash drives. In 2011, although rappers could register their music with the Bureau Sénégalais du Droit d'Auteur (BSDA)—the Senegalese copyright office, defunct since 2016—efforts to retrieve royalties, even when their music and videos were widely played in popular media outlets, were usually thwarted by corrupt relationships between the BSDA and television stations, where royalty "settlements" were paid in lump sums that lined the pockets of BSDA workers rather than the artists themselves. A rapper could watch his video play all year on major television stations and yet still collect minimal funds, if any, from the BSDA. While old-school rappers have been active in pushing for copyright reform, including successfully advocating for a new collective management society that was implemented in 2016 (the *Société Sénégalaise du Droit d'Auteur et des Droits Voisin*, or SODAV) it is too soon to evaluate the outcomes of the new legislation for hip hop artists.[12]

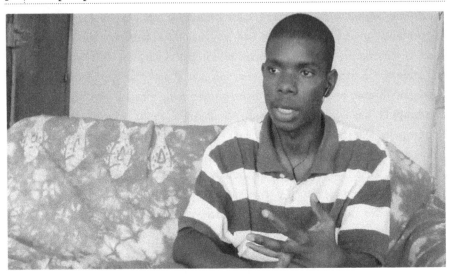

FIGURE 2.13 Amadou Fall Ba at the author's rented home in Mermoz.

In a rare moment of respite from the daily responsibilities of running the hip hop cultural center, Africulturban, Amadou Fall Ba stopped by my apartment one afternoon before he headed home so that we could film an interview (Fig. 2.13). Our exchange is riddled with humor, his responses curt and completely deadpan. Reflecting on his decades of involvement in hip hop, however, he is a bit grim:

> In terms of activity, for example, there's not a lot, because today I only know of four or three hip hop festivals here in Senegal: Festa2H, Hip Hop Awards, Rapandar, and another in Kaolack.
>
> You see, in a country of 12,000,000 people and 3,000 rap groups, which is to say, one rapper for every 4,000 inhabitants—that's also very strong—
>
> but in terms of success, in terms of money, in terms of economy, in terms of impact, it's not very—we can't measure it like this.
>
> Because, quite simply, there is no organization, there is no structuration.
>
> This can be something positive but at the same time something negative, because there is no cultural policy on the part of the state, there is no youth policy, in the town halls they don't try to work with hip hop people as in France, there is nothing, and yet hip hop exists.
>
> Even in the absence of cultural policy people try to do things.
>
> But, for this to become a business, legislation on the part of the state is necessary, to create laws and apply those laws so that everyone knows what they're about.

Today I'm the director of a festival but it pains me to say it . . .

because this simply doesn't pay, I don't earn a living from it, even if I thank God, but [*he snaps his fingers in the air*] it is very difficult because there is simply no trajectory, we don't know that if we begin at A, to arrive at Z we need to go via B, C, D; this doesn't exist.

We search for immediate solutions.

But I think, in terms of vision, today Senegalese rap has lost something, because before it was everywhere in Africa, but now if you want to travel, to see for example, in Morocco, I know that the biggest rappers in Morocco earn up to 10,000 euro.

Here, the most a Senegalese rapper will make in Dakar is between 150 and 200 euro . . .

Which is to say, in twenty years with 3000 rap groups, people know this culture well here, there is a social impact, I think we should be past where we are. I'm speaking of the economy, you see, there is no hip hop economy here.

Because people put out records that don't sell.

They play concerts, even in festivals it is difficult to pay them, because—I organize, I know what I'm talking about—because there is no money for this.

So we work for others, for the telephone and cigarette companies et cetera, and that's something else.

If we keep going like this we'll create a lot of candidates for undocumented immigration.

He talks about how much easier it is now to record albums, to make videos, to get a following on Facebook. And yet still there is no money.

It's like it's a taboo subject in hip hop—

when you say you want to make money, people will think you are whack, even though that has nothing to do with anything.

It's work; we've left school, people have left the university, there are many rappers who have children and wives, but if they don't earn money, how will they manage their families?

In Amadou's disillusionment, I saw how a mythologized concept of the underground clashes with the lived realities of Senegalese young people and their hopes to transition into social adulthood. Concepts of underground and commercialism imported from the United States don't easily map onto the financial realities of the Senegalese music industry or society, and can hold individual rappers back in their quest for the economic self-sufficiency whose lack they critique through their music. Even as aligning Rap Galsen with a mythologized underground hip hop may have helped youth claim the music as their own, that myth doesn't line up with the material necessities of their lives.[13]

This contradiction has guided Rap Galsen's shifting aesthetics and claims to voice over the past two decades. For although the street emerged at a particular moment of accelerated globalization, structural adjustment programs, and political transformation in the 1980s and 1990s, social change in Senegal began much earlier; in the coalescence and disintegration of African empires and the violent expansion of western ones; in centuries of religious conversion; in processes of urbanization and migration; and in the modernizing projects and cultural programs of the postcolonial state. The next chapter remaps the city through musical histories that predate hip hop, showing how hip hop myth intersects with indigenous oralities in contemporary Dakar. Whether in international rappers' engagement with Afrocentric narratives, which reclaim traditional performance from state and religious power (Chapter 3), or in the underground's claims to freedom of expression in the face of underdevelopment (Chapters 4 and 5), Rap Galsen negotiates social change at this intersection of musical genre, memory, and myth.

3

REMEMBERING THE GRIOT

EVERY SONG ON Positive Black Soul (PBS)'s 1996 debut album, *Salaam*, opens with a Senegalese soundscape or a snippet of local music that cedes to a globally intelligible hip hop beat. Listening again, ten years after I first heard it and twenty after its release, I find these opening moments, too, have become familiar. Leading into the third title, "Respect the Nubians," a Wolof folk song welcomes guests, wishes them peace day and night, describes sitting with them, conversing in a circle, in a togetherness so pleasant that the final lines include a preemptive counterjinx to ward off evil eyes and tongues. In a pattern that continues throughout the album, unison singing and clapping abruptly give way to a hip hop beat whose opening fanfare sounds like an old film score, something you'd expect in a Wu-Tang track. I'm momentarily distracted by the possibility, but when I can't find the sample on *Enter the Wu-Tang*, I soon give up, returning once more to PBS.

Duggy-T sings the verses in English, representing himself as "a brother man, from another land known as the Motherland" in one verse, riffing off Nina Simone to describe himself as "young, gifted, and Black, African," in another. Awadi provides the hook, his cadence evoking Jamaican patois: "Respect everyone, respect everyone, respect the Black man and respect the Nubian," Duggy-T responding, "La la la la laaay." Listening, I wonder if the celebration of fellowship in the opening folk song purposely prefigured these invocations of transnational Blackness, or if it just sounded good.

The album winds on, through songs where fragments of sabar and djembe drums are layered over the sounds of making tea and other daily activities, before we hear the sound of a *taalibe*—a mendicant Qu'ranic student—begging for lunch. This is "Return of Da Djelly (Return of the Griot)," the second and final English-language song on the album (the rest mix French and Wolof, although the titles come up on my computer with English translations embedded in the metadata). A pensive Fula flute and melodic kora establish a repetitive, single-phrase call and response, which Duggy-T interrupts once again with English lyrics:

> Flashback, it's time to check out history, lemme tell you this story, a bit of mystery
> The way I say it is musical, as they used to bust it back in the days in Africa typical

Speaking to the diaspora from the depths of an imagined past, through the voice of a resurrected griot (called *jeli* in Mandinka), he addresses an international audience of "soul people," whose history he will explain if they will just follow him back to their roots. He sings,

> I'm the symbol of knowledge, call me jeli

ANOTHER ORIGIN MYTH

Dakar is a bustling, sprawling city perched on the westernmost point of the African continent. Cutting through its aural barrage of cell phones, car horns, radios, and amplified calls to prayer, the voice of the griot sounds the city's precolonial history. Centuries ago, the earliest European travelers to West Africa "discovered" these bardic figures and documented their roles as historians, genealogists, social commentators, and royal mouthpieces. French colonial power was established; local Muslim brotherhoods emerged and grew in a constant counterpoint to European intellectual and economic colonization; independence ushered in the Parti Socialiste, which would rule until the turn of the millennium. And through it all, the griot survived, musically preserving the memory of life before modernity. In the contemporary urban landscape, griots are here as they were there—in the baptisms, naming ceremonies, and marriages that animate the twenty-first-century's concrete neighborhoods with the sounds and signs of indigenous celebration. The griot speaks. He plays. He sings. He reaches through the trappings of Europe's casually discarded modernizing project to reconnect his people with their past.

This is the griot's story. Or at least it is *a* story about the griot: the Master of the Word, a living source of ancient tradition, steadfast in the face of centuries of upheaval and social change. As its tellings and retellings circulate between Africa and its diaspora, this griot myth (re)traces historical connections and situates hip hop within them.

Stepping back from this globally imagined symbol of African orality, however, we find griots as human actors who, in precolonial Senegal, lived in inequitable symbiosis with members of the noble class. These roles necessarily shifted as French colonization and Islamicization worked in tandem to undermine indigenous social structures; they continued to change through the twentieth century, accommodating the postcolonial regime's codependence with Muslim leaders and the emergence of new cultural policies centered on revaluing African tradition and Blackness.

In the late twentieth century, two popular music genres—mbalax and hip hop—musically refigured the griot, their layered sounds indexing history, social change, and collective memory. Mbalax's signature mix of indigenous rhythms, Afro-Cuban harmonies and forms, and griot vocalizations layers musical signifiers of particular moments in urban Senegalese history. It sounds the cosmopolitan resignifying of social identities, religious practices, and publics that characterize life in Dakar. When the first generation of hip hoppers moved into the international spotlight in the early 1990s, however, they traced a different history, rerouting the mythologized griot through the diaspora and back to Africa via hip hop. Loosely citing a particular speech genre, *taasu*, they bypassed contemporary musical practices to layer globally circulating griot and hip hop myths.

It's hard to say who should be credited with elevating this narrative to an origin story—Western scholars and hip hop practitioners, African rappers, or maybe a combination of the three. French colonists were the first to dub the bards whom they encountered throughout West Africa *griots*, a word as invented as the tradition it came to signify. The term, a catch-all for a variety of distinct performance traditions, caught on with indigenous populations. In present-day Senegal, hereditary musicians from a variety of ethnic backgrounds, including Wolof *géwël*, Mande *jeli*, and Peul *gawlo*, are commonly referred to as *griots* when people are speaking French, in a conflation of colonial invention and indigenous practice that speaks to the griot's complex positioning in contemporary urban Africa.

Over time, the griot came to exemplify the binaries through which the colonizing structure functioned, representing a past, a tradition, and an orality that were juxtaposed with western modernity and literacy (Mudimbe 1988, 4). Postcolonial leaders (namely, the country's first two presidents, Léopold Sédar Senghor and then Abdou Diouf) adapted these constructions to their own purposes, even as Afrocentric intellectuals and artists in the United States began to claim the griot as a fount of African expressive culture. Attributing the visibility of the griot in the United States to the 1970s miniseries *Roots,* Thomas A. Hale (1998) traces the subsequent emergence of the griot as a ubiquitous figure in (self-) representations of African and African American arts and artists, one through which historical links to Africa could be reclaimed.[1] Hip hop in particular has inspired countless comparisons with griots in scholarly and media outlets.[2] US hip hop artists themselves have drawn these connections, from hip hop's "godfather," Afrika Bambaataa, to Kanye West (Keyes 2002; Tannenbaum 2006, cited in Tang 2012; Perkins 1996). In an interview aired on MTV in 2011, Q-Tip, of the US hip hop group A Tribe Called Quest, cautioned his fellow emcees, "Tell your own stories. We're griots, look that up. We're griots, man. We've gotta pass our own stories on. This is a part of our tradition, as African Americans predominantly" (Tardio 2011).

When the first wave of Senegalese rappers spoke of the connections between griot orality and hip hop, they did so in conversation with the Afrocentric ideas that were influencing some US hip hop at the same time, and with world music markets that were hungry for palatable experiences of musical difference. Senegalese hip hop groups began to produce international recordings in the mid-1990s, when artists associated with the Native Tongues movement in the United States, including A Tribe Called Quest, De La Soul, Queen Latifah, and the Jungle Brothers, were using jazz-based beats and Afrocentric imagery to create a self-conscious alternative to the gangsta images dominant in the hip hop of that era. And yet, the cycling of the griot trope between this first generation of Senegalese rappers and subsequent waves of western researchers and journalists has often elided the significant roles that griots continue to play in traditional life-cycle celebrations, in political campaigns, at sporting events, and as popular musicians. The dual epigraph to this chapter epitomizes this contradiction.

The griot has been *diasporically* constituted as tradition through Afrocentric intellectual and creative projects on both sides of the Atlantic. Tradition, here, signals neither codified musical practices nor timeless artifacts, but a locally invoked, discursive strategy in which the present invokes the past (Apter 2007; Scott 1999; Assmann 1997); something that is constantly (re)invented and (re)negotiated through human agency and intentionality (Yelvington 2006), constituted in social practice, and susceptible to reinterpretation as its forms and values are strategically linked in different ways (Erlmann 1991); and a practice of memory that calls upon the past in the construction of present selves (Young 2007).

To probe the gaps, elisions, and alignments between these musical histories and memories is not to claim that one is more authoritative than the other or to validate certain memories as true and others as inventions (Knapp 1989). Neither, however, is it to prioritize the mythologizing of musical practices to the point of ignoring the synchronic.[3] Instead, this synthesis of historical record and narrated myth reveals patterns of how the past is sampled in the present, in a shifting process of cultural remembering that is "as much a result of conscious manipulation as unconscious absorption" (Kansteiner 2002, 180). These points of connection and disjuncture reveal how musical practices work to remember—and sometimes revise—the past.

Flashback—it's time to check out history.

DISCOVERING THE GRIOT

A week ago, my friend gave birth to her first child, a boy, who was named this morning. Plastic bowls of millet porridge and sweet yogurt are passed around the house to be quickly cleared, refilled, and given to the next guest. The new mother departs to deliver a meal to her parents, returning in the afternoon to this, her mother-in-law's house, where she's lived since shortly after her marriage last year. Somewhere along the way, she's changed her clothes—the fabric, never washed, is stiff and gleaming, cerulean satin embroidered in white and yellow across the chest, studded with rhinestones, a pleated peplum emphasizing her hips, still wide from childbirth. The women cluster around her, a sea of colors and textures, bright robes and dresses in satin, silk, and printed cotton, or the billowing voile and crisp eyelet that are coolest in the summer heat. Some bang out sabar rhythms on large metal bowls, louder and sturdier than the hollow calabash for which they have been substituted. We enter the courtyard, géwëls, sisters, cousins, and neighbors alike milling about, momentarily coalescing into an uneven circle, overflowing again into every corner of the house. One woman, the mother-in-law's griot, sings loudly into a megaphone; soon others jostle in, taking turns to praise the new mother and her kin in the rhythmic, chanted call and response of taasu poetry that elicits short bursts of dancing. In this swirl of female bodies, even the few veiled women present (whose stricter interpretations of Islam usually lead them to avoid public displays of dance) begin to hop up and down, knees twisting impossibly from one side to the other with a slight pause on every third step, hips following. Without ceasing their movements, the singing women hold up smartphones and tablets, making shaky videos that they will watch over and over together in the days to come.

As the afternoon wanes and women take seats in the tent set up in the street outside the house, female griots—some affiliated with the matriarchs in the family, but most not—circulate among the guests with hands outstretched to receive money, wheedling, cajoling, and shaming those who withhold. They don't sing or perform. Most family members give as freely and openly as they can, exchanging money for a boost in social standing. Others proffer excuses and mutter under their breath about begging once the griots move out of earshot. My pockets deliberately empty, I finally go inside to escape the constant requests for money.

That day, I couldn't quite make sense of the shifting roles that griots and performance played in the various stages of the celebration. I had first encountered the griot in scholarly works about hip hop history and culture, as a (seemingly always male) repository of ancestral knowledge and agent of the mythical African power of the word. As a graduate student, I studied West African dance for pleasure with instructors trained by Senegalese choreographer Germaine Acogny; those teachers emphasized the griot heritages of the male djembe drummers from a variety of national backgrounds who accompanied the class.[4] Yet none of these early encounters resonated with my primary experiences with griots in Dakar, in the female-centric performance spaces of life-cycle ceremonies and in male-dominated performances of religious power. Nor did they hint at the complicated ways in which griot identity is variously claimed and elided in contemporary Senegal.

As people who work with their hands, griots occupy to the second-to-lowest strata in a system of social differentiation—often referred to as a caste system—that is common to many ethnolinguistic groups in the Senegambia region.[5] Senegal's ethnic diversity means that griot practices encompass distinct instrumental traditions, from Wolof sabar drumming to the Mande kora (harp-lute) and bala (wooden xylophone). With some exceptions, female griots don't generally play instruments, aside from the calabash.[6] Griot verbal performance practices across ethnic groups include various forms of spoken recitation—genealogies, epic poems, and declamatory speech—as well as praisesinging, which performatively bolsters social differentiation (Leymarie 1999, 100). Exchanges with practicing griots affirm the higher social status of those who patronize them; those same interactions, however, underscore griots' lower social status, and their uninvited presence at celebrations is often considered a nuisance.[7] Griot speech registers are sometimes characterized as crass and loud, in contrast with the restrained speech patterns of the noble class (Irvine 1973).

Indigenous social hierarchies have shifted in dialogue with colonization, religious conversion, and postcolonial political and cultural projects. In the four communes of Saint-Louis Dakar, Rufisque, and Gorée, the colonial policy of assimilation into French culture created new avenues for social advancement.

A small elite group of African residents and the growing métis community assumed positions of authority under colonial administrators; some were even granted French citizenship. And yet, because caste identity is embedded in surnames, it continues to inflect contemporary Senegalese culture. Griot families, for example, can be identified by last names, like the Wolof *Mbaye* or *Diouf* or the Bambara *Kouyaté* and *Sissoko*, although intermarriage and the abandonment of griot professions have muddied these distinctions.

In women's performance, divisions of Wolof society along the lines of age, gender, and caste are further exposed as contextually permeable. The taasu that I witnessed at the naming celebration is an improvised form of praise poetry that also takes on elements of satire and eroticism. Historically the purview of women, it is central to contemporary celebrations of individual women's life-cycle events (most notably marriage and naming new babies). There, both professional griots and amateur female kin will perform taasu, crafting relations of reciprocity that can raise the status of the person being praised, either through economic exchange (with griots) or social exchange (with family and friends), while strengthening or challenging female relationships within households (McNee 2000, 33–34). These verbal practices go hand in hand with instrumental and dance ones; the rhythms banged out on pots to accompany taasu are sabar drum rhythms, and the dance movements that accompany it are sabar dance movements.

Later that night at the *baptême*—a common, albeit not entirely accurate, way of referring to traditional naming ceremonies—I watch eagerly as young men carry sabar drums of varying sizes to the wide, sandy alleyway next to the house. They begin to play, one of them standing slightly out in front with the longest drum to lead the musicians from one rhythm to the next. In the dim, uneven light that leaks from the windows of the surrounding homes, a circle of women forms. One by one, they skip out in front of the drummers to dance—arms flailing, legs stepping, twisting, and kicking nimbly—before laughing and melting back to the edges. Their movements range from dainty restraint to exuberant abandon; women dancing toward the latter extreme let their skirts fly to reveal leggings or risqué crocheted wraps. Their movements bear little resemblance to the stylized, djembe-based movements I've learned to call "West African" dance in the United States.

This disconnect—between my prior experience with West African dance and the sabar circle at the baptême—reflected the contrast between the prevalence of Mande dance and music in the outward-facing cultural projects of many francophone West African nations and the processes of woloficization that have marked urban growth in Senegal.[8] The dominance of Wolof ethnic groups in the area, combined with colonial and postcolonial depictions of Wolof culture as

Senegalese (Castaldi 2006, 76), have led Dakarois of varying ethnic backgrounds to participate in and claim historically Wolof practices, including sabar, which is ubiquitous in the city.[9]

Sabar can mean an individual drum, the dance steps performed with sabar drumming accompaniment, or the drumming-dancing event in its entirety.[10] Sabar is traditionally a women's dance, while drummers are traditionally male. The leader of the ensemble plays the largest drum, the open-bottomed *nder*, which, in dialogue with the dancers, solos and signals changes to the other drummers. Sometimes he will signal a *bakk*: a rhythm, played in unison, that imitates Wolof's nontonal speech patterns (Tang 2007). At traditional wrestling matches, male fighters and their crews perform intimidating dances to their own unique bakks. Outside of wrestling, men increasingly dance sabar, a development perhaps traceable to the national ballet and the advent of pop-music and the advent of pop-music videos.

The most prevalent contexts for sabar, however, remain life-cycle ceremonies and women's social gatherings and revolving credit circles. In these spaces, women may, to a certain extent, step outside the bounds of gendered social norms to express their sexuality in ways that change continually as they age and marry (Castaldi 2004; Heath 1994; Kringelbach 2013; Morales-Libove 2005). This aspect of sabar has contributed to its uneasy and uneven relationship with local interpretations of Islam.

SOUNDING ISLAM

As the rhythms of the sabar drown out conversation for a blockwide radius, I notice the women with their heads together, smiling at me, raised eyebrows sending a playful invitation. I turn and creep back to the house before I'm pushed into the circle. Inside, the men of the family sullenly refuse to go out, criticizing the women for planning such a thing and complaining that a child named after a saint should not be celebrated with undignified dancing and music. Of course, the women could not have known that the child—called Baby until today, when his name was bestowed and announced—would be the namesake of Serigne Saliou, a local Muslim saint. Fathers—solely responsible for naming the first child from a particular union—have endless choices when it comes to naming a boy, while female babies' names are loosely prescribed by kinship practices in ways that strengthen bonds within polygynous families and matrilineages.

As I listen to the men criticize the drumming and dancing, I think back to a night a few weeks earlier, where in this same alley, in an unevenly lit tent, sabar drums had kept the neighborhood awake all night. One of the men in the family ushered me outside to observe. In a tireless display of Islamic devotion, a group of men sang, chanted, and danced themselves into a trance, jumping around the circle shirtless, dreadlocks flying. The rhythms sounded like dance rhythms, but the movements didn't seem to correspond to the sounds of the drum; their reckless abandon and frenzied energy, somehow so different from the playful dance I was watching tonight, made me uneasy. I flinched and turned away as they lifted slabs of rock over their heads and smashed them onto their own backs, with no apparent physical effect. The other men in the family watched from outside the tent, heads nodding, faces solemn.

In these two performances, and the gendered responses they elicited, I saw a wavering between alienation and uneasy symbiosis that characterizes the dynamic between instrumental music and Islam in Senegal, where Muslim brotherhoods wield significant social and political power (Leymarie 1999, 141). Most influential is the Mouride order, founded in the late nineteenth century by the local Sufi saint, Cheikh Ahmadou Bamba, also called Serigne Touba—father of the original Serigne Saliou (Robinson 2000).[11] Serigne Touba's trusted disciple, Cheikh Ibra Fall, founded the Baye Fall sect whose members I watched go into trance in the alley that night.[12] While strict interpretations of Islam reject music, dance, and drumming—particularly when they mediate indigenous spirituality, as in certain healing ceremonies in Senegal (Leymarie 1999, 141–142), in Mouridism, as in Sufism more broadly, music is used to induce altered states of ecstaticism in search of union with God (Avery 2004; Roberts and Roberts 2003). The Baye Fall's mystic practice incorporates sabar drumming, chanting, and costuming typical of a precolonial warrior slave caste known as *ceddo*, whose members are said to have comprised the core of Ibra Fall's followers.[13]

In my rented apartment in Dakar, as I flip through the very limited channels that our antenna provides, I pass over an American action film and what I guess is a Brazilian soap opera, both dubbed in French and frequently interrupted with advertisements for skin-bleaching creams and bouillon cubes. I land for a moment on a large religious gathering. There are no drums or dancing here—only men, sitting and chanting. Their leader, the *marabout*, sits in the center of the gathering, clearly distinguished by the respectful space around him and the sumptuous yards of satin damask he wears. As their prayers come to an end, a microphone is passed along until it reaches the inner circle. The marabout speaks quietly, almost as if to himself, pausing after each phrase so that the griot sitting to his right might clearly intone his words into the microphone for all to hear, while adding emphasis and ornamentation to the marabout's restrained speech.

I had read that griots served as mouthpieces for their noble patrons, ventriloquizing their voices, but I had never witnessed this phenomenon before seeing it that day on television, where the patron was a marabout (a Muslim holy man) rather than, or most likely, as well as, a member of a historically noble class. As colonial projects undermined local power structures and traditional leaders in the early twentieth century, Islam provided new models of social organization that were compatible with local norms of social differentiation and patronage (Behrman 1970). Gradually replacing the unstable indigenous ruling classes, the marabouts took on a new role as leaders to the unassimilated rural majority. Their involvement in the cultivation of the new commercial peanut crop made them an important asset to the French, who, in their need for liaisons with their rural subjects, directly contributed to the spread of Islam in the area (Klein 1972; Glover 2001; Robinson 2000).

The marabouts' rise to power in the twenty-first century inevitably affected griot practices. Relationships of clientelism and patronage that had centered on indigenous political leaders and nobles in the past translated easily to the Mourides' emphasis on the hierarchical relationship between the marabout and his disciples. Many early marabouts, in fact, came from noble lineages and were invested in maintaining those social hierarchies (Leymarie 1999, 142). At least as early as the 1950s, griots were praising marabouts in public meetings, even as they also sang God's praises and served as meuzzins, giving the call to prayer (Hale 1998, 21; Leymarie 1999, 143; Panzacchi 1994). In return, a marabout's disciples, rather than the marabout himself, financially rewarded the griot for praisesinging. While the griot-noble relationship still relied on an audience (why sing praises if no one will hear them?), now the audience became not just the arbiter of reputation, but also the patron for griot performances, compensating the griot for the praise of their religious leader (McLaughlin 2000, 196). To a certain extent, these adaptations to Islam marginalized female griots, who could not serve as muezzins or as authoritative mouthpieces for marabouts; they were, however, able to praise them as their male counterparts did.

The reliance on the Muslim brotherhoods that characterized colonial rule did not diminish with Senegal's birth as an independent country; if anything, the new African administrators, lacking the support of a major backing power on which their colonial predecessors relied, depended even more on the marabouts for political support, particularly in their issuance of public statements that served as voting guides for their disciples. The new state's reliance on maraboutic authority, particularly in the rural interior, was accompanied by state protection of the marabouts' material interests; today, they constitute one of the richest sectors of Senegalese society (Behrman 1970; Van Hoven 2000). Meanwhile, griots have continued to praise marabouts, while also serving the new patrons of the postcolonial Senegalese state: political candidates and factions.[14]

POSTCOLONIAL RHYTHMS

> The griot is by default a journalist, because the present is not legible except through the past, which can only be accessed through the present.
>
> DIOP AND DIOUF 1990, 278 (my translation).

When Senegal achieved independence from colonial rule in 1960, acclaimed intellectual Léopold Sédar Senghor took office as president.[15] Senghor's cultural projects built on a legacy of assimilation in which the "African" and the "western" converged in one community of people whose members would stand at the helm of the postcolonial state: the *evolués*, or elite Africans living in the colonial communes. In the early twentieth century, as the French grew uneasy with the increasing sociopolitical influence of the *evolués*, official colonial policy shifted to delineate a stronger separation between European and elite African populations. In a new policy of "accommodation," colonial administrators promoted the idea that Africans—now ostensibly distanced from their roots through assimilation to French culture—needed to be taught to live by their own traditions, an idea that appealed to the evolués, who increasingly viewed themselves as neither African nor European. As they turned to the ethnographic projects of European anthropologists for guidance, white "inventions" (Ranger 1983) of indigenous practices became the yardstick for cultural authenticity in colonial urban centers (Genova 2004, 95).[16]

The quest to reclaim and affirm an authentic and invaluable African essence was central to Senghor's particular version of the larger intellectual movement known as *negritude*. Senghor envisioned a Senegalese modernity that was dually French and African; he invoked his own rural roots as a symbol of his authenticity, even as he rejected indigenous lifeways—villages, ethnicity, age hierarchies—as antithetical to a modernity that he associated with French values (Diop and Diouf 1990, 270; Genova 2004, 153–156). The Africa of negritude was one imagined in rhythm and art, not one that necessarily reflected the lived realities of the indigenous population (Diop and Diouf 1990, 253; Genova 2004, 153). The griot was, above all, a memory to be harnessed in the evolués' self-appointed role of rediscovering African culture, in order to return it to Africans and present it to Europeans (Genova 2004, 149–150). Negritude was "a perception of history more than a history or memory itself" (Diop and Diouf 1990, 271).

This same duality marked Senghor's attempts to cultivate hybrid national musics in the immediate postindependence period; his elite outlook largely overlooked popular music, preferring to combine rural traditions with western art music forms. These compositions found little hold with local audiences (Benga 2002; Kringelbach 2013), who instead gravitated toward the vernacular musics that were emerging at the same time. In the early twentieth century, Dakar's racialized organization had worked in tandem with assimilation policies to maintain largely segregated urban audiences; local musicians in the city's nightclubs had faithfully reproduced ballroom, jazz, and Afro-Cuban music for French, métis, and elite African patrons.[17] In the decades following independence, Afro-Cuban music and the restrained couple dancing that accompanied it continued to symbolize a dignified, cosmopolitan leisure activity that reflected both French norms of social comportment and indigenous values of modesty among the generations who were young adults in the 1950s and 1960s (Shain 2009, 202, 2002, 92–93).[18] In the same period, the growth of an urban population less rooted in French assimilationism led to accelerated musical change.

In 2007, the entry fee to hear Orchestre Baobab play at the Just4U restaurant and nightclub is 3000 CFA francs (about US$6). Inside, a circular straw ceiling shields most of the patio floor, where the tight clustering of white-clothed tables conjoins discrete groups of patrons. Study abroad adventurers drink beers, their baggy pants collectively showcasing more African prints than a market stall. Draped scarves and rubber flip flops give way here and there to the crisp collared shirt and loafers, or clinging blouse and heels, of a Senegalese student, who nurses a soft drink that cost three times what it would in any one of the tiny boutiques that line neighborhood streets. Expats in loose linen tunics, leather sandals, and artisanal jewelry enjoy cocktails and three course dinners. Small groups of just-still-middle-aged Senegalese couples, the men in meticulously tailored suits, the women in flowing silk dresses and caftans, do the same. Oldest of all, the members of Orchestre Baobab take the stage after midnight, opening with a salsa that sounds as though it's broadcast from across the Atlantic. As they continue to play, sabar rhythms gradually break through the salsa harmonies. Patrons shift like sand through an hourglass, space opening up between the cramped tables as the area in front of the stage begins to fill. Young foreign women pair up with Senegalese men, bodies pressing together and breaking apart in ostentatious figures. They seem to move in double time as they weave around the older Senegalese patrons, who glide in a stately partner dance that looks more like a toned-down meringue than salsa; only their hands touch.

To listen to Orchestre Baobab that night was to hear the musical trajectory of indigenous performance, winding through intertwined histories of religious and political change, bringing us to mbalax. This music, which would remain Senegal's most popular musical genre until the present day, coalesced in the 1970s, when the primary accompanying rhythms of sabar drum ensembles overtook imported harmonies and rhythms. Political change in the decades that followed would render griot practices even more central to popular music.

In 1981, Abdou Diouf replaced Senghor as president, then won the first multi-party election in 1983. Diouf's *sursaut national* represented a nationalism grounded in the actual cultural practices of indigenous populations rather than a symbolic or essentialized Africanity.[19] This included revalorizing griot performance and its attendant social distinctions (Diop and Diouf 1990, 269; Leymarie 1999, 95). Under Diouf, the griot became prominent in national affairs; Diouf's personal griot sang his praises for national audiences, placing him in a royal Wolof genealogy, and became a celebrated radio commentator (Snipe 1998, 64). While official nationalist rhetoric privileged male performance genres, like epic poetry, women's taasu served as a popular, if unofficial, political medium in the presidential campaigns of the 1990s (Mcnee 2000, 8).

Another night at Just4U in 2007, but this time the entry fee is 15,000 francs—closer to US$30. Those who have paid double that fee are seated at the tables closest to the stage, eating dinner, while the rest sit in rows, behind a small barrier at the back of the room. Singer Youssou N'Dour finally comes onstage, his band playing an infectious blend of sabar rhythms on indigenous and western instruments, the rhythmic lines of the synthesizer and guitars doubling the interlocking beats of the sabar drums placed prominently on the stage. N'Dour's voice, clear and high, moves in the descending lines of griot song to land in globalized pop-style refrains. In front of the stage, men wearing pants cut generously in the crotch grasp the extra material and hold it out in front of them, emphasizing the end of their improvised dance sequences with exaggerated pelvic thrusts. Patrons' dancing ranges from the wide, flailing gestures of sabar dance to a more grounded movement, hips swiveling while the knees open in opposite directions, one hand grasping clothing at the waist and perhaps, in the case of women, lifting it slightly to tease a glimpse of stomach, while the other hand waves and jabs in the air.

This was no localized Cuban music, no stately reminder of jazz clubs from decades ago. While maintaining the harmonic structures of international popular musics, mbalax's early backing bands for singers like Youssou N'Dour, Thione Seck, and Omar Pene took sabar rhythms and transposed them to electrified western instruments. Mbalax came into its own as a musical genre when its elements drawn from griot performance—rhythms and vocal styles, as much as instruments—finally overshadowed its influences from imported popular music.[20]

Because many early mbalax singers were griots, and because the foundational rhythms of mbalax are those of griot drumming, it was only natural that griot verbal performance—particularly praisesinging—was transposed to this new popular music, a practice that continues to this day.[21] In the late 1970s, when griots' praisesinging of politicians became so exaggerated that it was finally censored from the radio, popular music provided a ready alternative for the financially rewarding practice, which was made all the more attractive by the difficult working conditions that musicians faced in the decades following independence (Benga 2002, 297; Panzacci 1994, 205).

In the 1980s, mbalax's primarily Wolof musical and linguistic features helped establish it as national music at a time when Diouf's administration was pushing a new, inward-focused nationalism that deliberately propelled the processes of woloficization that had begun earlier in the century (Kringelbach 2013, 100). With Diouf's strategic revalorization of precolonial cultural values over the integrationist dreams of Senghor, popular praisesinging took even greater hold. Popular music became an alternative site for the griot as national culture.

As a semiformal music industry developed in the 1980s, state and private radio and television programs provided a forum for mbalax, while the (often pirated) local cassettes sold in Dakar's downtown Sandaga market circulated throughout the country.[22] As the fleeting, contextually dependant event of praisesinging was inscribed, disseminated, and mobilized for commercial purposes, its audiences—and hence, its patrons—were extended indefinitely. The burgeoning music industry provided a potentially enormous audience whose new practices of patronage revolved around buying recordings that praised particular Muslim spiritual guides. Mbalax's commercial appeal relied on both its musical characteristics and this newly transformed praisesinging, so that musical fandom centered as much on those being praised as it did on particular musicians (McLaughlin 2000, 575).

Even as mbalax musically shored up political and religious hegemonies, however, it also became a medium of social engagement. During Diouf's administration, Senegal entered into an extended period of social and political unrest. In the 1980s, violent protests on the part of students and other youth had accompanied the uneasy shift to a nominal multipartyism. In the early 1990s, at least for a time, youth moved from political demonstrations to hands-on beautifying projects in their city. Under the banner of *Set-Setal* [to be clean-to make clean], they cleaned up trash, revived public parks, and renamed streets after local wrestlers and scholars, in a grassroots shift that reinscribed national identity through local memory (Diouf 1996, 247). Mbalax, particularly Youssou N'Dour's album *Set-Setal*, provided a soundtrack for the movement; its very sounds aurally inscribed local memory in the urban landscape.

Despite its global components, mbalax's heavy Wolof rhythms are decidedly local. Its limited international success has depended on Youssou N'Dour's strategic westernization of its musical elements to accommodate the world music craze of the 1980s, which capitalized off the hybrid musical styles of non-western musicians who mixed musical markers of difference with relatable harmonic progressions and song forms (Taylor 1997). N'Dour's international releases rework the grittier, rhythmically complex version of mbalax that permeates daily life in Senegal. They simplify indigenous rhythms, emphasize a clear 4/4 meter, and cull the dense instrumental overlays that characterize the music in its local setting to produce a thinner musical texture.

In many ways, N'Dour himself embodies the coming together of griot histories real and imagined; despite the fact that only his mother comes from a griot lineage (in a society where patrilineage determines social identity), his international success is directly tied to globally circulating mythologies of the griot. Across a wide range of media, he has been credited with representing "the ancient tradition of the griot, the West African story-teller" (Brown 2004), described as "A Modern Griot: Youssou N'dour" (*Another Africa* 2010) and praised for "[extending] Senegal's griot tradition of social conscience and praise singing into pop aimed worldwide" (Pareles 2014).

REROUTING THE GRIOT

Spin it back. Layer these histories on themselves and into hip hop; stretch and distort them; chop and reorder them; slow them; speed them. Rapper Nix takes up the narrative, telling stories about stories within stories (Fig. 3.1).

FIGURE 3.1 Nix waits for our interview to begin.

Now when you watch wrestling, for example, you see, the rhythms, you see, of the wrestlers, even the way of—

the bakk, for example—

you see, the taasu—

this is traditional music.

It was here before mbalax.

It is old, you see?

And for example, I have an uncle who told me back then, when he was really very small, he would go see the wrestlers, it wasn't like today, mediatized and all that, it was much more—

and so back then they would go see the wrestlers and there was always a session, the wrestlers in fact spoke over djembe rhythms, and that's something that really evokes rap!

You see?

Because in fact, because in fact, it's an ego trip.

It's an ego trip, in fact.

You big up yourself as the best, you balance your words, staccato, over a rhythm, you see?

You see?

It's a strong rhythm—

"Oh, yeah?" I ask, caught up in his narrative, pulled to respond.

—that takes you on a trip.

Yeah!

And that exists since way before.

[*Eng.*] It's old.

[*Fr.*] You see?

And that's traditional.

So, voila.

That's all I can tell you.

We laugh together at his emphatic ending, and then he tacks on a coda,

So that's why today, when you see that the youth love rap, it's normal, it's in their genes, you see?

It's something that we are since then, I think, but in another form.

In a way, hip hop history in a given site is always already an extension of hip hop's history in the United States; hip hop history in Senegal begins, in one telling, at the moment that hip hop arrives there from elsewhere (see Chapter 2). This was the moment of the country's nominal shift to multipartyism, its second president in twenty years of independence, accelerated urbanization, rising discontent among the city's youth, and a revalorizing of the griot, both in national politics and popular music.

Some of Rap Galsen's earliest figures circumvented mbalax's history to remember a parallel musical past that shifted what the griot meant to them in the present. Tracing a mythologized griot through the sounds of hip hop orality, likened to taasu, they rooted their claims to hip hop authenticity in the same inventions of tradition that informed postcolonial policies and cultural projects while they were growing up, even as they joined a decades-long transatlantic dialogue about aesthetic and historical connections between Africa and its diaspora. As they converted hip hop from a globalized US music into a diasporically local one, they claimed the authority of tradition and memory, rerouting it through diaspora to sidestep postcolonial power.

Sitting with me in the front courtyard of his home, Xuman, of the early, internationally successful group Pee Froiss, was telling me about traditional music and led himself to taasu, saying,

Taasu is like hip hop.

It's like rap.

Taasu is exactly like rap.

Which is to say there is someone with percussion who is going to speak quickly. He is not going to rap but he is going to speak very very quickly, he is going to speak about things to amuse people—

[*Eng.*] you know, just [*Fr.*] to amuse people.

Exactly like a rapper.

But he isn't going to attack people, he is not going to say, "yes, the government is doing this," no.

But he is going to talk about society, about funny things.

So it is all this that makes the difference.

Hip hop myth is implicit in Xuman's telling; it is hip hop that *will* attack people, that is going to say, "Yes, the government is doing this." And here is the contradiction inherent in this myth of griot origins: Taasu, while invoked as an ancestor for hip hop, is accessed through contemporary performance practices in which griot orality props up those in power. To claim taasu is to elide questions of caste status and griots' reputations as loud money seekers who often show up uninvited to events to harass guests with unsolicited praisesinging. It is to silently regender a woman's performance genre. It is also to bypass the obvious "modern" griots— mbalax singers. But while underground rappers would later conflate taasu and mbalax (see Chapter 4), in the early 1990s, taasu was not widespread in the preeminent popular genre, and it seems unlikely that the rappers who first noted the aesthetic resonance between taasu (rhythmic chanting over cyclical percussion) and hip hop (rhythmic chanting over cyclical instrumentals) would have associated taasu with mbalax.[23] And as the story of taasu and griot origins grew and took hold, it shifted quickly into myth and became about the telling and retelling more than any claim to equivalence.

To reimagine griot orality in and as hip hop was not to deny the music's African American roots, but rather, to position them within a larger story about diasporic lineage. Sitting with me in his studio, DJ Awadi likened traditional music and hip hop to "the grandpa and the son." He said,

> We are connected.
> There's a real lineage.
> In any case, me personally, I can't speak for the others, I can't cut this link
> [*Eng.*] between my roots and what I am—I cannot—
> Even if I want to, [*Fr.*] I can't do it.

Awadi knows intimately the debate behind my question; years earlier, the emerging hardcore had gleefully taunted him and other rappers over this question of griot origins. He pushes back, even as he refines the question,

> The proof: the big hits—I take the example of the United States—
> the hits, in rap, were the reprises of George Clinton and James Brown because [*Eng.*] those were also the roots,
> [*Fr.*] those were the roots,
> for example, East Coast American rappers are going to listen to, are going to take "Funky Drummer" you see—

FIGURE 3.2 Baïdy describes hip hop's transatlantic journey.

"James Brown," we say in unison, and he continues,

—and they rapped well over it.

You see?

The West Coast people are going to take George Clinton, because that's the music they listened to since they were little.

How to argue with this aural recognition of self in hip hop? With the idea that local sounds—James Brown on the East Coast, taasu in Senegal—are there to be heard if you only listen? This is a deeply personal question of perspective, one that places Senegalese hip hop in a diasporic history where African roots are not a foundation as much as they are one of many layers—layers that can be heard but not isolated.

One day, I sat with Baïdy, of Bideew bou Bess, at his family home in Parcelles Assainies (Fig. 3.2). His brothers, the other members of the internationally touring group mentored by Youssou N'Dour, were not around. I said, "There's people who say there's an old relationship between rap and Senegalese traditional music, like taasu and stuff like that." He replied "Yes!" his voice high, "I tell myself this is true!"

Because no matter what we say, the Afro— the Americans who are in the United States are *Afro* Americans, because it was slavery that drove them there, and when they parted, there were the genes of that music there, of that music, that which led to soul, to gospel, to music—

to Black American music, so that came from Africa.

In Africa, there were a lot of things that were similar to rap—

taasu, bakks, talmbat—there were a lot of rhythms that were similar to current rap music, so I can say that that comes from there somewhere, Africa is the source.

And there you have it, with slavery and all that, there were genes [*he runs his finger along the veins in the opposite arm*] that were transported from Africa to the United States, which led to rap music and the Black American music we see.

He pauses.

That's *my* idea, there are a lot of people who don't think that it's like that,

who say that rap is something American.

But I'm speaking in regards to the genes.

I'm speaking in regards to the birth, earlier.

It's clear that there's a, well, there's a moment, where there was a break, a rupture, because when Africans were deported from Africa towards the United States there was a rupture, but the genes remained.

He gestures again to the veins in his forearm.

They sang in the fields of the plantations, those were African rhythms.

Until now that's why Africans love what they hear from the United States, because that reminds them of their culture and everything.

It's a culture that just traveled, joined the United States, to yield something else, but the base remains African.

Baïdy speaks not of retentions, but of the music's genes, mixed and mutated over centuries. Nix says that youth recognize a version of themselves in hip hop. Awadi also speaks of lineages. Origin narratives reinscribe a history of diasporic connection while allowing for dynamic change in taasu's transformative transatlantic sojourn. For while taasu might sound superficially like hip hop, it doesn't typically convey the kinds of social commentary that Senegalese rappers—underground or mainstream, across generations—associate with a mythologized hip hop, rooted in the South Bronx and speaking to socioeconomic marginalization. Remembered through African American history, contemporary griot orality is transformed into something socially useful and musically global.

Speaking to me about the likeness between rap and taasu, Xuman catches himself, and I see in his face, in his quick move to clarify, a wariness of the griot origin myth and its detractors.

It's not the same thing. That's to say, at the base—

It's like if you say rap comes from Africa, because someone who created rap came from Africa. He who created rap went to the United States, it was Jamaicans who left Jamaica, who first came from Africa, who were forced to move to Jamaica, who came to New York, and so he who developed rap was a Black person.

That developed, that developed.

The form of rap, with rhymes, et cetera, et cetera, is not the same thing as taasu. Taasu, there are rhymes, but it doesn't respect the same norm.

The norms that rap uses are not the same norms that taasu uses.

The rhythm over which we are going to rap isn't the same rhythm as taasu.

But the flow, the manner of speaking quickly, is similar.

But I want to say, it wasn't the original taasu that was imported, that went to the US to directly become rap.

The fact that they are both spoken is the similarity.

It's like, the example that I can give you, when you take coffee.

It is grown here in Africa, in Côte d'Ivoire for example; coffee, cultivated in Africa, is exported to the United States and Europe.

It is processed, and when it comes back here, it is called Nescafé.

Leaving, a kilo of coffee will cost 500 francs, about one dollar; when it returns in a kilo jar, it costs ten dollars.

Rap is the same thing.

It's certain that our ancestors, upon leaving, knew our traditions, they had among them people who spoke quickly.

The slaves had celebrations and they had it in their blood, they had the rhythms in their blood.

But it was there a long time until, when it came back here, it wasn't called taasu anymore.

It had become something else; it became rap, as we hear.

And this is why there is a big difference.

The first difference is in the construction, how we construct phrases, the content we put in these phrases.

Because taasu is something that is very, very rhythmic.

Taasu—indigenous verbal performance—is recontextualized within the mythologized history of hip hop, itself emerging from a history of extraction and enslavement. Like coffee, taasu returns not in its original form, and importantly, not with its original meaning.

It had seemed, and still seems at times, that this narrative was about separating performance aesthetics and social function, about allowing the sound of griot speech to outweigh its contemporary role. But ultimately, this wasn't about any kind of equivalence between taasu and rapping, or griots and emcees. It was about telling a story that they knew to have happened, about layering a mythologized hip hop and a mythologized griot, placing them in a shared history, remembering them together, as a single memory. And this engagement with Afrocentricity would emerge as much through musical narratives of connection as through verbal ones.

SOUNDING AFRICA

On a Friday night in September, 2011, I arrive at Cinema Awa in Pikine, where young artist Sister Dia has asked me to film her performance as one of the opening acts for Daara J Family. We square off with the doorman; he is skeptical of a young girl claiming to be a rapper. One of the men involved in organizing the concert finally intervenes, and we enter, making our way to a wooden bench in the front row of the repurposed movie theater, still empty, the crowd waiting outside. The concrete floor slopes up toward the back of the room, wooden benches giving way to rows of flip-up seats about halfway up. Faded wallpaper wraps the theater in partial fleurs-de-lis. I imagine the cinema in its heyday, the decade of independence, catering to the burgeoning urban population in this newly developed banlieue. I see its paper pristine and new, its benches filled with young couples and friends. I wonder if, when their film is done, they'll go out to dance to salsa, or to something that still sounds a bit like salsa, but whose rhythms are even more familiar.

The audience for tonight's concert enters; the specters of their grandparents fade. At the front of the cinema, where a large concrete stage abuts the blank wall, a projector silently plays US hip hop videos; they clash with the mix of Senegalese hip hop tracks coming through the sound system. Pikine's own hip hop acts perform to a somewhat indifferent young crowd that mills about, waiting for the main attraction.

It's grown late by the time Daara J takes the stage, their band tweaking tunings and levels as the audience swells to the front of the room. I give up my place just in front of the stage, where I had filmed the opening acts unobstructed. For a brief moment, the crowd calms to near-stillness as the sabar drums begin to sound, beating out their rhythmic rendition of the obligatory opening prayer to Cheikh Ahmadou Bamba—*yaa ñu moom, Bamba*—we are yours, saint. The ubiquitous rhythm gives way to a busy mélange of traditional and electronic instruments, local rhythms, and global harmonies. Daara J plays old songs and new hits while the young men and women dance in front of the stage. Between songs, Faada Freddy takes the mic and announces—When we say rap comes from taasu, they are the same history. Rap went from Africa to America to Europe to Senegal.

The concert, which opened with a drummed rendition of Muslim-inflected traditional speech genres, ends with their newest hit single, "Bayi Yoon," a pan-African sound collage that layers French and Wolof lyrics over South African choral singing and sabar and hip hop rhythms. The audience sings along:

> Ana Sutura bi fi ñoom maam bayyiwoon [Where is the self-respect that our ancestors left here]
> Jiko yu raffet yi ñu raañewooon? [The beautiful way of life that we knew?]
> Dafa mel ni dañu bayyi suñu yoon [It seems we've lost our way]
> Bëgg askanoo li ñu moomutoo [Loving a culture that isn't our own]

As they reclaim an African heritage over assimilation to western values, they remind the young people in front of them of a Wolof proverb: it is better to know yourself first than for someone else to tell you who you are. In their lyrics, I hear the echoes of a PBS song from fifteen years earlier, DJ Awadi's gravelly voice crafting the same expression into a rhythmic chant:

> Xam sa bopp moo gën ñu woo la wax la ki nga doon.
> Xam nga li nga doon.
> Xam nga ki nga doon.
> [Knowing yourself is better than them telling you who you are.
> You know what you are.
> You know who you are.]

A month before the concert at Cinema Awa, I was drinking tea with friends in Parcelles Assainies when I got a phone call from television personality Y.Dee, who needed help on a project. I offered a noncommittal, I'm happy to help, maybe this weekend? He insisted that it was urgent. And so, with a reluctant final glance at the sweet, minty third pot of tea bubbling on the gas, I declined the myriad invitations to just wait until it's finished, and picked up and headed to DJ Awadi's Studio Sankara in Amitié II.

There, I find Y.Dee and Awadi, along with Awadi's sound engineer, Masson, sitting in the comfortable recording studio on the third floor of the house. They are recording the English dubbing for Awadi's film *Point de Vue du Lion* [The Lion's Point of View]. As the opening frames explain, the film is titled for a proverb attributed to the Bantu: *Tant que les lions n'auront pas leurs historiens, les histoires de chasse seront toujours à la gloire des chasseurs*/As long as lions don't have their own historians, the history of the hunt will always glorify the hunters.

Awadi quickly explains the film: a historicized reflection on current social conditions in Africa, as told through the voices of African political and intellectual leaders. They are dubbing it in English before he leaves in two days for Europe to put the film into postproduction. My job is to tweak the English translations, coach the pronunciation, and fill in on some scenes myself, despite my increasingly frantic attempts to explain "lisp"; without the appropriate French vocabulary, my concerns over what they interpret as "accent" are cheerfully dismissed. For three days, I sit in Awadi's studio as voiceover volunteers come and go: Y.Dee and rapper N-Jah, with their carefully developed African American Vernacular English; Keyti, formerly of Rap'Adio, and Xuman, formerly of Pee Froiss. When we finish on the third day, Awadi drops me at my apartment on his way to the airport to bring the project to Europe for mastering.

DJ Awadi was the first rapper I ever met in Senegal. When I interviewed him for the first time in 2007, at the same studio in Dakar's quiet Amitié II neighborhood, he was in the midst of recording *Présidents d'Afrique*, an album featuring collaborations with rappers from several other African countries. Each track on the album samples the voice of an African leader. "We've included Martin Luther King"—he informed me—"because we understand the diaspora as a region of Africa."

Since the early 1990s, the now-disbanded PBS has situated themselves in a global ecumene of Afrocentric discourse. Awadi's former partner, Duggy-T, has described the time that he spent in libraries pouring over the Senegalese philosopher Cheikh Anta Diop's texts. He explained the group's early recording, "Africa":

We did "Africa" because we wanted to let people know all around the world what Africa really is . . . We are civilized! Modern. We are not that bad. We are not the image that they saw on the TV screen. All they show is that in Africa there are diseases, wars. That is the image we want to change. That is why we are named Positive Black Soul. Yeah! Everything that is black is associated with whatever is negative. Know what I'm saying? So we want to give them another image of Black people.

(SPADY 2006a, 640)

Awadi and Duggy-T came of age as students at Cheikh Anta Diop University in the late 1980s. Their group's name—Positive Black Soul—deliberately invoked transnational idioms of Black Power, while also tapping into a particular moment of local political unrest in which youth, particularly students, were closely involved (Diouf 2008, 365). In its abbreviated form, PBS, the name played on Senegal's political opposition party (Parti Démocratique Sénégalais, or PDS), at a time when multiparty politics had only recently been legally implemented, but when the country had yet to see any party other than Senghor's Parti Socialiste in power.

This moment of social change and upheaval, when youth sought to break from traditional age hierarchies and the corruption of postcolonial governance to assert their place in society, was ripe for a corresponding musical change. Hip hop stepped in with images and sounds of an elsewhere that was somehow familiar, even as it stood apart from the increasingly nationalized and localized sounds of mbalax; and yet, in its very form, it created space to draw on indigenous musics in new ways.

Daara J's Faada Freddy said,

We are a generation, the postindependence generation, that has been able to disengage from the French music or the Cuban music that colonial Africa only knew.

Today, we're at the point of rediscovering our value, because the borders are open once more.

I'm talking about the influence that we had from South Africa, the choruses that we had, the choruses that we did in the style of groups like Black Mambazo, the styles that we developed, styles like Fela Kuti's.

I think that today we've fulfilled the artistic, musical, polyphonic heritage that Africa has, and in this moment, I think we're in this dynamic, of revalorizing Africa, from whence the logic of taking these musics, as well as African instruments, and giving them more international standing.

Because hip hop is a like a platform, where, as it happens, all the generations of the world recognize themselves and can use it to express themselves in a very free way, but we've chosen to borrow African musics and African scales and to incorporate them in rap and to contribute to changing the culture of young Africans and the youth of the world.

And I think today, that's what people like Kanye West, or in any case composers, try to do: they try to find old samples of soul music, of Billie Holiday and Aretha Franklin, like that, and what we have is Salif Keita, Miriam Makeba, and Fela Kuti.

Over the years, Daara J (now Daara J Family) and Awadi (formerly of PBS) honed distinct musical styles that were united in their embrace of sounds from throughout Africa and the diaspora, merged with elements of hip hop and other globalized diasporic genres like reggae and R&B. If PBS's 1995 *Salaam* was a distinctly hip hop album, whose prominent musical markers of Senegal worked mostly as interludes and preludes, by the time Awadi's *Sunugaal* album came out a decade later, his sound had changed and mellowed into a seamless blend of hip hop and African idioms.[24]

The album opens with the title track, whose common play on words re-sounds Senegal as *Sunugaal* or "our boat" (*sunu gaal* in Wolof). The phrase is often said to be the actual origin of the country's name, deriving from linguistic misunderstandings between early French visitors and Wolof fishermen. Over a languid, kora-esque guitar accompaniment and gentle drums, Awadi raps in Wolof about a country that cannot carry its citizens, until they flee its constant power and water outages, its corruption and greed, boarding a different boat that will take them out into the dangerous waters and toward Europe. The song's last notes echo into silence, and the album takes a sharp turn into "Zamouna," a remake of a popular Cameroonian song from the 1960s.[25] A talking drum revisions the refrain as broadly West African. The album continues its retro imaginings of Africa with a salsa-inflected beat in "Le Cri du Peuple," a French-language echo of "Sunugaal" that decries the hardships of life in urban Senegal. The next track "Rosa," fills the room with sabar drums played by the legendary Wolof griot Doudou Ndiaye Rose.

The most hip hop thing about these tracks is the rapping; I'm six songs in before there's something with a beat anything like the songs I heard on *Salaam*. All these years later, speech (rapping) is what identifies these international artists' music as hip hop at all. No wonder, then, that their narratives of connection hinge primarily on verbal performance.

Listening to *Sunugaal*, things sober again with "J'accuse," where Awadi exposes the lasting effects of colonization as he riffs off Émile Zola's famed open letter to the French government, rapping his own French-language letter that accuses the presidents of the world's superpowers of crimes against humanity. Griot

Noumoucounda Cissoko sings the refrain and provides kora accompaniment. The rest of the album's eighteen tracks continue along these lines, combining the most modern production practices with musical signifiers of Africa, magnified through the names of globally recognized masters of the drum and kora.

"Oh, Africa," sings Daara J, on stage at Cinema Awa, "proud of who we are."

MUSICAL MEMORY

Tracing a musical history that begins with precolonial casted musicians and proceeds through religious conversion, colonial domination, urbanization, and nationalism, we find the modern griot in mbalax. Fronted by the social and aesthetic revision of localized Islamic praisesinging, over the accompaniment of indigenous rhythms, sounding simultaneously on sabar drums and the electrified instruments that still retain elements of the jazz and salsa that brought them to Senegal in the first place, mbalax layers musical markers of multiple times, events, places, and peoples to express the contemporary mélange that is modern, urban Senegal. Equally present in nightclubs and traditional life-cycle ceremonies, it musically encapsulates the historical trajectory of the postcolonial city—a hybrid cacophony of indigenous and globalized languages, architectures, religions, and fashions.

Yet if we follow the griot through colonial inventions to the work of midcentury Senegalese scholars and the Afrocentric projects of European and New World intellectuals in the twentieth century, a different history emerges—one that culminates in Senegalese engagements with hip hop that began in the 1980s. When Daara J or DJ Awadi fills the stage with an orchestra that juxtaposes electrified western instruments with local drums, when they incorporate local instrumental styles with R&B, salsa, hip hop, and music from elsewhere in Africa, and when they open their concert with a drummed Muslim prayer, they too create multilayered musical memories, sounding an alternative history.

What does it mean for something to become memory while it still exists, as is the case for both the griot and hip hop? Collective remembering interprets the past through the needs of the present, even to the point of sometimes reinventing that past or erasing parts of it in strategic ways (Wertsch and Roediger 2008, 320). In diasporic memories of the griot and of hip hop, however, it is not only the past that is rewritten or forgotten, it is particular parts of the present. For a diasporic community involved in reconstructing the griot, or for postcolonial nationalists mobilizing an "authentic," rural Africa, contemporary performance practices like mbalax are less compelling, less easily imagined to be history that can be meaningfully invoked in identity-building projects. These are left out of griot myths.

In a critique of modernity that is simultaneously within and without it, hip hop's griot origin myth engages Afrocentric discourse's "invocations of anteriority" (Gilroy 1993, 191), in which tradition links contemporary practices "with an African past that shaped them but which they no longer recognize and only slightly resemble" (ibid.). Claiming a mythologized griot who "grew up" in diaspora, rappers subverted nationalist discourse, which also mobilized the griot as a living link to African tradition and the past. Their layered origin narrative transformed indigenous speech in hip hop while rooting it in a past that ostensibly predates diaspora and globalization.

Mbalax and hip hop sketch aural cartographies of the griot's inextricable trajectories, sounding memories of social change in a city that emerges from the juncture of global economic, political, and cultural flows that are profoundly unequal (Fredericks and Diouf 2014, 10). This is the griot as rendered, through hip hop practice, as a diasporic memory. This is a hip hop that claims a place in the world defined not through colonization or globalization, but through diasporic connections, grounded in Africa and facing outward to the world. Musical memories, and memories of music, emerge in the dialogue of circulating meanings between Africa and the diaspora, and (re)trace alternative, multidirectional flows of global connection (Matory 2006; Piot 2001). As we will see, these musical histories and memories have shaped hip hoppers' claims to voice and agency vis-à-vis multilayered social hierarchies (Chapter 4) and are central to understanding the gendered dynamics of those claims (Chapter 5). They come together in hip hop's layered musical form to produce diaspora (Chapter 6).

4

VOICING GALSEN

AFTER PICKING UP rapper Coumbis and her manager and friend, Hawa, in Ouakam, it's a quick taxi ride to the upscale Almadies neighborhood, where the two young women lead me down a narrow path to the setting they've chosen for our filmed interview. Perched on massive rocks jutting out from a windy beach, breakers crashing just beneath us, we take more than a few vanity shots before settling down to discuss hip hop's history (Fig. 4.1). Coumbis whispers "Bismillah" as we begin.

I ask about her earliest encounters with hip hop, and she answers that it was through her brothers, then cuts herself off—"Are we starting?" "Yes," I tell her. She breathes a long "aaaah," and hesitantly starts over,

Sista Coumbis. Sista Coumbis.

She gathers herself.

Salaam Maalek, Salaam Maalek.
Sista Coumbis.
Ouakam represent.

Our course righted, we begin again, shifting back into French to trace her journey into hip hop. Her reference points are Daara J, Pee Froiss, Positive Black

FIGURE 4.1 Coumbis (left) and Hawa (right) at the beach in Almadies.

Soul (PBS); is she picking up the same thread of history, somewhere after those formative encounters with US hip hop in the late 1980s and early 1990s, or is this a new beginning altogether? Hers is an account of family and mentors, of the immediate human connections through which she navigates the world of Rap Galsen.

And then I ask about the origins of hip hop itself, its own story. Something about my apologetic delivery provokes mutual laughter, even as she begins to answer a question that I haven't quite asked,

No, for me, hip hop wasn't born in Senegal, for me. Hip hop wasn't born in Senegal. Because according to what they say, I've heard it said that hip hop was born thanks to the demonstrations of Black Americans, when they were tortured and hurt and all, they all went out, how to say it, to revolt and all, they demonstrated in the street, to say we don't want this anymore.

So, I don't really know, because I am very young, and what's more, I haven't been in hip hop a long time, but according to what I know hip hop wasn't born in Senegal.

Next to her, Hawa pipes up to clarify,

It's not a question of being born, but people say hip hop comes from Africa. That it was slaves who brought it there [to the United States], you see. There are people who see it like that. Because there are people who do—

She turns away from the camera to ask Coumbis in Wolof, "How do you say it? Taasu." Coumbis replies, "Mmm, *taasu* is what they say." Hawa picks back up in French:

—taasu, which resembles hip hop a little, you see, you do rhythms—

Coumbis adds, "and that's traditional, also," as Hawa continues,

Yes, and also, it's traditional. Maybe that's why people say that it's the same thing, that hip hop comes from Africa. Maybe it's that.

The three of us pause for a moment. I offer, "Yeah that's what I heard sometimes, some people are really against it, some people. . . " My voice trails into uncertainty, and Coumbis murmurs, "*I* don't think hip hop comes from Senegal." We laugh, and she continues at a normal volume, "Maybe from Africa but not Senegal. Because in Senegal we started getting into hip hop in like 1992."

Just two weeks earlier, in a quiet apartment in Yoff, I sit with Kalif and Kronic, members of the Undershifaay collective from the Guédiawaye banlieue. The two of them lounge on a large mattress as we chat with Lamine Ndao about our interview (Fig. 4.2). We've only just met, so I've skipped over the questions that I sometimes ask about taasu, afraid they'll hear an unspoken prompting to affirm hip hop's griot origins. But Lamine brings it up for me, and the conversation turns to a playful, yet somewhat heated discussion of the Senegalese and US scholars who have connected taasu, and the griots who perform it, to hip hop. "Liars!" shouts Kalif. I make a show of pulling back out my video camera to capture the action. As the guys banter back and forth, Kronic turns to stare directly into the lens and raises his voice over the others, speaking in an almost lecturing tone,

In regards to the resemblance between taasu and rap, for me these are false histories. Because taasu certainly resembles hip hop and is older than it.

But because it resembles hip hop is not to say that it is the true ancestor of hip hop.

FIGURE 4.2 Kronic (left) and Kalif (right), Undershifaay.

It is one thing that our ancestors did here, but hip hop is *another* thing that resembles taasu and that Americans created.

But that's not to say that taasu is the mother or father of hip hop. It's something that looks like hip hop—

Kalif, who has stopped chatting to listen, tries to interject, "Hip hop is hip hop—" while Kronic continues his thought without pausing, "—but it's not really hip hop." Kalif raises his voice, "—taasu is taasu. Hip hop is hip hop, taasu is taasu." Kronic's emphatic "Yeah!" is swallowed in Kalif's advancing rush of words—

I'm a hip hopper, not a taasu-er. I don't do taasu! Not at all!

As Kalif finishes his outburst and leans back casually on his elbows, Kronic resumes his careful exposition, unfazed by the interruption,

Because they say that hip hop comes from someone who organized reggae parties and spoke between songs.

And afterwards he started to speak over the instrumentals, and through speaking that became a style and took on a form.

And then he began to join words together that ended similarly.

And according to what I've heard, that's how hip hop was born.

So if it was born like that, it doesn't come from taasu.

Stories repeat, and the hesitations and qualifications and precisions that mark them repeat, and they are the same and they are different, over time and across generations. Kronic's exegesis is a careful retelling of hip hop's mythical genesis in the South Bronx. Coumbis lays a foundation of Black American struggle under the specific originating moment when Rap Galsen's own founding fathers, Positive Black Soul, first performed at the French Cultural Center in 1992. Reported speech gives weight to these narratives, marks them as performances, as storytelling, as the collective remembering of "historically conscious individuals" (Crane 1997, 1383). Incongruous within this frame of storytelling, their literal interpretations of the taasu origin narrative mark the increasing inability, or unwillingness, of many young people at the turn of the twenty-first century in Dakar to look past taasu's inarguable contemporaneity, to extract it from a complex of griot perfor-mance genres that are powerful in ways old and new. Griot performance, as we saw in the last chapter, belongs at once to a mythologized past and a material present. So, too, does hip hop.

Each generation of Senegalese rappers has laid claim to hip hop's mythologized history of racialized socioeconomic struggle in the urban United States. Coumbis cites the first, internationally successful wave of artists, who asserted hip hop's fundamental Africanity even as they rerouted taasu through the United States and African American musical history. The hardcore or underground rappers who released their first albums in the late 1990s, many of whom originated in the quartiers populaires (Medina and the neighborhoods that grew out from it, such as Grand Dakar, Fass, and Colobane) and the banlieues (Pikine, Parcelles Assainies, Guédiawaye, and Thiaroye), also traced hip hop's diasporic routes, but from an originating point in African America. The resonance between hip hop depictions of the US ghetto and their own realities became a stepping stone to a re-sounding of the street, rewritten as a specifically Senegalese experience of urbanity that is voiced through hip hop.

Are these really different stories, or are they the same story, begun at different moments? "Because they say that hip hop comes from someone who organized reggae parties and spoke between songs," says Kronic, as he explains why hip hop and taasu cannot be linked, and in his words, a displaced echo: Xuman's narra-tive of taasu's transatlantic journey and its pointed detour through Jamaica that transformed it into hip hop, something that is no more or less African than its creators in the South Bronx, linked but not the same (see Chapter 3). Whether this is one story or many ultimately matters less than what these stories do, each in its own way mobilizing diaspora—as myth, as historical migration, as lived ex-perience, or as some combination of these—in the service of voice. And voice, in turn, rests on genre.

Pulling apart these origin stories to reveal the relationship they establish between various genres of performance complicates voice and its associations with agency. Underground rappers care whether or not hip hop comes from griots because griot performance has actively reinscribed hegemonic structures for decades. Challenging this indigenous dynamic between voice and power, they mobilize a liberal idea of voice centered on ideas of free speech, in a juxtaposition of oral tradition and the agential voice that has been fundamental to discourses of modernity (Weidman 2006, 8). Claims to voice, then, are wrapped up in origin myths, which, as we began to see in the previous chapter, collectively remember and contest the present as well as the past. Through these practices of memory, hip hoppers produce the genres through which they may or may not speak; they wrest speech from indigenous orality and reframe it in hip hop, so that even as music produces different subject positions (ibid., 13), music makers produce the genres through which particular subject positions articulate as voice (Kunreuther 2014, 21–22).

It is precisely because of the ways in which voice and subjectivity depend on the production of particular genres (Barber 2007, 66) that hip hop's representational lyrical content remains significant. Yes, to consider hip hop as a practice of musical genre entails turning away from romanticized readings of its lyrics and toward its "phonic materiality . . . an act of not only self-expression, but also self-creation [that] is characterized by gaining value only through being heard" (Saucier 2014, 205). Yet to be heard in Senegal ultimately hinges on the relationship of content to form; lyrical content remains central to understanding if/how/why hip hop resists, not only metaphorically but sonically and socially as voice. In other words, voice in Senegal has to do with both what is said and how.[1]

And perhaps this is why origin narratives matter—because they are not just stories about origins, but claims to voice, different plots unraveling toward the same denouement.

FINDING TRADITION IN DAKAR

> If you are born in Senegal, if you are born here, you know mbalax, it's obligatory. It's obligatory that you know mbalax. Because it plays twenty-four hours out of twenty-four on the radio and TV. You can dislike it. You can detest it. But you can't not know it. You know it. You know it, you know the rhythms, because you are Senegalese. It is in the blood.
> DRYGUN, YATFU

A tent set up in the middle of the road in Medina fills with women of all ages as neighbors celebrate the birth of their first child. Crackling through the imposing sound system, mbalax hits old and new drown out the laundrywomen chatting on the corner, their children playing around them, and mask the horns and shouts of the brightly painted buses passing just two blocks over. A young man in smart, slim-fitting jeans, pointed loafers, and a rhinestone-encrusted belt entertains the guests, frequently interrupting his singing to break away from the microphone and perform a quick sequence of dance steps. The blaring music extends the celebration far beyond the insufficient space of the rented tent and into the surrounding homes, matching the sonic reach of the sabar ensemble it replaces.

At the beach in Almadies, Coumbis shrugs and shakes her head. "Mbalax . . . how to explain it. I can't say anything. We are all baptized with mbalax. We are born with it. We grow up with it."

Walk or drive down any street in Dakar and you will hear mbalax. It pours into the streets from taxis and buses, nightclubs and restaurants, tented weddings and baptisms, family homes and the tiny corner boutiques offering daily necessities like butter, eggs, soap, and matches. Kronic described mbalax's pervasive aural presence,

It's just our national music. We are born within it—well, I hope that I won't die in it.

It's a music that we found—

it's what the average Senegalese loves, but also you should say they love it because in general it's what they see on TV, sometimes you can—

you love it not because you really love it but because you see it every day on TV.

And to try to resolve the problem will be really difficult, because if they saw something else on TV maybe they'd love something else, but unfortunately this comes back to our problem of the difficulty of the cultural education of our population.

Not to be mean, but *I* would say that the average Senegalese has no musical culture. Because I listen to all music, even if I am more into rap and reggae.

But what made me love rap is my musical openness.

But I listen to world music, pop, rock, *voila*.

And that's what the average Senegalese is missing—He only listens to mbalax. He is not open to other musics. So it's a little hard to make him—

Kalif interrupts in Wolof—"mbalax in the morning, mbalax in the afternoon, mbalax all night," and Kronic continues, riffing off Kalif as he switches briefly to English, "All time, all day. 24/7, that's what they see on TV and the radios. Mbalax."

To be born in mbalax is to become a social being in the ritual of naming a week after birth, during a celebration traditionally accompanied by sabar drumming and now just as often infused with mbalax. It is also to be born into a particular historical moment in which the ambiguity of the word *mbalax*—the name of both the popular music genre and the foundational sabar rhythm on which it is based—reflects a slippage between modernization, urbanization, and woloficization. The commutability of sabar and mbalax imparts a particular understanding of tradition, music, and historical memory to those born in the final decades of the twentieth century.

Rapper Profete was in his early twenties when we met on a road trip to The Gambia with Sen Kumpë in June 2011 and struck up a friendship. A couple months later, I meet him at his home in Grand Dakar to take some pictures and do an interview. He leads me through a carefully curated series of backdrops not far from his house. As he poses against unfinished cinderblock walls that abut rusted, corrugated tin shelters, debris litters the ground around his spotless white sneakers. He stops again in front of a shack; the perennial duet of equatorial sun and seasonal rains has weathered its raw wooden planks into a patchwork of beiges, greys, and browns. We continue to an open plot of land, surrounded on all sides by houses and shops; he perches atop a pile of old tires and logs and discarded plastic mats, tarp-roofed shanties a short distance behind him (Fig. 4.3).

When the light began to fade, we climbed to the second floor of a partially constructed house (I wondered uneasily if we're allowed to be here) and sat, I on a folding chair, he on a wooden bench low to the ground. His friend had procured a small tank of propane somewhere, and they got the tea started before we began, emptying bitter green leaves into the small pot, adding a generous pour of sugar; it would be ready by the time we finished the interview. Not a minute into our recorded conversation, he stopped, stricken. He doesn't speak French, like many of his peers, even in Dakar, and despite the language's official national status. While not quite half of Senegal's roughly 11 million people are ethnically Wolof, nearly 90 percent of the population speak Wolof as a first or second language (McLaughlin 2009, 145). I felt increasingly competent in Wolof but was used to interviewing older rappers who spoke French; I was unsure that I could translate my questions on the spot. We agreed that we'd each speak the language we were more comfortable in, both confident in our understanding, if not in our speech. Reassured, we continued, and Profete's initially curt responses gave way to a freer reflection on hip hop's place in Senegal.

He laughs when I ask about mbalax, indirectly, by saying, "What's the most popular music in Senegal?"

Well I listen to *rap*, I listen to *rap*! Yeah, I don't even know.

FIGURE 4.3 Profete poses in Grand Dakar.

but we have our customs, we have our tradition, and when you're born you find it here, which is mbalax, you know?

Again and again, I asked rappers to describe Senegalese traditional music; again and again, they answered by describing mbalax. I shifted my question as I continued to probe for the ethnically specific musics—what rapper Gaston called "*traditional* traditional music"—that rappers almost uniformly described as predating, rather than coexisting with, mbalax's modern tradition (Waterman 1990); "*Besides* mbalax, how would you describe traditional music in Senegal?"

So I ask Profete to tell me about traditional music, besides the mbalax he's just spoken about at some length. His Wolof absorbs colonial language into an indigenous syntax whose primacy in Dakar speaks to the intertwined histories of indigenous and colonial conquest that shaped urban identities in the twentieth century. He answers me with refusal, a layered and repeating disavowal of something that, like French, he has not mastered [Fr. *maîtriser*].

That side of things, I haven't really mastered it well [*maîtrisewuma ko bu baax*]

Yeah, I haven't really mastered it well [*maîtrisewuma ko bu baax*]

Because, I don't listen to a lot of people who are doing what's traditional.

You know, what I listen to in that isn't like, a lot.

That was Souleymane Faye, you know, that was Idrissa Diop, because what they were doing was kind of close to our hip hop, they were speaking truth in their stuff, you know.

But I can't say anything about traditional music,

Because I haven't mastered it a lot [*parce que maîtrisewuma ko lu bëri*]

I don't listen to it.

Patterns of linguistic and musical change, inseparable from shifting conceptions of ethnic identity, mirror each other and reflect what it means to be a young person in Dakar at the turn of the century. The city's histories have produced a distinctly urban form of Wolof that invites critiques of cultural loss, of generations unmoored from their origins, speaking a language corrupted by colonialism and marked by absences and deformations (McLaughlin 2009, 156).

"Besides mbalax, how would you describe traditional music?" I ask then-rapper Mame Xa, on one day out of many spent together in his barbershop, named for his debut album, *Dor War* (Hard Work) (Fig. 4.4).[2] His limited abilities with French

FIGURE 4.4 Mame Xa stands outside his barbershop.

challenge me to sharpen my Wolof; he seems to enjoy stumping me with new words as much as I enjoy learning them. On the wall behind him, a mirror reflects a countertop, cluttered with hair products and a battered stereo that plays Damien Marley and Nas's song "Patience" on repeat. To our left, one of his friends shaves another's head. The buzzing clippers act like a drone beneath the hip hop track's staccato strings, vying for my attention with Mame Xa's low, wry responses. His speech forces French verbs into Wolof conjugations; he punctuates his resistance to the question with woloficized French adverbs, their consonant blends pushed apart into separate syllables, their silent terminal consonants sounded in an emphatic staccato [Fr. *trop*; W. *torop*; Eng. *too*]:

> Traditional music? Well maybe there's ngoyane,[3] there's something we call ngoyane,
>
> but there's not too, too, too, too much of it [*Mais bëriwul torop torop torop torop*].
>
> the young people aren't so into it, in general old people are the ones—
>
> there are also others,
>
> but I haven't mastered it too, too, too, too well [*Mais maîtrisewuma ko torop torop torop torop*].
>
> There are others, but I haven't really mastered it too well [*Mais maîtrisewuma ko torop*].

In this antiphonal refrain of abstentions and protest each time I tried to guide an exchange past mbalax, I encountered a persistent understanding of tradition as something that pertained, in an unspecified but assuredly precolonial past, to the various ethno linguistic groups that are now partially subsumed into this Wolof-dominated urbanity.

One day, during an interview in a comfortable home in Point E, I ask rapper Nix about traditional music. He stumbles over words, in a French that he speaks fluently,

> Well, traditional music in Senegal, I can describe it a little, even if I'm not, I don't know it very, very, very, very well.
>
> But I know that we have a traditional music, which is to say, with all that is, with instruments like euh, euh, euh—the riti,[4] the—all that is—djembe, euh, what's it called again, our xalam, all that, all these are our traditional instruments.

You see?

It's music—and this traditional music was here before mbalax, you see, because mbalax is a recent music, anyway.

It's what, at the end of the '70s, you see?

Mbalax was at the end of the '70s, to the '80s.

It's a mix—

it's a bit, it's salsa, at its base, that Senegalese musicians played and that they ended up modifying, modifying, modifying until that produced mbalax.

So—

and even before those musicians played salsa, there was traditional music, in fact.

And as he continues, his voice changes, brightened by his laughter, an apologetic overemphasis,

So, now, *I'm not an expert in this,* I'm not up to the task of describing it to you, but I know that these instruments were part—

all that is xalam, riti, euh, djembe, you see?

These are part of the instruments at the base of what made Senegalese traditional music, right?

And then, well, you also have music, you have ethnic music, it is also ethnic, music a little—

the Serers, for example, you have the Jola, you have the Peul, you see?

I think that all these ethnicities have their traditional music.

Another day, rapper Alou of Colobane's KTD Crew spoke hesitantly to me about traditional music, while his partner, Madou, sat to his right, looking away from us and from the camera, his disinterest clear. Scratching his head, speaking in careful French slowed only by his discomfort with the topic, Alou said,

[Traditional music] is varied. But not well known, eh?

Because, as I was just saying, the most mediatized music in Senegal is mbalax, even though there are other traditional forms of music—

I personally am not familiar with many [he raises his hand in an absolution of responsibility, eyebrows raised, head tilted apologetically] but I think that there are a lot.

Uh, it's like, as they say, there are how many ethnic groups in Senegal?

There are as many ethnic groups as there are kinds of traditional music, I think.

He shrugged.

Like, according to me.

Next to him, Madou, who had deferred to Alou's francophone responses throughout, finally chimed in, shaking his head and wagging his finger at me in comedic resignation, speaking around his toothpick as he quipped in Wolof, "I don't have many thoughts on *that*." Alou turned away in laughter (Fig. 4.5).

Madou's friend, Books, summarized traditional music's metamorphosis from ethnic plurality into the aural monolith of mbalax, saying,

FIGURE 4.5 KTD Crew Madou (left) and Alou (right) pose on a rooftop in Medina.

And now mbalax has become, I would say, "traditional music" in Senegal.

Because if you say "traditional music," there are people who don't know wango,[5] there are people who don't know the music of the Serer, the music of the Jola, the music of the Tukaleur, even the Sarakhule, you see.

Now there is a *melting pot* [*Eng.*] here and all that music is traditional music but we don't know it, we don't understand it.

We only know mbalax.

A repetition of disavowal—I don't know, I haven't studied, I haven't mastered it, I *think*—connected disparate narratives, spoken in localized French and urban Wolof and accompanied by invocations of youthful inexperience that marked tradition as something older than my interlocutors, older than us. So distant in time and experience that many rappers did not want to speak on it at all.

On the one hand, rappers' general reticence about traditional music invokes its supposed links to rurality and the past. On the other hand, their consistent portrayal of mbalax itself as tradition highlights tradition's dynamism and reminds us that tradition and modernity are coeval and coconstitutive.[6] My questions that evoked these responses—uncertainty, nervous laughter, apology, disavowal, stuttering, hesitation—assumed a distinction between "traditional traditional" music and mbalax's cosmopolitan hybridity, although surely I should have known better, should have recognized that, "[U]rban Africans could not have related to (adopted, adapted, mixed, preserved, rejected, revived) tradition—except insofar as tradition was copresent with modernity" (Fabian 1998, 73). As mbalax becomes tradition, it takes on a weight, a duration. It is not as old as the mythologized griot of negritude, but neither is it new; young people have heard it since infancy, and so have their parents.

"We are born in mbalax," says Kronic. "I hope I won't die in it."

SINGING SILENCE, VOICING DISSENT

When the city's youth began making hip hop in earnest in the early 1990s, griot performance, popular music, and political and religious power structures had long been deeply intertwined. So it was no surprise that when Rap'Adio founder Keyti was telling me about encountering a translated Public Enemy video for the first time, all those years ago, his story became, without my asking, a story about mbalax. And his story about mbalax was, as I had come to expect, also a story about indigenous cultural norms and their misalignment with the world he lived in.

That night I saw the video I couldn't sleep, you know, I just like, kept thinking about the translation and how it was really strong.

Because the music we were used to here was mbalax [*he claps*]

which is more about, you're coming from a royal family, you're a good person, you've been well educated, and for me as a youngster at that time, to see a video where they say don't believe the hype, don't believe the system, this and that, this is how the world is, that was amazing, you know, and I felt like, I want to do that.

Rappers reminded me that mbalax didn't just *sound* traditional in its reliance on sabar rhythms; it also functioned as tradition when it channeled indigenous verbal performance. Keyti noted mbalax's tendency toward praisesinging ("you're coming from a royal family, you're a good person"). Tigrim Bi's N-Jah (Fig. 4.6) connected it to griots' recitation of genealogies, saying,

Mbalax is like a tradition.

Most of the time when they sing on it they are trying to sing your grandmother and your great-grandmother.

They sing history, where history came from.

They try to give value to your traditions so you can give them money.

FIGURE 4.6 N-Jah sits for an interview.

There's a slippage in the verb *to sing* as rappers use it, in English and French, that seems to come from the Wolof usage of the verb (*woy*). Before urban popular music developed in the twentieth century (see Chapter 3), to be a *woykat*—a person who sings by profession—was to be a griot. The verb *woyaan* (often glossed as *woy* in daily speech) means to sing/to praise, and it is an action that generally only woykats do, although others, particularly women, will sometimes temporarily (and often playfully) take on this role in the context of life-cycle celebrations. Prior to the emergence of hip hop, popular music, as a refiguring of griot music, had been sung in both senses—physically singing and praising.[7]

In the mid-1990s, underground groups like Rap'Adio had explicitly rejected singing in their hardcore aesthetic, reacting to the soft musical style of international artists (Chapter 2). But they also conflated "singing" as the melodic vocal practice foregrounded in popular song with "singing" as a performative affirmation of interconnected historical and contemporary power imbalances. Their rejection of singing entangled global hip hop myth and local understandings of song (Appert 2015).

Keyti and I talk about how he started rapping, stepping directly into Wolof lyrics without detouring first through English or French, listening to and appreciating PBS on television, meeting the men who would form Rap'Adio with him, marking the divide between melodic performance and hardcore hip hop. He tells me how Rap'Adio pushed at the boundaries of musical and linguistic communication:

> What impressed people was the way we were writing—
>
> it was the first time they heard people write like that, with rhymes, images, metaphors, and the subject matter was related to what people were going through, not only in terms of politics but also daily life.
>
> I remember when we released our first album, people kept asking me, "How come you can talk about certain things I feel and you are just putting it into words?"
>
> That's one of the biggest problems with Wolof, the local language.
>
> The biggest problem with Wolof is to translate feelings.
>
> We are raised like that—
>
> we don't grow up with certain words.
>
> It's difficult in Senegalese society to see a mom or a father telling his kids "I love you" in Wolof, because we are taught to hide our feelings.
>
> When people are sad or when they suffer there are not even words to say, "this is what I'm going through."
>
> They might exist but I think over time we lost these words.

Someone might spend all night with things on his mind and in the morning you will ask, "Noo fanaane? How did you spend your night?"

And he will say "jamm [in peace]."

So, it's like, from the beginning we are really taught not to talk about ourselves and our feelings.

And the whole time we were in the underground that's what we were fighting for—this anger we had inside, this frustration we had inside, we had to find words to put it on paper.

And I think we succeeded in that first album and that's why it had such a huge impact on Senegalese youth here.

For a lot of people, Rap'Adio remains *the* rap group.

"But I think over time we lost these words," said Keyti, and again there's an echo of loss that sets me thinking about language, and if the use of Wolof in hip hop isn't about more than localization, class status, or intelligibility, although it is surely about all those things. I think of the power of the tongue to bring bad luck, of hastily muttered counterjinxes when I inadvertently drew attention to someone's health, wealth, or talent. I remember the Wolof value of *sutura*—discretion, privacy, not airing dirty laundry or exposing other people's actions. What kinds of utterances are possible in Wolof? In traditional music? What can and cannot be said, and by whom?

Language turns to speech, and speech sounds as voice, when I ask him why hip hop has continued to be so successful in Senegal in the years since Rap'Adio's first album.

I think it's related to what I was just talking about.

When you're in a place where you're denied freedom of speech—

it's not institutionalized, but it's like, it's here.

And people just don't talk about it.

Certain parts of society, they are not heard.

They don't got the right to talk.

The way Senegalese society is built is, and I think even back then it was like that, younger people, they don't talk, they just listen to the elders.

And what the elders decide, that's what everybody's doing.

But I think from 1960, the independence of Senegal, to the beginning of the '80s, there was only one regime here, the socialist regime.

And from independence to the '90s, the standard of living kept going down, you know. And it's like, the whole Senegalese society was frustrated, but people were scared to talk. And I think actually when hip hop arrived, in the beginning we didn't really straight talk about politics.

But yeah, rappers talked about it.

PBS's first album talked about politics, not 100 percent but on two or three tracks, and their position was clear, they were against the government.

Pee Froiss did the same.

The other groups, in the underground, they did the same.

And I think back then, Senegalese people were ready to hear such a message, a message of revolution, that we need to change this country.

They felt oppressed and couldn't say it.

The musicians in other genres that were here weren't talking about that.

And that is why when hip hop came and was addressing these issues, people were like yeah this is what we've been waiting for.

And I think that's mainly the reason why they adopted hip hop in Senegal.

Voice, the freedom to speak, is entangled in a web of traditional communicative norms that govern speech within and across social categories—of age, caste, gender, and kinship—and that encompass griot performance. For griot speech enacts power. At the level of everyday social relations, griot speech can ruin or make reputations; its force lies in how it represents, and in so doing, consolidates or even constructs, social identity in relation to others (Barber 2007, 109; Wright 1989, 52). Griot speech upheld the noble classes in precolonial Senegal, and it has mediated and propped up power in the postcolony, where indigenous hierarchies are unevenly displaced onto political and religious ones (Diouf 1996, 236). Mbalax emerges from and extends this complex web of speech and power. Hip hop seems to stand outside it.

Lamine Ndao once said to me,

If there is a problem with the government, something serious, it's hip hop that is there . . .

People might ask, where are the mbalaxmen?

Are they drunk or what?

They can't speak.

I think they can't speak because they are always busy singing the government to have money.

The praisesinging voice, imbricated in traditional practices of patronage and clientelism that foreclose the possibility of resistance, is not a voice at all, but rather a stifling silence, one that is partly a reality of sociopolitical structures, but is also partly constructed by rappers' own retellings of the griot, of tradition, and of mbalax.[8] For mbalax is to some extent reimagined here as well: if, in its long history, it has not always been socially or politically engaged, there have been mbalax artists who rejected praisesinging, protested corruption to the point of censorship, and worked for social change.[9] And what seems like rappers' wholesale rejection of mbalax becomes, at times, a bit tongue-in-cheek, as in the annual "Rappers vs. Mbalax/men" soccer match. Older rappers were more likely than their younger counterparts to temper their distaste for mbalax, and the narratives that emerged in interviews and lyrics aside, I've seen many rappers break out a playful dance move or two when mbalax music is playing in the privacy of their homes or among friends.

Drygun cautions me that rappers may hate mbalax and its messages, but they can't pretend not to know it. He evokes its ubiquity, its presence in the blood, as though to be Senegalese is to know intimately its rhythms, inescapable as one's genes. We are born in mbalax.

At two o'clock in the morning in mid-June 2011, Simon takes the stage in front of a sizeable crowd of perhaps five hundred teenagers outside of Kennedy Highschool (Fig. 4.7). Television personality Y.Dee is the master of ceremonies for tonight's show, and I'm disoriented for a moment when I realize that his voice, booming out over the crowd in an extended introduction for his "brother from another mother," is prerecorded, part of the backing track for "Rap Legnou Wax." As

FIGURE 4.7 Simon performs at Kennedy Highschool during the Orange S'Cool Tour.

the heavy string ostinato abruptly drops into silence, Y.Dee's gleeful laugh ushers in the beat, which immediately locks into the first hook. Simon raps in the seamless mixture of French and Wolof that has come to stand as a linguistic marker of urban identity, as the audience answers in a call and response after each line, "Rap Legnou Wax [We say *rap*]."

Bayyileen beleen bele yi [Stop talking without saying anything]—*Rap Legnou Wax*

Naafeq yi taxaawe ne [Hypocrites, get lost]—*Rap Legnou Wax*

Publique bi lu leen soxla? [Audience, what do you need?]—*Rap Legnou Wax*

Degguma [I can't hear you]—*Rap Legnou Wax*, Degguma—*Rap Legnou Wax*

Sponsored by the cellular provider Orange, the concert stretches for hours, with rapper after rapper taking his turn to perform over prerecorded tracks. As I stand backstage, half asleep on my feet, suddenly the young girls clustered in front of the stage start shrieking, and I jerk awake. Next to me, Books scowls at the scene in front of us, where a familiar blend of synthesized instruments, rhythmic chanting, and piercing pressure drum riffs dispels my confusion even before he speaks. "Mbalaxmen!" he spits, his lips curling as we watch the dancing feet of the current performers in the tiny sliver of stage visible to us, their bodies blocked by the backdrop. Y.Dee stalks back to where we're standing and tells me in English—I'm out. They paid me to work a hip hop show, not this mbalax bullshit.

Bayyileen beleen bele yi. Stop talking without saying anything. Into the silence of mbalax's ubiquitous sound steps hip hop, whose utility, its promise of action, emerges in opposition to indigenous music. Rappers' claim to a liberal construct of voice and free speech works against the power of generational difference in the context of a modernity in which youth is attenuated and disempowered.

On the rooftop in Medina, Madou is explaining why so few women participate in hip hop when he abruptly cuts himself off. "Catty are you understanding what I'm saying?" I assure him that I am. While setting up, we'd discussed another interview where I struggled to understand my interlocutor. I say it's fine, that the problem was that the guy spoke Serer. He and Alou respond at once, "Really, Serer?" "No, I don't even know," I confess. I watch it dawn on them, the unexpected but distinctly Dakarois joke that conflates my lack of comprehension with hearing a non-Wolof indigenous language, and then they laugh in surprise. Alou explains to no one in particular—"She couldn't understand him!"

I continue, asking why, despite hip hop's undeniable presence in Dakar, mbalax remains the most popular music. Madou has been reticent to this point. Now reassured, he rushes in, "Let me speak first on that one." His Wolof is sprinkled with French words, nearly every sentence ending with "like" or "you know." He says "music" in English, rather than in French (*musique*); the repetition of the un-expectedly elongated first syllable throws his sentences slightly off balance.

> Because, as they say, mbalax is found here—it's our culture, first off.
>
> You understand.
>
> It's a culture, you know.
>
> And you know, we all find it here because we are named with it.
>
> You can say we are named with it.
>
> And that person and that person are named in mbalax.
>
> Because mbalax is our culture, that's what we find here . . .
>
> But if you see mbalax now it's about nothing.
>
> Guys do whatever they feel like in mbalax.
>
> They say that mbalax is music, you understand.
>
> But music has to follow a path, it should be significant.
>
> But here, if you look at what rappers are saying and what mbalaxmen are saying, it's two different things, they're not the same.
>
> If you look closely, what rappers are saying is much more conscious compared to what mbalaxmen are saying . . .
>
> Now, I don't listen to mbalax.
>
> For me it's useless compared to hip hop music.
>
> Hip hop is the music I can listen to and take a lot away from it.
>
> For me that is music.
>
> Music needs to be useful.

Just minutes later, Madou would repeat the same speech about taasu and rap-ping; rappers often slid this way between taasu and mbalax, taasu and traditional music, traditional music and mbalax. But Alou spoke first, hearing the unspoken question that I thought to have purged from my inquiry about taasu and obliging,

> Most Senegalese rappers say it's the ancestor of rap.
>
> But it's not scientifically proven.
>
> We can never know.
>
> It's a little close to the way we rap, but I wouldn't say it's similar.

It's far from being similar.

When someone does taasu, he pays homage to someone or talks about things that don't have any sense, while when we do rap we make efforts that it be logical, that it has a certain form, whether that form is loved or not, and that there is content.

That is the logic.

It's truly different.

Maybe if the origin, even originally, when Black Americans did rap it was for their revindication.

Here they don't do taasu for revindication, I've never heard of that.

It's just for fun, to pay homage or give history, but I've never heard a *taasukat* [person who recites taasu] talk about a politician or denigrate the regime via his taasu.

Never.

For me that's the difference.

Hip hop, in what it says as much as how it says it, becomes a foil to the modern traditions of taasu, praisesinging, and mbalax, and questions of origins are answered even when they aren't asked because these pervasive narratives tacitly frame our conversations.

Discarding the aesthetic resonance at the heart of earlier origin stories that traced taasu through the diaspora and back to Africa (see Chapter 3), the underground insists that referential content creates an irreconcilable difference between these speech genres. As I discussed traditional music with Gaston, he continued,

It's true there was, that there is a nuance between rapping and taasu. Taasu is to make your words staccato, rap is to make your words staccato, so you see, there is a nuance between these two worlds, but I think it's not at all related, because taasu, more accurately, pays homage to someone, while rap music exists to denounce, to revolutionize, to inform, to raise consciousness. So at the base it's two different worlds, but in terms of form, there is a nuance between these two.

We will see that hip hop's pull is not just about its lyrical content; it is about the form that content takes as being diasporic rather than "African" (Chapter 6). Still, verbal referentiality is central to how these performance genres are produced in relation to each other (Barber 2007, 66) and through them voice and subjectivity. Hip hop creates the possibility of new kinds of utterances in Wolof, so that to use

Wolof is not just to localize hip hop or make it locally intelligible, but to challenge the social limits of indigenous language by mobilizing it within a new form. In a corrective push to consider hip hop as sound and as music, it can be tempting to set up a binary between lyrical and musical considerations. Hip hop, however, is both a vehicle for content *and* a form that is meaningful, and these two things are inseparable because of the ways in which certain kinds of utterances are made possible through and in particular genres. And genre, in turn, is produced through origin myths that link and delink time and space.

TIME AND URBAN SPACE

If traditional oralities are characterized by topical content as much as aesthetics, and remembered in ways contingent on their function in the present, then the same is true for hip hop, whose usefulness in the present is grounded in a particular remembering of its past. And this too is a narrative of origins that works to produce genre.

"Because the history of rap, even if I don't know it all, I know a bit," said Books. "I know where it comes from . . ."

It doesn't come from Africa.

It doesn't come from Africa.

It doesn't come from us.

It doesn't come from us.

We are influenced by Americans and this comes from American ghettos.

Origin myths bring us again to the street, the hip hop ghetto as a metonym for a specifically Senegalese experience of urbanity, heightened in the banlieues and quartiers populaires (see Chapter 2). This is the ghetto that sounds in Pikine-based Tigrim Bi's "Rongognou Guetto [Tear of the Ghetto]," which asks those in power to acknowledge the daily struggles of life in the banlieues, including blackouts, malnutrition, poverty, and lack of access to medical care.

Ni am lekk desal bay tuur nañu gëstu ñi lekkagul ba suur [Those who have eaten and have leftovers should look for those who haven't eaten enough]

Xiif, mar, raflek, tumuranke; woop ak raag, ñak angi sanke . . . [Hungry, thirsty, lacking, destitute; diseased and malnourishment, poverty claims its victims . . .]

Xoolal fi ci ghetto, metti ñipp a koy yëgando [Look here in the ghetto, we all feel the same hardship]

Tear of the ghetto, rongogn ñipp a toqaando [Tear of the ghetto, everyone cries together]

The street (re)sounds in 5kiem Underground's "Joyu Askan Wi [Tears of My People],"[10] whose verses detail the struggles of daily life in Dakar's quartiers populaires, returning each time to the refrain that demands that a plural "you"—politicians, religious leaders—pay attention to the people's plight.

Dafa mel ni gisuleen li ñuy daj bes bu nekk [It seems you don't see what we encounter every day]

Deggluleen: Askan waangi joy [Listen: the people are crying]

Xanaa yeen yëguleen li ñuy jankonteel [Aren't you aware of what we face every day?]

Yeen, seetluleen: Askan waangi joy [Look closely: the people are crying]

The refrain repeats, the words shift. "It seems you don't see what we encounter each day in the street."

"We say what's happening in the ghetto," said then-5kiem member Baye Njagne, in his home in Medina. "We're obligated to do what Americans are doing because we live the same problems, the same difficulties. Underground rap there talks about how life is hard, daily problems. It's like here in Dakar, in a quartier populaire." Around the corner, on the sidewalk outside his home one afternoon during Ramadan, waiting for the afternoon call to prayer that would announce the end of the day's fast, Baye Njagne's partner, Djily Bagdad, described "Joyu Askan Wi" to me in the fluent English he picked up during a brief stint studying in Atlanta, Georgia, in the early 1990s,

[The song] is about the masses, people in the ghetto, how they are living and the hardship and everything.

Tears of My People.

Things were better when colonization was here.

The farmer sold his product and the white people bought it and paid them in due time. But since independence, people are doing whatever they want.

Our own leaders, who should care about the people, it seems like the white people cared more about us than our own leaders.

It talks about what people are living on a daily basis. While they are building monuments, people are dying of hunger, begging for money in the street, and while the situation is getting worse the rich are getting rich and richer and the poor are getting poorer and poorer.

Sitting with Djily in Medina that day, I thought about how often this particular neighborhood was invoked as an example of "the street." I listened to him paint the ghetto as a direct consequence of corrupt postcolonial regimes, highlighting the tensions between lived experiences of underdevelopment and superficial markers of development—like the notorious Monument de la Renaissance, completed in 2010 under the direction of then-president Abdoulaye Wade. Overlooking the city of Dakar, the towering, remarkably Stalinest statue has been a topic of controversy; many Senegalese citizens protest not only the gross financial expenditure, but also the short garment that the bare-breasted woman wears, an affront to local norms of modesty.

Hip hop's origin myth, its specific moment of emergence in the South Bronx, mediates local realities, the street that is born from the union of colonialism and neocolonialism, an index of underdevelopment, a metonym of urban youth experience. This is hip hop's *usefulness*: it voices these experiences in ways that traditional music cannot, and this is why origin stories matter.

My own knowledge of hip hop origins was often tested, as men in Dakar's hip hop scene flipped my questions back on me in a formulaic litany that went something like this:

HIP HOPPER: Do you know American rappers?

The question itself gives me pause. The verb they use—*connaître*—is ambiguous, and it's unclear if I'm being asked if I personally know famous American rappers (not an odd question—I know famous Senegalese rappers), or if I'm familiar with their music. Finally, I respond—Yes. Of course I know their music. Right on cue, the name-dropping begins, a canon of East Coast artists whose careers peaked in the 1990s or, less often, the early 2000s.

Him: Do you know Das EFX?
Me: Yes.
Him: Salt-N-Pepa?
Me: Yes.
Him: Nas?
Me: Yes . . . yes . . . yes.

Sometimes the test is less leading, a double question leaving no room for pretense: Do you listen to hip hop? What rappers do you like? I recall Books's advice, one day in the courtyard of his family home in Medina, as I complained mildly about their questioning—Tell them you know everything about "les anciens," but that you don't really listen to new hip hop. That will end the conversation. It's none of their business what you listen to, anyway; they don't need to know that you listen to all this new stuff.

In another Medina courtyard, rapper Almamy's aged mother greets me, smiling, without the curious calculation that I encounter in women of her generation in the other homes I visit for research. Almamy and I have taken a break from our extended interview to eat the rice and fish that he asked his sisters to prepare, knowing it's my favorite; having finished, we venture outside to thank them and chat with his mother before returning inside to finish our conversation. We're old friends by now, in the busy neighborhood where I spend most of my time, and I don't hesitate before following him to his room, whose familiar furnishings include a photo of his uncle, Rap'Adio's Iba, pinned to the wall above the computer. We pick up where we've left off, discussing US hip hop and its influence in Senegal. His nostalgic reflections quickly turn dismissive, even contemptuous,

> In the beginning, we were familiar with engaged songs like, euh, LL Cool J, Wyclef and his group, the Refugees—we listened to their songs a lot, you see, we loved their ideas, there were people that gave us a lot of very positive ideas, for example you listened to Tupac, there were his texts, they brought you to seventh heaven.
>
> I appreciated these texts.
>
> Biggie, you listened to his texts, his texts were really well written, it was extraordinary. But today's generation, like you hear–
>
> [*he switches to English*] you know I've got my swagger on—
>
> seriously I don't have time to listen to this kind of music.

Down the block from Almamy's house, Lamine Ndao too complained that hip hop in the United States has deserted its commitment to social consciousness in favor of celebrity and financial gain:

> I'd say that American hip hop is overall a good hip hop.
>
> But more and more, I would say I don't know what we hear in American hip hop, it's increasingly a hip hop that's losing its value, as they say.

What it defended, a lot of rappers have changed, and now they speak of material things, "yeah I have nice cars, yeah I have a nice house, yeah I've got dough, I've got bling bling, I've got a girl, I've got hos." For me, it's a bit vulgar.

In these recurrent refrains of loss, I heard that hip hop had changed, that it had become commercial, vulgar, *easy*. Stories about hip hop could stand in for stories about mbalax: all about girls, dancing, money, fame. Not *real* hip hop. Not *tradition* tradition. The romanticized precolonial griot, lost to mbalax. The mythical old-school hip hop, twisted to conspicuous consumption.

"I'm very young and I don't know," Coumbis told me when I asked her about hip hop's history. Hip hop too becomes tradition, myth; its youngest practitioners note their distance from its beginnings, back in the day when their elders were young.

When the same question, or a version of it, is turned on me, the internal battle begins. Don't tell them you listen to all this new stuff, Books had advised. My mind recites the litany that will bring a satisfied nod from my interrogator. Das EFX. Redman. Method Man. Nas . . . But maybe today there's time to kill, or maybe I'm feeling mischievous, or maybe I'm just tired of staying in character for so long, and so I respond that lately (this was 2011, mind you), I've been really into Lil Wayne. The appalled disproval is immediate—Lil Wayne doesn't rap about anything. Drugs and hos. It's not real hip hop. It's not conscious.

I knew what I was in for when I answered the way I did, and I'm ready to passionately defend my position, for the fun of it, if nothing else. I lay it on thick—Hip hop is art. It's poetry. If it wasn't, *you* could just make political speeches instead of making your music. Lil Wayne is brilliant; his lyrics are like a hip hop concordance. The referentiality is remarkable. The lyricism is so clever. It inevitably turns into a dispute, but in the end, I receive the same satisfied nod I would have with my list of old-school East Coast artists.

Knowing hip hop as poetic expression and as music comes up against myths of how and when "real" hip hop speaks, from where and to what ends. Lil Wayne—the epitome of what rappers referred to interchangeably as crunk or Dirty South music back then—was a foil to a hip hop myth rooted not only in the past but also in a distant place of origin: New York, and more specifically, the South Bronx. Dakar rappers frequently transposed this spatial mythology onto hip hop's changing lyrical content over the last few decades, in a narrative of moral decay that echoed a globally circulating "moral panic" about the commercial cooption of hip hop as it spread from its inner-city origins (Perry 2004, 192).

About a ten-minute walk from Almamy's house, on the other side of the major road that cuts through the Medina, Djily Bagdad narrated hip hop myths of commercialism and consciousness, layering spatial distance (between the East Coast and other US hip hop scenes) over temporal distance (between old-school and new-school rappers):

> Shit.
>
> Right now, it's like, 'cause to me it's like two different types of hip hop in the mind . . .
>
> When you go the West [Coast], like listen to like, I dunno, like, Snoop Dogg, like that kind of hip hop it's like more women, drugs and money, bling bling, and you go to the Midwest, like—
>
> Like I've been down South in the States, like Ludacris and them, and all that type of, Lil Jon stuff—it was like bling bling, money, and stuff—like, I'm not into that hip hop. Because even lyrically, lyrically East Coast hip hop is like, it's like they got better rhymes, better metaphors and punchlines than like—
>
> what Lil Jon and other people are doing, I could do it!
>
> My English is not very good, but I could write "They say put your hood up, like whatever mothafucka I ain't scared!"
>
> It's very easy, there is no message, they just, they just talking.
>
> So, but, to me there's two different types of hip hop, the conscious one, the lyrical one in the East, in my opinion, like, in the East, and in the West they're just bullshitting partly, like I said.
>
> But um, right now it's changing too.
>
> Like, even the East Coast rappers, most of them, they tend to be more commercial.
>
> It's like the essence is not there anymore, like, you know?
>
> Hip hop right now, American hip hop, is too commercial, to me.
>
> It's like too, it's only entertainment, now, it's only fun, entertainment, there's no more message, no knowledge, not really.

His phone rings, and he stops to answer it. Once he's hung up, he asks, "Is it good? Yeah man, did I answer?"

On the balcony of his quiet apartment overlooking Parcelles' wide beach, after several interruptions from young women walking below, the light was fading by the time Thiat settled back into his seat and I repeated my question about US hip hop (Fig. 4.8). He said,

FIGURE 4.8 Thiat on the balcony of his apartment.

> The difference between American and Senegalese rap is that today, in Senegal, the people who do conscious rap are more respected than those who do other things.
>
> While in the United States, those who do other things have more media exposure . . .
>
> I had the chance to go [to the United States] and I saw you don't see a lot of New York rappers [in the media] but those from Atlanta.
>
> That's deplorable.

Like the mythologized tradition of a rural African past, hip hop myth relies on a slippage between temporal and spatial distance. And just as early international rappers circumvented mbalax to claim a mythologized griot (Chapter 3), underground rappers have circumvented contemporary US hip hop to claim its imagined tradition. These hip hop claims to voice create particular—and at times peculiar—temporal elisions between present-day Dakar and the South Bronx circa 1990.

In the apartment in Yoff where I interviewed him and Kalif together, Kronic continued to shift back and forth between French and English as he told me,

> What an American rapper lives is necessarily different than what a Senegalese rapper lives.

And so, what a young American lives is different than what a young Senegalese lives.

It's not the same culture; it's not the same lived reality; it's not the same references.

An American rapper—

[*Eng.*] because of the American dream, you can wake up one day and sell one million albums and have a lot of money.

[*Fr.*] But here in Senegal, that's practically impossible.

All you can hope for is to one day make a song that sells internationally; there, you can have a lot of money.

What an American lives daily is not what a Senegalese lives.

Americans—

in my view, euh? I'm not *chez toi*, but this is what we see on TV and in music videos, and music videos are very expressive—

is [*Eng.*] *drinking, money, drugs, bitches, cars, nice cars.*

[*Fr.*] In general that's what it is.

Us?

[*Eng.*] Nice cars, we don't have them yet. It would be hard to have nice cars by selling your [albums] here. Because [*Fr.*] the buying power of Senegalese people doesn't generally allow young Senegalese people to buy an album.

He says that while he may want people to buy his album, it would be a foolish waste of money when there isn't enough to eat. He says that this is what it comes down to—we don't have the same worries, the same texts, the same lives. The music may sound the same, but the realities are different, and hip hop should express local realities. "You need to understand that difference," he tells me. "Life in Senegal is not dreams and gold."

Contradictorily, US hip hop's apparent corruption is in some ways a testament to the genre's power to effect change. Rapper Dex, speaking in French on behalf of the other members of his group Niamu Mbaam in Pikine (Fig. 4.9), said,

We are at the same place where American hip hop started.

If American hip hop isn't conscious anymore it's because they've fixed their problems: their social problems, their economic problems.

Before in the United States there was racism and slavery and they spent all their time clashing with whites to have liberty and now they have their *blow* [*Eng.*].

FIGURE 4.9 Some members of Coalition Niamu Mbaam: (l–r) Dex, Jamil, and Latif.

Everyone should write what he lives and they live this: they live luxury, they are millionaires.

In Senegal this doesn't exist . . .

You should tell people the real life that you live.

Americans, I get it.

They've achieved that liberty.

But we aren't there yet.

If hip hop myth makes sense of urban Senegalese realities vis-à-vis the rest of the world, then placing the street in the US past and the Senegalese present tells a story about underdevelopment, the backward progress that Djily Bagdad invoked when he suggested that life was better under colonialism. In this strategic invocation of hip hop's origin myth, the distinction between old-school and contemporary US hip hop comes to signify a distinction between Senegal and the United States that is temporal as much as—or more than—it is spatial, and that locates a potential for development within hip hop as an agent of social change.

SCHOOLING THE STREET

We're trying to show Senegal that it's not just the government, it's the people. We are citizens . . . Now rap is part of the development of the country. Rap plays a role in development.
BAYE NJAGNE

FIGURE 4.10 Gotal on the roof of Def Dara Studio in Parcelles Assainies: (l–r) Coumbis, Sister Dia, Hawa, Toussa, Anta and son.

On a rooftop in Parcelles Assainies, the five members of the women's collective Gotal arrange themselves in a line in front of my camera—Coumbis, Sister Dia, Anta, Toussa, and their manager, Hawa (Fig. 4.10). I ask the group what hip hop can do for youth in Senegal. There's some brief discussion among themselves, and then Hawa answers the question as I asked it, in French:

> I see that for some people it's just hope, for certain people.
>
> For others, it's just a means of traveling outside the country. That's what I see.

Coumbis starts speaking over her—"*Non*"—and then switches to Wolof. "No, she isn't going there, do you know what she asked? What does hip hop bring to the youth, the people who are listening to it, for example." Hawa objects, "She isn't saying the people who listen, she's saying the people who are in it." Coumbis faces me and returns to French, "For us?" Dia adds, in Wolof, "The rappers?" as Coumbis continues, "The rappers, or the people who are into it?" Toussa steps in, her French full of pauses and small slips,

> For the audience, hip hop is something positive.
>
> It's in hip hop that we revindicate things.
>
> It's in hip hop that we say things we feel like saying.
>
> So we have a freedom of speech.
>
> We have freedom of expression in hip hop.

So what others don't dare to say, it's rappers who say it.

So that's a positive side for the Senegalese audience.

So we do it like this—for example—there is the political that comes in here.

Our president should cede power, you see?

But among the people, there are people who don't even know what the people are being subjected to.

So it's the rappers that show them, here there are flaws, here the president is supposed to step down; so they are the ones who explain this through their songs, you see.

"What others don't dare to say, rappers say it." Speaking of, from, and to the street, hip hop voice challenges the ghetto as a manifestation of underdevelopment, not only commenting on experiences of urbanity but also contesting them. In other words, hip hop voice is speech *as* action, unlike griot speech which, although powerful and empowering, leaves social action to the patrons whose power it upholds (Wright 1989). Voice as action is encapsulated in the multivalent trope of education that runs through hip hop narratives: "So they are the ones who explain this through their songs."

On the rooftop, silence. Coumbis quietly urges, "Anta, come on. Dia, let's go." Finally, in her quick Wolof, Dia explains how hip hop is important for the youth, how many young women have "woken up" through hip hop. She says that she started rapping at the age of fifteen, that at that time she was getting into trouble, that things changed for her when she began to rap.

There are things that hip hop did for me, my dad didn't do it for me, my mom didn't do it for me, but rap did it for me.

("Those of us who are in hip hop, it brings us a lot of things," Toussa had said, moments earlier.)

So I'm thankful to God, because rap is why I really know where to place my feet, rap is why I know—

I don't even know everything, but there are things I know.

The little experience that I have is through rap.

("Because," Toussa had continued, "hip hop has given me a lot of experience. In a way, it's played a role in my intellectual life.")

In Toussa and Dia's testimonies to hip hop's formative role in their lives there was a faint, distorting echo of nationalist discourse that, since the 1960s, has mourned a crisis of values and weakening traditions of deference to elders as parents went to work outside the home (Diouf 1996, 241). Working the same trope, repeating it louder, Dia's friend, rapper Dex of Niamu Mbaam, said,

> We rap to raise consciousness, to let people know that today they are the ones who hold the power, you understand, they are the ones who can run their own country by their own hand.
>
> Because currently, there are no longer parents, dad or mom, who can stay at home to educate their children, because of the cost of living, of putting food on the table.
>
> So if Dad leaves, Mom leaves, just the children are left, there is no longer anyone to raise them.
>
> Now it is only music, more specifically hip hop, that can raise the children.

Their words layer widespread refrains: of hip hop as a mode of education, an adaptation to the ways in which urbanization and modernization have destabilized traditional family structures. There is an ambiguity here, in the French word *education* that Dex used, which can mean either "upbringing" or "formal education." Urban Wolof often links these two meanings; a person who hassles a foreign woman in the street, for example, might be described as someone who "*ñàkk* [lacks] *education*," implying that they were not raised right, but also that they are uneducated, and probably of rural origin.

Lack of education, in both senses, relates to the same colonial and postcolonial power structures that govern urban space. Colonial designations of areas of Dakar as urban or non-urban, depending on whether European or Africans lived there, did not only discursively exclude indigenous populations from modernization but also manipulated the educational system to limit African residents' social mobility; in marking areas like Medina as "rural," colonizers ensured that only trade schools would be established there (Nelson 2007, 236). Even as access to education broadened after independence, the quality and consistency of education did not; today, there is a widespread sense among educated young people that they've been cheated by the government, as they earn their degrees only to find unemployment awaiting them.[11]

Senegal's first president, Léopold Senghor, upheld a commitment to the French language and educational system that had served elite Africans during the colonial period (Castaldi 2006; Diaw 1993); in the twenty-first century, the public education

FIGURE 4.11 Lamine Ndao poses for a picture on a trip to Gorée Island.

system continues to effectively disenfranchise a large part of the Senegalese population. Although French is the official language and the language of governance, few children speak it at home. While a small economic elite sends their children to private (mostly Catholic) schools, and some families of lower socioeconomic status manage to scrape together tuition, the majority struggle in public schools, where they learn to read and write in a language that many of them rarely speak outside the classroom. This leaves young people ill equipped for formal employment and for exercising their rights in an ostensibly democratic system. Consistent strikes on the part of schoolteachers, whom the government often fails to pay, further destabilize the educational system, an issue that extends all the way to the universities, where the students themselves often strike when their government stipends are late to arrive. Lamine Ndao, at the time a student working towards his Masters degree at Cheikh Anta Diop University (Fig. 4.11), told me,

There are even Senegalese, I want to say, frankly, Senegalese who don't know the Senegalese constitution.

Seriously.

I'm at the university.

When I studied English, and when I studied American civilization, the professor gave us documents about American civilization, and I told myself, "Hold on!

I am in Senegal and they provide documents on American civilization and the American constitution, even though since I've been here at the university no one has *ever* given me this kind of document."

For me it's a question of communication and it's also a question of advising.

Because, every government in place, a new regime, should have all the materials, or rather, all the documents, necessary to inform the population and tell them, you should do this and that, your rights are this and that, you should act like this and do this, your rights are limited here, my rights are limited here.

For me there's a bit of anarchy.

Because if you can educate a population, you should give them the details, or the documents, to know how the current regime works.

"To lack education" takes on yet another meaning—one that positions education as a right of citizenship, and its absence as both a consequence and a tool of corrupt governance. Voice as action plays out through this trilogy of meanings of *education*. It addresses the dilution of kinship in modern, urban Africa. It confronts the colonial heritage that lives on in contemporary issues of uneven access to schooling. It informs people of their rights as citizens, so that they may take those in power to task.

As the 2012 presidential elections approached, more and more songs emerged directly criticizing the government, as they had before every presidential election since the turn of the millennium. Simon's song "Abdoulaye" indicted then-president Abdoulaye Wade for his hollow promises of "change" and his projects that seemed to place a shiny, transparent veneer of development over the people's struggle to survive. "New cars, new streets, new roads, new lights. The people are dying of hunger . . . [Abdou] Laye." Books's single "Wakhal Sa Baye," released in late 2011, urged Wade's son Karim—without explicitly naming him—to "wakhal sa baye [tell your father]" that the people are tired of injustice, of corruption, and of poverty:

Degg naa sa baye a moom dëkk bi [I heard that your father owns the country]

Ba fu la neex nga dey ci biir ët bi [To the point where you can shit wherever you want]

Ku la jaay nga fey may ko oto bi . . . [You give a car to whoever sells himself
to you . . .]

Dawal wakh sa baye [Run and tell your father]

Askan bi cry nañu na ñu na bayyi [The people are crying, let him leave us be]

Through hip hop, Books and Simon—and countless other artists—speak directly to power, to "you, Laye," to "you (Karim)." "Listen!" 5kiem Underground
admonishes, "The people are crying." There is no disguised speech here, no sutura;
this is speech as action in its directness, in its truth.

In such moments of heightened political stakes, action sometimes exceeds the
musical boundaries of hip hop voice.

June 23, 2011. I arrive home from the Africulturban cultural center in Pikine,
where I've been filming the breakdancing, graffiti, beat boxing, and deejaying
workshops at the annual festival, Festa2H. Exhausted from being on my feet all
day, and daunted by the file transfers ahead of me, I flop onto the couch and
turn on the news. I'm startled by the gruesome footage—fire, tear gas, crowds,
police in SWAT gear with guns. A presidential mandate has forbidden all public
demonstrations, yet the city swarms with Y'en a Marre T-shirts, many handmade.
A giant poster reads, "Wade da fa doye [enough of Wade]." As the same violent
images play over and over, I watch, stunned, as buildings burn and rocks fly at cars
and police. The cycling footage is suddenly interrupted, as rapper Simon hobbles
into the newsroom, his pants ripped, his face swollen, eyes blinking without his
glasses, wearing a Y'en a Marre T-shirt. He explains, first in French and then
again, when asked to, in Wolof, that he and his friends have gone to peaceably
demand that the police liberate rapper Foumalade, arrested earlier today at the
Place d'Independence. He lifts his shirt to reveal the marks on his back where
police nightsticks struck him.

It's clear that Simon hasn't even gone to the doctor; he's come straight here to
the news station, and he's carefully told his story in French on a primarily Wolof-
language newscast, ensuring that it will be understood beyond a local audience.
I pick up my phone to call Books in Medina and see what they know, if Simon is all
right. The image cuts to a montage of footage from today's demonstrations. Youth
throw stones at trucks full of police holding guns. Fires fill the streets in Medina,
and smoke pours from windows. Fancy cars are destroyed. Six police beat an un-
resisting young man to the ground in front of a massive handwritten banner that
reads, "Wade assassin de la constitution."

The June 23 demonstrations and the larger work of Y'en a Marre activists leading
up to the 2012 presidential elections constituted a striking reversal of Rap Galsen's

efforts in 2000 to elect Wade and effect the first change in political party in the forty years since independence. Yet, as Baye Njagne said of Wade,

> What he told us and what he promised us, up until now he has done nothing.
>
> And we'll continue to tell the truth.
>
> We live without electricity and without water.
>
> There is no development, no economy, there are even millionaires who waste things.
>
> We need someone who can fix our problems.

Despite concrete, measurable signs of progress under Wade—including the construction of a new airport and highways that mitigated the country's horrific congestion—widespread corruption in his administration and the daily trials of power outages, flooding, unemployment, and educational strikes had led the same youth who had supported him in 2000 to turn against him by 2007, when he ran for a second term. Again, they turned out the youth vote and wrote songs criticizing the government, but this time to no avail. Wade's reelection struck a blow to hip hop, even as the election process brought Rap Galsen more firmly into national and international view.[12] Y'en a Marre built on this longer history of hip hop's engagement in electoral politics and joined in a widespread surge of demonstrations and protests that preceded and exceeded it, so that at times, it was difficult to clearly distinguish Y'en a Marre from the larger youth unrest that marked the year leading up to the 2012 elections. (Fig. 4.12).

And yet, although these moments of explicit political engagement threw hip hop into sharp relief against the backdrop of Senegalese society, it would be a mistake to view Y'en a Marre and the movements that prefigured it as paradigms of hip hop voice. Hip hop networks facilitated Y'en a Marre's work, and hip hop histories emboldened its actors; but the power of hip hop as voice lies precisely in how hip hop genre renders speech into action, rather than in how it is instrumentalized in extramusical political mobilization. As rapper Gaston told me in a reluctant but capable French spoken solely for my benefit, as we sat together on the roof of his recording studio in the Parcelles Assainies banlieue,

> When it comes to me, I'm not part of the Y'en a Marre movement, but I think that the fight is the same, because their fight is how to make Abdoulaye Wade step down, and me, too, my hope is how to make Abdoulaye Wade step down to change the regime.

FIGURE 4.12 Simon (far left) and Almamy (far right) talk with vendors during a Y'en a Marre canvassing march in Colobane Market.

But each has their strategy, each one has their way of solidifying their ideas.

So they have chosen to have a movement, while I remain a musician.

I am a musician and I will remain a musician.

If I have a personal opinion I should put out, I return to the studio and I do it in a song, and that remains there.

If I should inform my audience, I make a song—

in my album there is a song called "Go Vote."

So it's like this.

My idea is that I'm not in any movement.

I'm not in the Y'en a Marre movement, I'm not in Bibson's movement, I'm not in any political movement that is here in this moment in this country.

I make music. I am a musician.

And I will stay a musician.

Long-held understandings of hip hop itself as a genre that generates voice have led many rappers to reject the role of extramusical political activists. Their *music*, they say, represents political and social action that stands on its own, without demonstrations and speeches to accompany it. Their voices sound materially and metaphorically to negotiate social change, if not always to effect it.

While underground artists do rap about topics like romantic love, religious devotion, and family, and while most can't resist recording the self-aggrandizing tracks known as *egotrips*, these topics rarely emerge in Rap Galsen's self-narratives, inconsistent as they are with its origin myth. And yet of course all of these—desire and heartbreak, piety and faith, platonic love between siblings and friends, play and humor—are also part and parcel of youth experience. Perhaps simply to *speak* in the face of generational difference and indigenous communicative norms is to voice youth experience, not only as it emerges in and of the street, but also as it precedes and surpasses it.

THE LIMITS OF VOICE

In America, when they started rapping, it was just to defend society. I heard Louis Farrakhan said one day that the rappers of nowadays have the same responsibilities as Malcolm X or Martin Luther King. Those things they were defending, rappers nowadays have to defend the same thing. That is why I can say that rap is more important than taasu, because it represents society. We have the habit of saying we represent the people who don't have the opportunity to face the microphone and say what hurts. You have to be in the body of the people and know what's wrong and then translate those things that are wrong into your music. You have to represent those people who don't have a mouth. This is our rap in Senegal.

N-JAH, TIGRIM BI

Summer, 2011. At breakfast time, I walk down from the second-floor apartment I share with two American students and out into the morning sun. My neighborhood, Mermoz, is calm at this time of day, at most times of day really, lacking the noisy bustle of the quartiers populaires where I spend so much of my time. My Medina friends sigh in sympathy when they think about how lonely it must be. I pick my way across the open space in front of my building, avoiding the plastic cups and bags that litter the dusty ground.

At the opposite corner of the building is Abdoulahad's boutique, a long, narrow room with a counter running down the middle and a bench along one wall, where men from the neighborhood sit to drink spiced coffee and watch the small television set perched on the counter toward the back of the shop. Assalaamaalekum—I murmur as I walk through the door. Almost in unison, they turn their heads from the television to look at me curiously, in silence. Abdoulahad, a tall gray-haired man in long Mouride robes, responds with a clear—Maalekum Saalaam; their belated echoes follow. I hover behind children ordering things for their mothers, hands reaching up to place coins on the counter as they recite—50 francs of butter, half a kilo of sugar, two bouillon cubes. A woman pushes past me and the children with her own demands. Finally, Abdoulahad looks at me, his words measured and polite—What would you like?—I'd like a baguette and two eggs.—Cooked? or Uncooked?—He speaks slowly, and waits to see if I'll remember how he taught me to describe hardboiled eggs in Wolof.—Cooked!

Behind me, a man seated on the bench asks where I'm from. America— Abdoulahad responds—they are students. The man turns his questioning to me, and I explain briefly that I'm here to do a project with the rappers in Senegal.— Rap music! The man sitting next to him chimes in—You know the rappers these days they are doing important things for the country—That's true, the first man agrees. Abdoulahad interjects—But they shouldn't be burning and ruining things. We all nod somberly in agreement, remembering just last week, when some youth barricaded our street by burning a bus at its intersection with the main road; it's quite unlikely these were rappers, but it all seems to run together these days in the news.

Later that week, I hail a taxi in Medina, steeling myself as it pulls over in front of me. I'm going to Fann Residence. The driver doesn't hesitate a second before pronouncing a grossly inflated charge. That's the white person tax! I protest with a smile, wheedling him to accept a lower price. He objects in turn, citing the cost of gas these days, the closure of the main road over the canal, the traffic jams at this hour, but finally we come to an agreement, and I climb into the taxi. Our haggling capably and amicably concluded, the taximan chatters away; I struggle to decipher his words over the Muslim chants crackling from his tape deck. He grows excited when I tell him why I'm here—Hip hop! I don't really know much hip hop music, but the rappers are doing such important things. Do you know Thiat? I'm not sure what he's asking—if I know Thiat personally, or if I know who he is. I tell him yes, we are friends. He continues—This Y'en a Marre movement. It's not the first time. Already rappers were a big reason that Abdoulaye Wade was elected in 2000. Now they are doing important work again for our country. Advocating a new kind of Senegalese person who is respectful of our country. It's very good. Hip hop is good. Thiat is good.

It is not surprising that rappers view hip hop as something that carves out a space of social legitimacy. In mobilizing for political and social causes, they earn begrudging respect from elders who are skeptical of hip hop as a globalized US cultural product, but who can't deny the value of their children's efforts to improve their country.[13] There is a growing public sentiment that hip hoppers are the ones holding the state accountable to its citizens. Kronic said,

Look at rap—

Before, no one liked it, they said it was rude aggressors who did rap.

But now, even our parents know that rap is something interesting that wakes their youth and that wakes their society.

And at the same time [*Eng.*] it's like a police, [*Fr.*] a stabilizer—sometimes the government wants to do something, but it thinks, "if I do this the rappers are going to say something."

[*Eng.*] So we are here like guards for the government sometimes, guards of the population.

But although hip hop has in many ways carved out a space for, and then amplified, youth perspectives, its freedom of expression is still limited. Rappers have on occasion been jailed when their voices got too loud for comfort. And when, at a Y'en a Marre rally in 2011, Thiat called then-president Abdoulaye Wade a liar (a serious insult in Wolof culture, regardless of its veracity), he was widely criticized by old and young alike, with the latter demographic holding discussions on Facebook about the need to respect elders.

And so, intergenerational relationships and cultural and religious norms continue to check hip hop voice.[14] Djily Bagdad said in English,

95 percent of the population are Muslim, and when you Muslim you're not supposed to say any obscenity or any bad words, you know, and stuff like that.

When you rapping, you have to respect the people who are listening; when you're rapping, you might think, my parents are listening, or somebody might be listening to me, and you cannot be cursing on records like, as Americans do.

You know how American people, they very explicit.

It's very different, 'cause they have more freedom of speech in America, way more freedom, but right here you kind of have your tongue tied, like, you cannot say anything. Maybe sometimes in concerts, like between us—young audience and young people—when you freestyle you might say some obscenity, some stuff, and people are gonna laugh, just for fun.

But when you're putting out a record you cannot, like, curse in the record, really, 'cause people are not gonna respect you, you cannot curse in the records, you cannot say bad words, you know, in respect of the Senegalese values.

That's the main difference.

Like, American hip hop, like out here you put out a video, and you put girls in swimsuits you're gonna be criticized like "Oh look at what he's doing" and people are doing worse than that, like in the national mbalax music, but like when a hip hop person does it they're gonna be like, "Oh, they're copying America people, those people with no morals" and stuff, you know, you know, all that speech they're gonna give you.

But it's the big difference.

Like the religion and the society don't allow you to say whatever you want— you can say whatever you want but you cannot say it however you want it, like you have to measure the words.

Drygun, of the early hardcore group Yatfu, described how these same constraints limit hip hop's capacity as a medium of free speech to men,

Well, for women, I'd say that we are in a 95 percent Muslim country.

There is a custom that relegates women to—

well it's true that the youth now, they are very, they evolve in their minds, they are very western we'll say, but at the base we have a tradition and cul- ture, that brings women—

to be obligated to—

not to veil herself, but to respect her body, to not go to certain, certain places for example, you see, to be respected, to make herself respected, to respect her body, to not do certain things . . .

And that is why some women are ashamed to go on stage for example and do hip hop because that is more given to men, hip hop.

And so, they even prefer to play the traditional music from here, which is mbalax.

Young women's efforts to make a place for themselves in hip hop—and to reap the same benefits of agency, articulation, and acceptance that their male counterparts enjoy—are doubly constrained by the same traditional norms that male rappers seek to circumvent via hip hop practice, and by the very masculine overtones of (Senegalese) hip hop itself.

If indigenous speech and musical genres are inseparable in their association with a particular endogamous group that by nature excludes nongriots from verbal performance (at least in principle if not always in practice), rapping is a speech genre equally inseparable from its instrumental beats. It stands as a performance medium whose counterhegemonic potential pivots on its non-Africanity, on its origins as a speech genre emerging from outside a closed system of performance that encompasses speech, singing, and instrumental music, and on an imagining of diasporic connection that is urban and experiential. Yet in terms of lyrical content, political expression, imagery, and gendered participation, the freedom of expression that hip hop provides youth is still largely limited by local cultural and religious norms. Hip hop may voice youth experience, but it does so selectively and conditionally.

We are here to fight the movement, to promote female rap. Because here you could say female rap isn't very well done and there aren't a lot of people doing it. Girls don't like rap here. We felt that forming a collective was better than each one sticking to her own corner.

TOUSSA

5

GENDERING VOICE

IN EARLY SEPTEMBER 2011, I head to Parcelles Assainies to meet Toussa at Gaston's Def Dara Studio, in an unmarked apartment building that I recognize from the last time I saw her. I hesitate on my way up the stairs, try to be inconspicuous as I peer around an open door and determine that, yes, this is it, call out a tentative Assalaamaalekum as I enter. To my right, in a small kitchen, people kneeling around a bowl of gumbo and rice invite me to join them. I'm full, *bon appétit*—I call, and hover in the hallway until they finish. A woman with a toddler in tow cleans grains of rice off the floor, collects the spoons where they've been dropped, piles them neatly on top of the covered bowl. Toussa introduces her as Anta.

As I resign myself to the long period of waiting that I've come to expect in any hip hop space, the collective's other members arrive, punctual and ready to go. Hawa and Coumbis announce themselves at the door, chattering as they shake the others' hands, stilling their boisterous Wolof to greet me carefully in French. This is Catty—Toussa offers. Sister Dia arrives, trading girlish pecks on the cheek with Coumbis and Hawa, grasping hands with Anta and Toussa, offering me a measured *ça va* and a neat handshake. We file into the studio space, where I'm dismayed to find the young man who had insistently professed his love to me in the street just minutes earlier. He greets the producer and Toussa familiarly, squeezing onto the bench where we sit facing the sound booth, and picks back up where he left off. As the girls band together to scold him for hitting on a married woman, I begin to feel guilty. Now I don't know how to confess that I'm not married at all.

Later, Coumbis and Hawa will laugh when I come clean, then shrug it off.

Anta hands her son off to Sister Dia and heads in to record, trading four-bar segments with Toussa. When the engineer gets caught up in conversation, Toussa bangs on the glass separating her from us until he turns his attention back to the console. Dia goes next. Before Coumbis can take her turn, the engineer abruptly gets up and leaves.

All these years later, I catch myself calling them *girls* and think about what it was like to be an unmarried woman in my late twenties in Dakar; how it grated to hear people refer to married teenagers as *women*, but not to me; how friends' and neighbors' good-naturedly mocking calls of *jank bi* (maiden) called attention to my aged youth without ever mentioning it. We were all girls, in Senegal, not just the still-teenaged Toussa, but also me, Coumbis, Hawa; all of us grown, and yet none of us adults.

With the engineer gone on his mysterious errand, we head up to the roof for a group interview. After each woman introduces herself, I ask in French how they formed Gotal. They all turn to Anta, who, after a moment's pause, speaks up in a rapid Wolof marked by slang and frequent punctuations of "quoi"—similar to the American use of "like"—

There, I'm the one to answer.

How we started Gotal is that I was sitting thinking that here, there are a lot of *sistas* in rap, but each one, if she sees her peer, won't greet her again until they see each other when there is a concert or a soirée.

So that's what I called each of them about, to tell them about how it would go and to get them to come together and be part of it, to work bit by bit.

Since then we're working.

As she trails off, next to her Toussa murmurs in Wolof, "She wants to know when it started," and Anta picks back up with her narrative, "Ah, it didn't start that long ago, soon it will be a year. We're working. But also, the main reason that the work is a bit hard is that there's no money here."

As a group and individually, these young women told the same story of Gotal's origins. At the then-annual hip hop festival 72 Hours of Hip Hop in 2010, Anta was in attendance. Born in the Pikine banlieue, she had listened to hip hop since the late 1990s, coming up on the likes of Daara J, Gaston, Rap'Adio, and Waa BMG 44 (she notes, in particular, their one female member, Fatim). After watching her brothers perform at school concerts, she herself began to rap at their urging in 2005. Only a week later, Coumbis would relate her own almost identical story.

They are young, among the youngest hip hoppers I've spent time with; their journeys into hip hop began with Senegalese artists who were already well established by the time they reached adolescence, not with Public Enemy (and I wonder if all these young men, some not much older, could really have begun with Public Enemy, or whether they are just faithfully retelling what they know to be the story of Rap Galsen). They came to hip hop under the watchful eyes of their older brothers.

Five years after she began rapping, Anta noticed a glaring absence of female performers at this festival purporting to represent Rap Galsen. She worked her way through the crowd, collected phone numbers from the few women there, and organized a preliminary meeting. Gotal was born. While the group's makeup fluctuates, in 2011 it included Anta, Sister Dia, Toussa, and Coumbis, with Hawa as manager. Each member worked as a solo artist and as part of the collective.

Sister Dia picks up from Anta, in quick, impassioned Wolof,

If you see also, we created Gotal because here in Senegal, you see, women in rap are really underestimated.

You'll see one, or two, or three on the TV.

Today, when a stranger comes from somewhere else saying "I'm looking for women who rap," they'll tell her about one girl or two.

Our fight is to make it so they recognize every girl in Senegal.

We started the connection, we went on the radio and called girls, all the girls doing rap in Senegal, and gave them our phone numbers so that whoever wanted to be part of Gotal could come and be part of it.

As Dia finishes speaking, I hesitate, recognizing myself as the stranger—or one of many strangers—in her story, hearing her claim to local visibility expand to encompass the tenuous and often-unfulfilled promise of global visibility that drives underground rappers to entertain foreign researchers. There's a moment of silence as I fumble with my notes. Coumbis jumps to fill it.

Gotal is an association that was created—

the original idea came from Anta—

it was created to promote female hip hop.

Because we saw that here, in Senegal, a girl who raps is not well viewed, and beyond that they don't invite us, they always ignore us.

Even if a stranger comes to Senegal and asks if there are girls who rap, they just show you one or two even though there are truly a lot.

This is why Anta called us to try to promote female hip hop.

We try to make female hip hop more visible.

I won't realize until later that she was only summarizing in French what Anta and Dia have just told me.

There's a lack of polish to these interviews that betrays youthful inexperience, that clashes with the smooth competence of men who have been giving interviews since these women really were just girls. Yet they have a story that they want to tell. At its center is a struggle between presence and invisibility that exceeds hip hop to comment on their place in the world, and to perhaps claim a different one.

Sample the stories that women tell about themselves and about hip hop. Layer them over and under men's stories of the same. Listen to the narrative that emerges, (re)producing youth, voice, the street, and hip hop itself.

We have seen Rap Galsen lay claim to modernity and voice through constructions of hip hop realness that center on the street and the underground. These claims work through a marked gendering of musical genre that reconstitutes a globalized hip hop masculinity in relation to local performance practices. US hip hop has often valorized a particular, exclusive masculinity in which Black male subjectivity, in response to hegemonic depictions of and violence toward the Black male body, plays out on the bodies of Black and Latina women (Perry 2004, 118; Pough 2004, 11). In their assertions of hip hop realness, male underground rappers in Senegal pointed to the sexualized images of women's bodies that they saw in music videos as a symptom of US hip hop's moral decline (see Chapter 4). They held up their own respectful treatment of women, their refusal to depict women in bikinis or miniskirts (although one might argue that the skintight jeans and leggings common in Senegalese hip hop videos themselves challenge local norms of modesty). Yet the underground's hardcore musical aesthetic and rough physical posturing had effectively closed off hip hop spaces to young women from the late 1990s onward (see Chapter 2).

Rap Galsen's distinct masculinity engages US hip hop at the crossroads of local and global musical histories, indigenous and religious social values, and traditional and popular performance genres. It is informed by a multilayered patriarchy in which colonial Victorian codes of femininity, Muslim values that inform and are encoded in law, and indigenous norms of social interaction work together to place women in a subordinate position to men and contain their movements through public space. It relies on an unquestioned gender binarism that is increasingly the only accepted conception of gender in Dakar. And these are all part and parcel of Senegalese modernity, as constituted in dialogue with the rest of the world.

Blending imported hip hop tropes of realness with local constructions of gender, male hip hoppers categorized popular music through a series of dichotomies, aligning with mbalax and hip hop and respectively coded as feminine or masculine: traditional and modern, old and young, local and global, home and street, commercial and underground, easy and hard.[1] To ask men about women in hip hop was almost invariably to return the conversation to mbalax. To ask about traditional music was to bring us back around to women.

The women of Gotal harnessed these same tropes to contest exclusionary inscriptions of hip hop as a male space, which mirror larger, equally gendered struggles over presence and voice in urban Senegal. They claimed the street and the underground, revealing how these constructs have always been gendered, even as they attempted to neutralize them at times by layering them with tropes of home, family, and work. Their interactions with male hip hoppers were but a single node in a complex of significant relationships that included their connections to their parents, their interactions with strangers, their own investment in certain religious and cultural values, and their friendships with other women.

GENDERING PUBLIC SPACE

About a month after Toussa introduced me to Gotal at the studio, we all convene a second time at a beach in Almadies, not far from where I interviewed Coumbis and Hawa. They've called me to come take their picture, group and individual shots that they can use to promote the collective online (Fig. 5.1). The girls tease and joke, jostling for their individual turns, stealing off to the side one at a time to change their tops or accessories, until we break briefly so that I can talk one-on-one with Anta (Fig. 5.2).

We speak Wolof, and yet this does little to coax her out of her reticence. She tells me again about how she started Gotal, working her way through the crowd of a hip hop festival where no women were performing, taking the number of every girl she found watching. I ask why there were so few women, and she says,

The problem is that, there are those who want to [rap].

But sometimes there is a man there that doesn't want them to.

Or they get married and they have to stop.

FIGURE 5.1 Gotal poses for a group shot: (l–r) Toussa, Anta, Sister Dia, Coumbis.

FIGURE 5.2 Anta on the beach in Almadies.

If you have a husband who does hip hop, or who wants you to do it, then he will support you. But if it's just you alone, without means, you'll have to leave it.

Here, you don't have your place.

There's an ambiguity in Anta's words, in her wistful claim to a *here* that may be hip hop or may be Senegal. Where is young women's place in these nested worlds?

A week after our oceanside interview, I arrange to meet Coumbis and Hawa in Ouakam so we can go together to the hip hop soirée where Gotal is performing. Caught up in the excitement of going with the girls, I greet them at Hawa's house promptly at 7 p.m., freshly bathed, made up, and wearing a tank top with bits of lace at the shoulders. They compliment my flat sandals, drab and practical next to their lamé heels. They tease me about my figure, pleased with how my jeans fit, torturously tight in the summer heat. They ask if I've brought my camera. Four hours later, they are finally ready to go, and I'm in desperate need of another shower.

The venue, called Cafeteria, is in Hann. We get there quickly at this time of night, Anta meeting us as we descend from the taxi. Inside, lightbulbs nestled in the peak of the sloped ceiling strain against the dim expanse of the room; young men in T-shirts and sneakers idle in its shadowed corners. Others shuffle from one foot to the other in the middle of the dance floor, arms neglected at their sides, a cluster of colorful baseball caps bobbing out of time to the grainy hip hop tracks that force their way through the reluctant sound system. We settle into one of the booths that line one wall, then wait for another hour before the venue begins to fill with young male rappers and their friends. Sister Dia, the youngest of the group, shows up with her father in tow; who else could he be, in this crowd, with his grey hair and solid build, his subdued suit and loafers? The other women greet him politely, some adding a quick dip of their knees as they shake his hand, and then move on, wandering around the space in pairs throughout the night, chatting occasionally with the young male rappers, but for the most part keeping to themselves.

Gotal's performance that night was also an (almost) unchaperoned late-night venture into public space—one that challenged how young women's virtue, and, by extension, the movement of their bodies outside the home, is surveilled by both elders and strangers. We have already seen how youth navigate new kinds of relationships and mobility with the loosening of indigenous social formations in Dakar. But, for all we hear of hip hop as a youth culture, the category of youth is a recent one in Africa, and one that has unevenly included women, as gendered relations of power have shifted and coalesced into new structures of oppression and possibility over the past century.

Although Wolof society was historically matrilineal, the confluence of Islam and French patriarchy weakened women's social position and effectively barred them from upward mobility in the new colonial order. The union of colonial and religious leaders undermined local social structures, in which women's power derived, in part, from their relationships to male political leaders. Agriculture was commercialized to the enrichment of the Muslim marabouts, leaving women to tend to subsistence crops (Creevy 1996). French colonizers implemented an educational system that created new paths of social mobility that largely excluded women, enforcing a gendered divide of public and domestic space as they prepared boys for public lives and girls for domestic ones (Creevy 1996; Mcnee 2000, 88; Assie-Lumumba 1997).[2] The relegation of women to the domestic sphere—often considered a "traditional" practice, even by Senegalese people—was part of a western project of secular modernity as much as or more than it was a remnant of African cultural norms or Muslim values (Scott 2017).

After independence, the economic consequences of structural adjustment programs in the 1980s, including waning government subsidies of secondary education, saw boys' schooling consistently prioritized over girls' (Morales-Libove 2005). Well into the twenty-first century, girls enrolled in school are often expected to do domestic work before and after classes, while boys have free time to play and study; pregnant girls are suspended from school, while the boys who impregnate them are not (Assie-Lumumba 1997, 311). Since the 1980s, even educated young people face widespread unemployment; lacking the means to transition to adulthood through marriage, they are snared in a semipermanent state of youth. The resulting gap between childhood and becoming a wife/mother has created new experiences of adolescence for Senegalese women, particularly in urban areas (Antoine and Nanitelamio 1991). However, women still generally marry significantly sooner than men do, often in their early twenties in urban areas and even younger in rural ones, and women's participation in marriage is crucial to men's transition out of youth into adulthood.[3]

Years before I would meet the women of Gotal, I sat with Lady Sinay in Sen Kumpë's home in Medina. She told me how she had begun rapping with Rap'Adio in 1996, only to abandon hip hop when she married in 1999. Now divorced, in 2008 she was just coming back into the hip hop scene, sharing the stage with the Jolof4Life artists who had been part of Cartel Underground with her back in the day. She said, "It's difficult, because we're already in a Muslim country. We are not called to—Women, generally in Senegal they say that they should stay in the home, occupy themselves with their children, something like that."

And here is the unelusive key to the scarcity of women in Rap Galsen. Like men trapped in an extended time of youth, women take up hip hop during a liminal moment of girlhood. But they pass through this moment more quickly than men, and their transition into adulthood is a transition into new, and even more rigid, restrictions on their movements outside the home. Xuman of Pee Froiss, speaking from the perspective of someone who had been in the hip hop scene for several decades, said,

> Before, there were [female rappers].
>
> But there is a problem in Senegal.
>
> A girl should get married.
>
> And once she is married she has other responsibilities and she occupies herself with her family.
>
> Before, there were a lot of girls, but once they got married, if the husband didn't want her to do rap then she couldn't.

The question, then, is not one of women's interest or initial participation in hip hop. It is one of cumulative presence, of the gendered nature of youth and of hip hop coming together to belie the idea that hip hop is a youth music at all. To date, men have not aged out of hip hop, even when they have moved out of youth by filling social expectations for marriage and becoming the head of a family. Some of the earliest rappers—Xuman among them—have enjoyed musical careers that span decades, while women cycle in and out of Rap Galsen in ways that mirror local gendered patterns of youth and adulthood. The distinction between nonexistence and fleeting visibility becomes crucial here, and the young women of Gotal were eager to make this clear.

Sister Dia herself, although among the youngest in the group, had married an industry figure in her late teens, had a child, and then divorced and picked back up with her career. She explained,

> There are a lot of women, but they aren't famous, because their careers pass too quickly. Sometimes they get married and have to leave it.
>
> Sometimes they get pregnant and have to leave.
>
> Sometimes they flee after seeing the violence at concerts and soirées.

Even as social and economic changes have created new female experiences of adolescence, women participating in hip hop continue to face myriad obstacles, as long-standing gendered constructs of public and domestic space intersect with familial obligations and with conceptions of hip hop space as particularly physically and socially dangerous for women. A month after my interview with Gotal, during a one-on-one conversation in Toussa's home, she explained,

> In our generation, in Senegal, the adults see hip hop as something bad. Like when I started doing hip hop, here at home they didn't want me to. I negotiated it, I made an effort to make them understand what hip hop is and I convinced them. But when people see their children involved in hip hop they say, "That's something bad!" They see rappers walking with their sagged pants and whatnot, and we have our language that the parents and grandparents don't accept. Hip hop is something of the street, and it's hard for the home to accept what comes from the street.

In the group interview with Gotal, Toussa had said almost the same thing word for word, concluding that "it is a little difficult to combine hip hop and family."

The question of hip hop's incompatibility with family arose only in conversations with or about women in hip hop. Male rappers claimed that older generations resisted hip hop because of its westernness and its dissonance with religious beliefs and local norms of comportment. Women—and sometimes men, when speaking specifically about women—cited these same reasons, but wrapped them in familial expectations for women's behavior and life trajectories. Several young women described their ability to continue to make hip hop as contingent on their mothers' support. If Senegalese rappers have fought an uphill battle to win the tenuous acceptance of older generations, that acceptance extends unevenly to young women.

Paradoxically, then, the very same social processes that men critique in hip hop are those that allow them to do it in the first place, and that limit women's participation even as they may briefly and temporarily enable it. Poverty and unemployment produce the overabundance of leisure time in which young men hone hip hop skills, at times converting this imposed leisure into labor through hip hop's strategic "self-commodification of play"(Kelley 1997, 44–45).[4] Yet the traditional social structures that men ostensibly subvert through hip hop place the burden of domestic work and social reputation on women, so that the possibilities of leisure are not only gendered in terms of who can move where, when, but also in how they depend on women's labor in domestic spaces.[5] The extended youth that results from these factors leads to discrepancies in the average age of marriage that extend male experiences of youth far beyond female adolescence. Young men don't only have more time to devote to hip hop on a day-to-day basis, but may remain rappers through decades of youth. Men's transition out of youth depends on

FIGURE 5.3 Sister Dia performs at Cafeteria.

women, and vice-versa; unlike women, however, men's passage into adulthood is not necessarily a passage out of hip hop.

At Cafeteria, the women move around the open performance space, encircled by young men, trading off bars on a joint track. There aren't enough mics to go around (Figs. 5.3 and 5.4). As I watch them navigate a constrained visibility on the margins of the hip hop scene, the youngest generation, the least audible, I wonder if this is a hip hop adolescence—a shadow world to their immediate social realities, and one that will simply fade away when they move inevitably into adulthood.

MUSIC, PUBLIC SPACE, AND SEXUALITY

On a rooftop in Medina, I ask Alou and Madou why there aren't many women in Rap Galsen. They both laugh. Alou responds, mixing French and English, "*Ça c'est le* big question. That's the big question." He continues in French,

I don't know.

First, unlike the United States, it's not in our culture.

FIGURE 5.4 Toussa rocks an air mic at Cafeteria.

Here, even if you're a boy, when people see you rapping they say you are wasting your time; it's not something that you should be doing as a Senegalese or a Muslim.

It's not ours—

It's not in our culture.

For me that's all the difference.

When you see a girl rapping it's quickly seen as negative ["Yeah"—Madou says] even though that's not the case.

It's not a negative thing for girls to rap.

It's like doing mbalax or playing a musical instrument.

For me it's that simple.

But the difference is that it's not in our culture, contrary to your country, to the United States, it's not come into our culture to see a girl rapping or doing something we judge to be so masculine.

Madou jumps in, speaking Wolof. "Yes. Girls here have a lot—Already girls here, even for me it's that." He stops, clarifies, "It's not a question of clashing them or anything," and we all laugh again as he continues,

For me, hip hop really belongs more to men.

When you see girls who rap, once they get started, they can't advance in it.

Because for me, what a man should truly live, a woman can't live.

And already, people, with our culture, you know how it goes.

You come into it, and even if you're a man, guys will bring you problems . . .

If it were another kind of music, that would be a little better.

Alou and Madou remind us again that even male rappers have struggled to win over parents, who see hip hop as a western import at odds with local cultural values. And yet, it is this very distance from tradition that defines hip hop voice, imbuing it with a freedom of speech that defies indigenous norms of communication between youth and elders (Chapter 4). Like Alou, many male rappers are sensitive to the cultural constraints that women face. But when they construct hip hop as inherently masculine, globally modern, and necessarily nonindigenous, they align themselves, however unwittingly, with dominant discourse that binds women to tradition in the face of modernization.

Where, then, is women's place in Rap Galsen? Discussions about women's place in US hip hop often highlight female sexuality as a response to or cooption of misogynist tropes.[6] Recognizing Rap Galsen's masculinity as locally contingent, however, means considering the ambivalent association between women's sexuality and tradition. In Dakar, indigenous performance already allows for socially sanctioned expressions of female sexuality. Women dance, make music, and improvise verbal performance, including taasu, in the context of *tours* (monthly meetings of revolving credit cycles), *tanbeers* (organized sabar dances), marriages, and naming ceremonies. Their overtly sexualized words and movements reclaim female eroticism in a context where colonial prudery and Muslim conceptions of modesty have exacerbated the policing of women's bodies in public space (Castaldi 2006; Heath 1994).

Yet these are not private spaces, nor are they officially segregated along the lines of gender, although often the only men present may be drummers.[7] Rather, they constitute a different kind of public space, a "privately public" one (Morales-Libove 2005, 112) in which the restrictions on women's behavior are loosened in ways dependent on class, caste, age, and marital status (Kringelbach 2013, 90).[8] Through their changing participation in these spaces across different stages of life, women explore Wolof notions of gendered personhood (ibid., 86). They also build and sustain social networks through the exchange of money and goods (particularly cloth) in practices that developed over decades of "conversion, colonialism, capitalist accumulation, migration, wage labor, and trade" (Buggenhagen 2011, 715). Senegalese men, both in everyday conversation and when speaking from positions of religious and political power, have often subjected women's activities in these spaces—from their seemingly extravagant displays of wealth to the apparent lewdness of their dance and poetry—to intense moralistic critique, and dismissed them as outdated traditions (*cosaan* in Wolof) that stand in the way of modernization (ibid.).

Women's privately public spaces have only become more important since the mid-twentieth century, as economic decline, accelerated urbanization, and demographic growth have dramatically changed Dakar households, in turn provoking increasingly restrictive moral standards (Morales-Libove 2005, 136). With widespread unemployment afflicting men, women (with their husbands' permission) have become entrepreneurs in a variety of formal and, more often, informal pursuits outside the home. To a certain extent, they experience increased independence by having their own income, which Islam dictates is their own to do with as they please (Hainard 2001). Popular discourse, however, continues to assert women's place in the home and their subordination to their husbands; women involved in public and political life—as politicians, entrepreneurs, and of course musicians—often emphasize their submission to their husbands as a counterbalance to the moral risk of their engagement in these spheres (Kringelbach 2003, 84).

When women emerged as pop stars in the 1990s, their newfound visibility, labor outside the home, and international mobility invited negative public perceptions of their character. Popular female singers like Kine Lame and Fatou Guewel preempted such criticism by praising the mothers of local Muslim saints like Serigne Touba and Cheikh Ibra Fall in their music (Tang 2007, 158). In doing so, they emphasized women's importance by placing them in a position of maternal authority over male religious icons, a move that also reinforced the propriety of their performance and public visibility by "conforming and simultaneously subverting normative Islamic gender ideals" (Castaldi 2006, 87). In present-day Dakar, however, the relationship between women, indigenous music (including mbalax), and the public sphere remains fraught. The news media protest women's dance as a symbol of moral decline; female sabar/mbalax dancers have even been jailed for indecency when videos of them dancing suggestively in revealing costumes were released online (Kringelbach 2013, 112–113).

Male rappers have implicitly endorsed these critiques by conflating depictions of female sexuality in mbalax and in commercial US hip hop and positioning both as a foil to hip hop consciousness. Most told me that Rap Galsen does not objectify women; they celebrated motherhood as the pinnacle of female virtue (a familiar trope in US hip hop, as well). But these representations are, of course, distinct from women's self-representation, whether in mbalax or in hip hop; when female rappers eschew dominant norms of modesty, they disrupt Rap Galsen's self-mythologizing.

In 2016, young rapper Déesse Major, like sabar dancers before her, was arrested for her supposedly provocative clothing. Although several male rappers, notably older ones like Keyti of Rap'Adio, came to her defense on social media, younger male artists had publicly critiqued her behavior for years prior. Rap Galsen's moral claims, then, reinforce traditional gender norms as they juxtapose girlhood, public space, and the moral risk of uncontained female sexuality with motherhood and the domestic sphere. And marriage, domestic life, and motherhood, we remember, are where women's youth—and their time in hip hop—ends.

"Hip hop really belongs more to men," cautioned Madou.

If it were another kind of music, that would be a little better.

But in rap music, I can't see a woman who begins and continues.

Those who have entered, if you look today they've been left behind.

Because what we live, and the spirit we have, with the way parents hide girls away, you know, because guys were saying gangsta things at one time, so it starts to not be easy.

His tone changes, as though he's speaking to someone hard of hearing. "*Catty do you understand what I'm saying?*"

I did understand, beyond the level of language comprehension that concerned him. Without a family of my own, I moved around the city and stayed out until all hours of the night. I came and went under the watchful eyes of neighbors who pointedly asked about the male friends they saw visit on occasion; I took tangled detours when male strangers followed me in the street; I guarded my address from most of the men I met in hip hop spaces.

On the rocky beach in Almadies, Hawa, Coumbis, and I continue our interview. "Are you welcome in the rap scene?" I ask. "Yeah, of course," Coumbis replies quickly, even as Hawa qualifies—"By some people. But certain people think we've come to be sluts. That we are here for the boys." Coumbis nods and adds, "Also we have problems because certain people see you and say, what can a girl do in hip hop? It's just to get laid. That's all. So when they see you, they don't think about helping you advance. They think, 'now I will try to call Coumbis, we'll become friends, and then we'll try to go out together and we'll see.' Even though this isn't our objective. We want to move things forward and to truly integrate ourselves, even as girls." I think about how I've traced male hip hop networks through relationships of collaboration and mentoring that cross-cut neighborhoods; I remember that young male rappers come up as hype men for established ones, eventually getting their own verses on their elders' albums (Chapter 1).

As we walk home, Hawa several meters ahead of us, placing one foot in front of the other on the raised stones that edge the street, arms floating to the sides like a gymnast on a balance beam, Coumbis and I discuss our weekend plans. I have a follow-up interview to do, and she shoots me a warning glance—Careful with him! Boy, does he like white women. I lift my eyebrows, rolling my eyes toward her; I already know. We share a look of commiseration and walk on.

Coumbis and I had learned firsthand that free movement through public space via hip hop raised questions about our unmooring from cultural norms of modesty and chastity, so that as young women, our reputations were at stake when we attended or participated in hip hop events.[9] These assumptions were sometimes exaggerated in my case due to my foreignness; as a white woman, I was immediately visibly exempt from familial oversight (Appert 2017). But they were infinitely more damaging when directed at young Senegalese women, whose reputations would determine their life trajectories long after I returned to the United States. Sister Dia said,

It's so difficult, because if you go to concerts at 2, 3, 4, in the morning and you're a woman, it will be rough.

A lot of people won't understand if you are going to work or going to spend the night somewhere.

When you're a woman, if you go to a concert, as soon as you perform then you need to take your taxi home, not letting anything bad slow your way . . .

But honestly, I don't see any bad women in rap. The women I see go, do their work, and then quickly take their taxis to go home.

I nodded as she spoke. I wasn't going to tell her this, but more than once, men in Dakar's hip hop scene had warned me about spending too much time with young women rappers, making barely veiled insinuations about their alleged promiscuity and their pursuit of white men. The irony here seemed lost on my well-meaning advisors, as I thought of all the interviews I'd postponed or cancelled, the footage ruined by men shouting painful nothings in my ears as I tried to film at concerts. Sometimes I thought wistfully of the quick Wolof acquisition that I could have expected from a home stay, which I exchanged for the freedom of movement that came with the apartment I rented. I considered staying out at concerts until the first call to prayer before dawn, often without another woman in sight, and regretted that no matter how hard I tried, like Sister Dia, to mark what I was doing as work, the fact that my work went all night seemed to identify me, too, as a "bad woman," certainly as far as my neighbors were concerned, and likewise for many of the young men I encountered at concerts. Freedom of movement came at a price.

The issue, then, is not just one of access to public space, but of a socially sanctioned access that might amplify women's voices rather than drawing censorship and criticism. Like popular musicians in other genres, the women of Gotal neutralized hip hop space and public space—or rather, neutralized hip hop negotiations of public space—by invoking the respectability of family. Describing their collective as a familial one destabilized the dichotomy between home and the street. It challenged the idea that female movement in hip hop spaces was contrary to social norms of female behavior. "And now we can even say we are sisters," Coumbis told me, describing her entrance into Gotal. "We are the same family. It's not a connection but a family and we love each other."

If young men negotiate the postcolonial city through hip hop networks, converting an imposed social marginalization into a purposefully assumed underground that ultimately increases their visibility and amplifies their voice, young women reimagine the street—that is, the colonially inflected class distinctions that mark the geography of the city—through narratives of home, family, kinship, and respectability. In doing so, they expose the underground—that is, the ways in which youth negotiate their relationship to urban space and the social relations that constitute it—as an already gendered construction, in how it is imagined vis-à-vis- public and domestic space and various genres of music making.

In the studio with Gotal, their hook plays on repeat:

Hip Hop industry [Hip hop industry]

Yaangiy jaay last criy [You're selling last year's model]

Gotal affaire de street [Gotal, a street thing]

Dox ci game bi free [Walking freely in the game]

MASCULINITY AND WORK

> There was a girl group formed by Rap'Adio, and they rapped seriously, like men.
> LAMINE NDAO

I heard that there used to be more women, back in the day, before hip hop was *hard*. "In the beginning, there were women at hip hop concerts," said Falsower.

But that was the time, the trend.

Hip hop is a truth.

But something that's trendy is something that's going to pass.

If you do something that's not serious, everyone will come.

But when you do something different, then people will only stay if they're brave. People will [only] listen to things that don't edify, like the texts of the mbalaxmen.

People love things that are easy here.

We don't have time to do the Youza [a popular mbalax dance in 2011].

Before, there were only love songs.

And women are naturally sentimental, and now rap is harder than it was.

For years, underground rappers categorized international Senegalese hip hop, mbalax, and contemporary US hip hop as commercial musics whose lyrical content (about love, bling, girls) was as soft as their melodically effeminate music. They spoke of hip hop's global masculinity, reminded me that *even in your country*, there are more men than women in hip hop. And yet, they ultimately explained hip hop's gender question as one that was deeply local. "It's not hip hop's fault, but Senegalese culture," said Books.

Often, here, if girls want to enter into the arts or the musical world, they prefer to sing than to rap. Because we didn't know hip hop culture here. But now we are starting to see, little by little, the girls starting to rap . . .

Now there are girls who rap but more in the banlieues. I don't know any girls who rap in Medina. It's because of Senegalese culture. They prefer to sing or dance because they don't really know what hip hop is, they just know mbalax and traditional dancing.

Women are linked, again and again, to tradition, to mbalax, to dance; and we know already how these stand as the counterbalance to hip hop's modernity, consciousness, *voice*.

"You find some girls who love hip hop and will come, but most of the time they're kind of scared," said Djily Bagdad.

And the national mbalax music, all the girls listen to it. Mbalax is so easy; they aren't saying anything in their lyrics, it's easy to understand. But most of them, they say hip hop is too hard to understand. And in our music, people aren't used to thinking about what you're saying, they're used to just hearing melodies, it's way too easy, anyone can be a musician when it comes to mbalax, our national music. And girls are so used to that easy thing.

Easiness was a gloss for commercially successful musical styles, often rooted in tradition; it was a dismissal of topical themes that didn't challenge the status quo. Easiness was an indictment of lyrical content and musical sound. And easiness threatened to exclude women from hip hop realness and, by extension, voice.

One day, I sit with four men: two rappers, a deejay, and another friend, listening to them criticize a young rapper for being too "manly" in her dress, body language, and style of rapping—She shouldn't try to act like a man—they agree. I know the young woman in question and protest that I'm pretty sure she's just acting like herself—Could you imagine her wearing makeup, or primping and prancing around in a frilly dress? What do you want her to rap about, going to the market and cooking lunch?—They reluctantly cede the point.

Like a loop on repeat, these narratives shape women's place in Rap Galsen: voice sounds through real hip hop, and real hip hop is masculine, yet women should not be masculine, so they cannot claim hip hop realness or voice. Hip hop hardness is defined against femininity, a femininity that women for the most part cling to, even as they contest their marginality in hip hop. Coumbis told me, "You didn't become a rapper to become a guy. And the guys will mock you for dressing like a guy. We are born girls, so why change because we do rap? We are girls before being rappers and we should guard this femininity. I have no desire to be a hardcore rapper and be like a guy."

The gender binary at the core of Rap Galsen's narratives of genre, tradition, and modernity writes out queerness as it historically existed in the region and as it is found today, even as mbalax's association with femininity sometimes leads to accusations of homosexuality against its male singers.[10] The level of secrecy that surrounds same-sex desire, and the danger of violent repercussions at the hands of the state or civil society, mean that queer identities are largely invisible in present-day Senegal.[11] Yet, perhaps spurred by recent accusations from African leaders that homosexuality is a western import designed to contaminate African cultures, Rap Galsen has become increasingly vocal in its hostility toward gay men since 2011.[12] This antigay rhetoric is touted as a form of social consciousness and political intervention—one that warns political leaders not to capitulate to western pressures to decriminalize homosexuality. Social consciousness reinscribes normative masculinity as a marker of hip hop realness.

While leaving questions of queerness to the side, the women of Gotal subtly clapped back against masculinist constructions of hip hop authenticity that would dismiss them through tropes of easiness. They reframed conversations about women's role in Rap Galsen in terms of work and visibility, implicitly rebutting the stories that they knew or anticipated men would tell.

When I asked why I saw so few women in the hip hop scene, Lamine Ndao told me,

> Maybe they would say that men are more popular in hip hop, which doesn't encourage them to continue.
>
> But there are girls who are really good and rap in different languages.
>
> Maybe they're afraid; maybe they would say that people are more interested in [hearing] men than women in hip hop.
>
> Also, a lot of girls don't have the flow they should have, and so they'd have to work a lot to get to the same level as the men.
>
> Sometimes you hear an American woman who has a good flow, and you say she is more hip hop than the men, even though she's a girl.
>
> There are American girls who have imposed themselves more.
>
> But here, there aren't girls who make the effort to impose themselves—they think men should come to them to support them every time.

Back on the roof at Def Dara, Sister Dia interjects in French, "We also want—" she pauses, and starts over in Wolof,

> We also want them to believe that it's not because we're women that they should help us; we don't need that.
>
> Help us in our work.
>
> Don't anyone help us because we're women.
>
> I don't want that.
>
> Rap is just rap.
>
> There's no woman, there's no man.
>
> Work is just work.
>
> What men are thinking of and sitting down to write, women can think of and sit down and write.
>
> Don't say you should support her because she is a woman, you should support her because she is pretty; we want to work, to show people this is why you should support us, not that we're women so you should support us, no no no.
>
> Don't help us because we're women.

Lamine tells me, "It's the work, and if it's good, there aren't further barriers. If it's well done, people will listen." I ask him what keeps women from doing that work, and he answers that maybe they are busy, or maybe they aren't patient enough. I think back to the day that I interviewed Gotal at the studio, where the engineer first flirted and chatted instead of recording, and then left in the middle of the session to do something else. I try, and fail, to imagine the same scenario happening at a studio session with Books. When Gotal and I went back downstairs after our interview, Gaston, the studio's owner, arrived and demanded to know why the session still was not finished. Without mentioning his mysterious errand that had paused the session in the first place, the engineer explained that I had taken the group to go do an interview. My eyes widened, and a chorus of protest arose from the women, who insisted on finishing their session.

A few weeks later, Coumbis and Hawa would drop Coumbis's single at a radio station and bring me along, their foreign researcher whose interest in the song might pique the radio personality's own interest enough for him to play it on his show.

Lamine says they don't take the time to impose themselves, that if you hear someone who is really popular, you will know it's because they've worked a lot. "Only work pays." I wonder aloud if women have the same amount of free time as men do. He reflects for a moment and then admits that yeah, maybe men are more available, their movements less closely surveilled, their families less concerned with what they are up to. Maybe women can't just wander around until all hours of the night.

"Help us because our work is well done," said Sista Dia, "because our work is good."

> Because we also want to make products that are quality, that anyone who hears it will know it's real hip hop.
>
> So that whoever hears, knows we aren't playing, we're working.
>
> So that whoever supports us, doesn't support us because we're good [people] or because we're women, or because of this or that.
>
> Whoever would help us, listen to our song, and if you accept it, support our song.
>
> If the work is bad, without quality, say "Hey, go work!"

Framing hip hop as work, these young women moved to neutralize the negative connotations of their hip hop forays into public space, and to contest the conflation of femininity and easiness in Rap Galsen. They described their desire to make financial contributions to their parents' households as a primary motivation for the time they spent on hip hop; in doing do, they leveraged shifting cultural attitudes towards women's labor outside the home to establish the respectability of their efforts as rappers. At the same time, in their insistent description of hip hop as work—rather than as leisure or even idealistic social activism—they emphasized the seriousness of their music, marking it as something that was as real, if not more so, than anything male rappers were doing.

BETWEEN HOME AND THE STREET

> Rap is rap. Female and male rap are the same thing. Rap is open to everyone. It's a freedom of expression. There's no rap for this person and rap for this other person. Rap is rap.
>
> TOUSSA

I heard that there used to be more women, back in the day. I heard that we don't know what happened. Maybe they got married. Maybe they didn't want to do the work. Maybe, maybe . . . I heard that there *were* women, in Rap Galsen's mythical old school.

I never got to know rapper Nix very well, but I vividly remember our candid conversation about hip hop voice and its gendered limits. In French, he said,

> In general, rappers have a freedom of expression here, which, I don't know how it would be seen if women did the same thing, especially here in Senegal, where we still have these barriers, so maybe women who do rap here now aren't as free. It's not like in the United States where you have women who do rap and say things that, if you listen to Lil Kim, Nicki Minaj, you can't imagine a female rapper here saying these things, although if it were a man you could imagine it.
>
> I don't know if that's why we don't have a lot of women who rap here.
>
> But I think we did have a good number before, but maybe they had a hard time really imposing themselves and building their rap careers.
>
> And here, every woman wants to be married and have children one day, and once she does that, it's hard to have a career.

"That's complicated," I offered, and he laughed humorlessly. "Yeah, it's complicated. Welcome to Africa."

The freedom of expression that men have historically located in hip hop is one that draws on a nonindigenous performance genre to contest the powerlessness of youth and to flout the age hierarchies implied in their relationships to political leaders. Yet we've seen how these intersecting power dynamics are infinitely more restrictive in the everyday lives of young women, limiting not only the duration of their careers but also the time they have to develop their rapping skills on a daily basis. More than anything else, this gendering of youth—as a hip hop time, a time for hip hop—works against women's claims to voice, because, as we will see in the next chapter, hip hop realness depends on how hip hop sounds as much as what it says.

In the street outside his family home in Medina, I asked Djily Bagdad why there aren't many women rappers. I still thought, then, that this was the question to ask. He responded,

> There are women rappers but not a lot and their level—they don't have the same level as men.
>
> In the States, a long time ago you might hear Lil Kim, Foxy Brown, Eve. In Senegal, there's a few female rappers but they aren't that great, they don't have the same level as male rappers.

"Why aren't they as good?" I asked. He responded honestly, "Because they are just in the beginning, they are just starting, it will take some time."

It seems that in Rap Galsen, women are always just in the beginning. The particular historical circumstances of female adolescence in Dakar mean that the question to ask is not, how many women are making hip hop, but rather, how hip hop claims to visibility and voice are gendered in ways that emerge from and at times uphold the same structures of power they contest. Djily's response aside, the fact that many female rappers simply aren't as skilled at their verbal craft as the men whose careers exponentially outlast their own often becomes proof of hip hop's masculinity. "A lot of girls don't have the flow they should have, and so they'd have to work a lot to get to the same level as the men," said Lamine Ndao. And Thiat, on the balcony of his beachfront apartment in Parcelles, told me,

> You know, women's problem in hip hop is first of all their voice.
>
> I know some, they are from rural areas and their problem is the family. Some, they finish their *Bac* and should come to Dakar to study and that wrecks their hip hop career.
>
> Others are forbidden by their families to do rap, because, according to a lot of people, it's too masculine.
>
> The ones that are in Dakar, I don't know what they're missing.
>
> Because back then, we had Fatim, we heard her, we had Sister Fa. We have young girls that are here but there's a lot missing.
>
> We had Alif, Jafaroy, we had Lady Sinay and now she is in Europe.
>
> I don't know what's going on with the girls but that's what it is.

It's a very macho, a very masculine hip hop, Senegalese hip hop.

And you need to be honest about that.

There's something poignant in Thiat's recitation of this litany of female old-school rappers, now gone. He says he doesn't know where the women are; he muses about family pressures, rural values, and hip hop masculinity. But first, he tells us, women's problem is *their voice*. There's an ambiguity here between the aesthetics of the gendered, sounding voice (whose masculine hardness marks hip hop as real), the cultivation of a skilled verbal flow, and the freedom of expression that hip hop promises. We remember that this freedom of expression is constructed in explicit opposition to traditional speech genres and to the musical styles and genres with which they are inextricably paired. We remember how, they said, Senegalese culture locates women's place in music in mbalax—that is, in tradition—and not in hip hop.

Remembering tradition, we come back to taasu, and we recognize how origin myths gender voice. Keyti, in describing Senegalese traditional music, told me,

But usually Senegalese traditional music is just praising people.

Your grandfather was a king, your grandfather was a good man, your mother was a nice person—usually that's the subject matter.

Or it's sexual.

You've got a lot of this taasu for example, which people are saying rap comes from taasu blah blah blah.

Taasu, a lot of taasu is mainly sexual.

It was used, for example, when people were getting married and women had to go to their husband's house.

The taasu they used in the moment had a lot of sexual connotations in it.

That's why I think hip hop was really the first genre in Senegal coming with real, real, real subjects people could relate to in their daily life, people could relate to in terms of politics, economy . . .

Painting hip hop as an inherently masculine practice, while claiming it as a speech genre integrally linked to voice, men inadvertently relegate women to what they have rather forcefully argued is the voicelessness of traditional music. However, traditional music doesn't exactly render women voiceless. Rather, the somewhat reactionary opposition of hip hop and taasu hinges on a gendered rendering of social consciousness that underestimates—or completely devalues—how taasu negotiates kinship and other social relationships among women in domestic settings. Taasu is only *not* socially conscious if *social* means the male-dominated public sphere and *consciousness* denotes a very specific idea of resistance centered on a liberal construction of the agential voice and tied to political interventions at the level of the state.[13]

Nevertheless, the young women who were members of Gotal in 2011–2012 were singularly focused on asserting themselves in hip hop, leveraging their layered invisibility to lay claim to hip hop realness and its potentiality of voice. (Some, like Coumbis and Hawa, were mildly skeptical about hip hop's potential connections to taasu. Others, like Toussa and Anta, said sure, they could be linked. I wondered if the distinct lack of feeling had to do with the fact that as women, they surely participated in taasu-centered moments of performative collectivity in which men might be present, but marginal.) Griot myths and hip hop myths pushed women to the margins, forged diasporic connections through the imagined traditions of male griots or the masculine resistance of hardcore hip hop. Yet these women cared little for grand narratives and origin myths. They busied themselves with work, challenging what it meant to be feminine and to be women in the face of significant social change since their mothers and grandmothers were girls.

On the roof at Def Dara, Coumbis explains the song that they've been recording downstairs, which talks about how they should be united, how they are five people and one at the same time, so that if someone invites one of them to a show, another can swap in to represent the group. "If you see Coumbis you see Gotal." As Toussa picks up the narrative, she enters into a kind of call and response with Coumbis, saying,

> She talks about how we each come from a different neighborhood to become one.
>
> In my verse, I even valorize what we are, say that we can do this, and trample a bit on the others.
>
> And when I say the others, I don't mean other girls.

Coumbis clarifies, "They're the guys," while Toussa continues,

> I'm speaking of the guys, because they're here for a very long time and can't even bring hip hop anywhere.
>
> They're here for years—

Coumbis insists, "They've done nothing"

> —and they've done nothing.

"They've done nothing," echoes Coumbis. Toussa goes on:

I would say their work has run aground.

So it's time for them to cede their place, so that we can show what we know how to do. Because when you have a profession and after years it hasn't worked, you should look for something else—

Coumbis repeats, "Another thing, yes—"

—Or, they have a problem of not wanting to do research in the work.

So that's missing.

So that's what we're doing to share our work.

So the song is also kind of an ego trip . . .

Coumbis quiets, satisfied. Toussa says,

[Hip hop] doesn't advance because the people who are ahead don't want to make space for young talent and they don't help them at all.

They organize VIP concerts among themselves, what we often see on the TV, with no underground at all, and this is not at all normal.

And they know that the underground is stronger than them.

Because they no longer represent anything, they are just there to squabble and create drama among themselves even though this is not hip hop.

Hip hop is peace, love, and harmony. I think that the guys say they are the best, the first here, but they don't understand hip hop.

Women's invisibility becomes their own claim to realness—the mark of a new underground vis-à-vis mainstream society and Rap Galsen, where their relative youth means that they relate to many male rappers as elders rather than as peers. In the face of a hip hop masculinity that mobilizes gendered constructions of labor and consciousness to exclude women, these rappers flip the script to claim that they work harder and better and are therefore not only as legitimate as men, but more so. Claiming a place in Rap Galsen, they further insist on a place in the world. Hip hop, unlike mbalax, is particularly suited to being deployed in this way; the very idea of a hip hop underground, the do-it-yourself nature of hip hop, and the rise of hip hop cultural centers all create a musical scene in which amateur participation is fairly welcome, at least on a certain level.

Yet music was not something that they filled their time with, but rather something they made time for, and they linked this to their desire to make money, support their families, and effect material change for women in society. This—and not a lofty and at times vague ideal of social consciousness—was what it meant for them to have a voice.

Still on the roof at Def Dara, Coumbis said,

> In fact, the concept of Gotal is to show another facet of women.
>
> Because here in Senegal, in Africa in general I would say, there is a tendency to put women off to the side; they are here to get married, to have children, or to be home watching the children.
>
> Gotal is here to show another facet, to show that a woman has the right to go on stage, to do her music, to work in an office, and other things.
>
> We also want to show guys in hip hop that women are here and what's more, we can do what they do, better than they do it.

Sister Dia jumped in,

> I would add that it's not just being a woman in hip hop.
>
> Everything is difficult.
>
> You're a woman in a business, you have difficulties there.
>
> You're in a house working as a maid, even when they pay you every month, you have difficulties.
>
> Women are the ones with little power.
>
> Here there are those who really underestimate women.
>
> But our fight is how to make it so that whoever is in a marriage, her husband takes good care of her . . .
>
> Our fight is about the way female students and their teachers behave.
>
> Our work is how to make it so that woman has a voice here in Senegal, that she be well respected: in rap, where she's working as a maid, in the office, everywhere.
>
> If you're a woman, to make it so you know that anywhere you go, you have a voice, and that they respect you like they respect men . . .
>
> To know, wherever she goes, that no one gave this to me, no one offered it as charity, it's my right, it's *mine*.
>
> That's our fight.

I love [sampling], too much even. Things that
represent a little bit of scratch—I represent
the real hip hop chicka-chicka-chicka.

BOOKS, SEN KUMPË

6

PRODUCING DIASPORA

MAY 2011. AS I approach the gates to Magic Land, I see Lamine Ndao waiting to guide me to the concert venue hidden away in the amusement park's interior. I follow him past rides like the ones that I worked up the nerve to try at church carnivals in New Jersey when I was a child—tilt-a-whirls and bumper cars and miniature roller coasters, here eerie in their stillness. In the deepest recesses of the park, we come to a pavilion; Books sits inside, while Simon performs just out of sight. Offered a lawn chair, I study its legs before lowering slowly into it; and we're up and moving again, back through the looming rides and out the gates, haggling a taxi, rushing across town, arriving at the Liberté V bus terminus only to find the Orange S'Cool Tour concert has yet to begin. Books wanders off to find coffee, and I take my cup gratefully when he returns. In the tent that serves as a backstage, my plastic lawn chair wobbles as I sit, then sinks into the earth; I shake my feet from side to side to dislodge the sand, eyeing the men's sneakers with envy. Arriving rappers and their entourages greet us. Those who know me call me by name, offering a warm handshake or a quick peck on each cheek (I'm American, not French—I chide them). Those I've never met abruptly dampen the brightness of their Wolof exchanges as they turn to me with a measured, *Madame, ça va*? I've learned to recognize the exaggerated courtesy of their distant greetings as a response to whiteness and, perhaps, attendant anxieties over French.

Each new arrival hands a CD of instrumental tracks to Simon, who beat us here somehow. He rattles a set list off the top of his head to a friend, who notes it on a sheet of paper. Eventually, the concert begins; when I hear 5kiem Underground's songs, I move to gather my camera, but I'm trapped by a stranger intently practicing his English on me as I dodge the smoke from his cigarette. When I'm finally summoned to film Sen Kumpë and Simon, I rise in relief and head to where they want me to stand, just in front of the stage.

Synthesized strings and rapid, driving sixteenths on the snare and high hat set up their duet. Books and Simon move across the stage with wild abandon, taking the crowd with them to the left and then to the right. I like this beat; it reminds me simultaneously of listening to the radio in LA traffic and of bouncing from side to side with Lamine outside a late-night show in a small club in Dakar as this same song played inside. Now, with effort, I keep my body and camera still.

When Nix comes on, moving across the stage in a fitted red T, sunglasses, and a silver chain, I again recognize the song. A lone balafon plays its rhythmic ostinato, its tight compression betraying its origins in a sound bank. Low, synthesized strings enter, sustaining a single chord underneath. The strings move together, sweeping downward to usher in the high, tight snare rhythm and syncopated chords that once again coax a Dirty South bounce from my shoulders, even as I force them, once again, to stillness. The driving chords, the elongated strings, the hyper snare drum articulate against the balafon's steady pattern, locking into a rhythmic counterpoint that juxtaposes aural signs of a traditional Africa and a global Blackness. Nix's voice marks this sonic zoom, reaching across the Atlantic to a US hip hop tradition indirectly spoken in the African American Vernacular English that bookends his litany of place—Whattup—yes—DK—Galsen–Africa–That's your boy Nix.

Beats, sounds, language, and flow work together to locate us in time and space. In a performance of diaspora that is at once an assertion of and a challenge to local belonging, musical layering *sounds* the transatlantic connectivities that link postcolonial urbanity to the US inner city. This is what I call *a practice of hip hop genre:* a self-conscious engagement with hip hop production practices that is as much about how, where, and when voice sounds as it is about topical content. Refracting earlier chapters' claims about speech, voice, memory, and history through this lens of musical form shows how musical practices performatively enact these (sometimes conflicting) narratives of diasporic connection in ways that change over time. This practice of hip hop genre ultimately undermines distinctions between commercialism and consciousness, music and text, mainstream and underground, global and local.

In hip hop genre as imagined and inscribed in Rap Galsen, two understandings of time—as musical meter, and as history, memory, and myth—come together in the palimpsest of sound and meaning that I call *hip hop time*. First, hip hop time marks a particular stage of life (prolonged youth), at a particular historical moment (the last three decades) in a particular place (Dakar), while reimagining these through transatlantic hip hop myths. Hip hop time is a way of engaging the past; it is a retemporalization and spatialization of diaspora—or rather, a series of reconstructions of the past and present in and as diaspora—that shift, conflict, come together, and diverge again. Subverting the invented traditions of colonial and postcolonial projects, international rappers circumvented contemporary griot performance to reroute tradition through the transatlantic slave trade and African American musical history and reclaim it in hip hop. Challenging indigenous dynamics between speech, music, and action, underground rappers mobilized hip hop narratives of the ghetto to voice their experiences of postcolonial urbanity and underdevelopment as they spoke from, to, and for the street. These projects were not mutually exclusive; they depended on common understandings of hip hop—as a resistant social force and transformative musical practice—and a shared desire to challenge local realities.

Rap Galsen's constructions of time, history, and memory have, from the outset, been tied up in debates over aesthetics, genre, and commodification. Early hardcore rappers eschewed the commercial viability of their international counterparts' R&B and reggae-inflected refrains, and rejected their collective memory of indigenous verbal performance. Instead, they tapped into a globally circulating mode of hip hop realness, whose direct topical content and hard musical aesthetic marginalized them in mainstream media and society. While their local and global visibility increased in tandem with their engagement in electoral politics, their claims to voice actively gendered music, speech, and youth itself, producing a hip hop that remains, at times, masculinist and exclusionary.

Second, hip hop time concerns the rhythmic temporality of hip hop music, its characteristic layering, and how it is constructed and produced as a musical genre whose form is ultimately as meaningful as the messages it carries. Hip hoppers reminded me that they *knew* the story of hip hop, where it came from. They told me a story of ghettos and oppression, but also of sound systems, deejays, and breakbeats. They remembered how these generated practices of sampling, quotation, and signifying that made the decentering and recentering of other musics a definitive quality of hip hop. In hip hop's layering of music from different times and places, they heard the echoes of days past and spaces far away.

And they, too, practiced such layering, lifting tradition—as a coherent configuration of aural signs (Bakhtin 1986, 103; Barber 2007, 22)—from its original musical and social contexts in griot performance to incorporate it into hip hop instrumentals. There, it continued to evoke locality and history while acquiring new meaning, form, and function (Baumann and Briggs 1990; Briggs and

Bauman 1992). By separating the instrumental and vocal elements of traditional performance, hip hoppers have laid claim to musical markers of local place, even as they have deliberately detached them from traditionally inflected social relations. These practices of musical intertextuality render musical genre—as imagined in discourse and practice—a social practice in which musical narratives work alongside discursive ones to remember and reinvent histories of connection, and to mobilize them in the pursuit of immediate and material social change (Appert 2016b).

PRODUCING THE LOCAL

The first time I went to Senegal, in 2007, I met Gaby, a musician who lived amid his collection of handcrafted traditional instruments, many tuned to western scales to facilitate collaboration with foreign musicians. We sat in front of two small wooden xylophones as he picked out a short, syncopated ostinato on his instrument. He began to sing, a haunting melody that rose and dipped in waves—*oooo—eeeyah-oooo—eee–yah* . . .

But I know this song already, from Positive Black Soul (PBS)'s *Salaam* album, one of the few Senegalese hip hop recordings commercially available in the United States and, in 2007, the only one I've heard. There, it comes as a musical interlude toward the end of a song about drinking tea with friends, sung over the same balafon line that Gaby wants to teach me. He knows it as part of a puberty ceremony from the Casamance, where it is sung as boys go into the forest to be circumcised.

Four years later, I will recognize Gaby's circumcision song in the refrain to Simon's "Borom Xél," accompanied by djembes. I hear it yet again on ResKp's *Dafa Jot* album, where it bridges sections of a song based on subtle pressure drum rhythms and punctuated with kora and traditional singing.

One day in 2011, a taximan asks me where I've traveled in Senegal, and I confess that I spend almost all my time in Dakar, with occasional trips to the cities of Thies and Saint-Louis. He admonishes me that I need to get to the regions outside the city, and I wonder idly to myself if, in any of my spheres of existence—fieldwork, ethnomusicology—my village-shunning, spoon-using, jeans-wearing, *chaise anglaise*–preferring, pop music–focused experience of Africa will ever count. The taximan is still talking, and I focus on deciphering his rurally accented Wolof as he continues—Casamance, in the South. That is the place to go if you want to see tradition.

Another day, another taximan picks up the same thread, raving about the wonderful cultural performances to be seen in Casamance. He wants to know if I know the Konkoran. I recall a snapshot of my friend from southern Senegal, smiling as he poses next to a giant living figure of bark and straw. This must have been a folk-loric performance featuring the UNESCO-designated representative of humanity's intangible cultural heritage; from what I've gleaned, the real Konkoran is a fright-ening spirit central to Mandingue male circumcision rituals in the south and taboo to women and girls.

Tradition appears once more as something deeply local, precolonial, and nonurban—and thus, to a certain extent, non-Wolof. Something that cannot be accessed in the gridlock of traffic that bogs us down as we traverse the city. Something and somewhere else than here.

Years later, beside a main thoroughfare in Parcelles Assainies, after the sun has already set, a woman snatches up the toddler playing at our feet and runs inside. I look up, startled, to see a Konkoran bearing down on us, a mob of chil-dren running behind it at a safe distance, alternately shrieking and laughing. It passes us, stops, and leans against the closed door of the neighboring shop, where it freezes in a quivering stillness. Unnerved, I steal glances at it out of the corner of my eye while trying to follow the lead of the women around me. They carry on as though it's not there, but their looks in my direction communicate as clearly as fingertips held to lips. Without warning, it springs away from the building, striding out into traffic, the feeling of foreboding fading into darkness with it.

In a museum in The Gambia in 2017, I snap a picture of a Konkoran mask to include in this chapter. But the lifeless, diminutive husk is not a Konkoran at all.

On the other side of the Gambia, far from Dakar, the Casamance has long served as a symbolic fount of culture, its non-Wolof sounds invoking a distant past. Remember that Senghor's earliest nationalist projects privileged rural Senegal's performance traditions, particularly Mande ones, folkloricizing them as preco-lonial history and presenting them to the world as a testament to the value of African culture (Kringelbach 2013, 39–40). Likewise, musical instruments associ-ated with Mande cultures were among those that most commonly appeared in underground hip hop tracks in the first decade of the twenty first century. These include the kora (a harp-lute), the balafon (or *bala*, a wooden xylophone with gourd resonators), the djembe (a goblet-shaped hand drum), and the *tama* (a small pressure drum played under the arm, shared with the Wolof and similar to any number of pressure or "talking" drums in West Africa) (Charry 2000; Hale 1998). Sampled in hip hop, these sounds of tradition speak newly, differently to youth experiences of modernity.

The sound of the tama embedded in the instrumental of Sen Kumpë's "Aythia Gnu Dem" is forever linked, in my memory, to the music video's images and to the blossoming of a friendship between me, rappers Bourba and Books, and their manager, Lamine Ndao. When Lamine gave me the file shortly after we met in 2008, I was living in a homestay, without access to television or, therefore, much exposure to local music videos. After transferring the file to my computer, I watched, enthralled, as an already-familiar cast of characters moved across the screen—Bourba, Books, Simon, Keyti (but in retrospect, I don't know if they were all familiar then, I think they can't have been, not yet). Then Books sticks out his left elbow and hooks his left hand under an invisible tama, which his right hand beats in rhythm with the short, escalating bursts of drum rhythms whose ascending pitch punctuates the instrumental track. With his visual cue, I recognize the snippet of indigenous percussion otherwise buried in a beat indistinguishable from one I might hear in the United States.

I start to look for other examples, and I find them, although never more than a track or two per album, not when it comes to the underground.[1] Traditional music shows up as samples, as studio-recorded additions to hip hop beats, and as digital re-creations. Listening to 23.3.'s song, "Guem sa Bop [Believe in Yourself]," from their album *Sugnu Thiono Sen Nioflaye*, I focus on the looping kora phrase, which rises, falls, and repeats; under it, I hear the hand drum rhythms—synthesized, from what I can tell—accented with snare hits. Strings and flutes fill out the texture.

After an interview with members of Coalition Niamu Mbaam, I take their new album, *Guddi Leer,* home to listen. Four tracks in (I glance at my computer and see this is "Sa Yoon," meaning "Your Way/Path"), the sounds of a lute catch my ear; I can't say whether it's a Wolof *xalam* or a Mande *ngoni*. Its descending melody layers over a balafon; they proceed in unison while singer Pape Diouf vocalizes over the top. A drum kit enters, and the xalam (ngoni?) quickly fades to the background. The balafon continues, though, trading overlapping phrases with a kora.

Between these poles of subtlety and prominence, Books's air tama on one end and the thick layering of Niamu Mbaam's track on the other, a musically inclined Goldilocks might be pulled toward the many examples that fall somewhere in the middle. I hear tradition ebb and flow in Gaston's "Khikeuma," emerging as prominent layers during musical breaks, receding into a mixture of synthesized western instruments and drum machines during the verses. A string-heavy hip hop beat quickly overwhelms the hand drum rhythm that opens the song. Again, a new layer—kora—fades back into the beat after several bars, reappearing in the final verse. Then Baye Fall praisesinging juts up against electric guitar melodies, finally giving way to the same kora from the beginning, which continues alongside the strident guitar lines in a combative layering until the song ends.[2]

Listening to 5kiem Underground's "Joyu Askan Wi"—a lyrical critique of government corruption and underdevelopment through the lens of the everyday suffering of the people—I fixate on the kora, whose first simple melody continues to loop underneath the korist's layered improvisations; beneath it all, sustained, synthesized strings ground the beat. As Djily Bagdad announces, "This is the cry of the people" in Wolof, I hear a hand drum enter under the kora. The first verse begins, the simple melody picked up in the strings, the kora continuing its descending runs, the hand drum competing with a drum kit's hip hop beat, building to a dense texture of voices and sounds in the refrain, where the kora recedes and reemerges in the mix. In the remaining verses, we lose a few layers, and the kora and hand drum fade in and out of the beat. After the final refrain, the kora returns in force, echoing the melody of the refrain; the strings continue in unison, the hip hop kit and hand drum work together beneath the kora's now-unfettered improvisations.

Djily's former partner, Baye Njagne, says that the kora came after the lyrics were written; it was played live over the beat in the studio. He says that it was meant to amplify the song's lyrical message; that the suffering of the people, their tears, should come through in the music. "If I write a text, I'll see a kind of beat, drums, bass—this is the first thing," he tells me. "Afterwards, I go to the studio and I tell the technician to program what I tell him. It's not up to him to make my beat, I do it in my head. If I do 'tum tum tak,' that's what he does."[3]

Content and form remained intertwined; localized beats conjoin with lyrics. Musical meaning emerges from the layering of sounds and words. Traditional musical elements emphasize the self-evident themes of 23.3's "Believe in Yourself" and Niamu Mbaam's "Your Path." They underscore Gaston's treatment of religious wisdom and local Muslim saints in "Khikeuma." The circumcision song from Casamance grounds ResKp's "Diar Diar," in which he describes his journey through hip hop, from an early group called Ninjki Nanka (named for another mythical creature from southern Senegal) to his emergence as a solo artist, and links his personal history to the rootedness and locality of tradition. It does the same for Simon's lyrics about knowledge of self in "Borom Xel."

Several weeks after helping to film the music video for 23.3's song "Get Up," I head to Falsower's house in Grand Yoff. There, on a mattress on the floor in his small room on the roof, we watch the video with rapper and friend Don Zap, and I wince when I see my name—or a version of it—as the video credits flash on the screen: "Images: Caty." We talk about the different scenes—the shoemakers and stadium in Medina, the small obelisk and larger stadium in Grand Yoff, whose large SENEGAL graffiti figured prominently in the video (Fig. 6.1).

"We use [traditional music] just to show your identity," said Djily Bagdad, on the sidewalk in front of his home in Medina. "To show that this is where I'm from. For example, when you go back to the States, if you hear a beat with kora or sabar you

FIGURE 6.1 Almamy (Nigga Mee)(right) and Falsower (left) shoot 23.3's "Get Up" video.

might know it's from Senegal." Layers of belonging, of locatedness, sound through hip hop, from the experience of the street and attendant neighborhood pride on display in 23.3's video, to a wide grasping at belonging, at a rootedness that eludes urban youth, that is temporal and spatial at once. Indigenous music grounds hip hop in an imagined past, audible in the present. This is instrumental music, the authoritative tradition of male griots—what Gaston had called "*traditional* traditional music"; neither the feminized modern tradition of mbalax, nor indigenous verbal performance more broadly. This is the mythologized past that has stood as a marker for hip hop's shifting engagements with tradition over decades. Music of another time, paradoxically saturating the present.[4]

HIP HOP TIME

At Cinema Awa in Pikine, Daara J is still performing, their backing band's skilled combination of traditional and electronic instruments, local rhythms, and global harmonies evoking cheers and dancing from the young people pressed up against the stage. Several rows back, I enjoy the open space of the half-empty hall and the chance to just be a spectator, now that Sister Dia has finished her short set. A young man who works at Africulturban, the hip hop cultural center not five minutes away, leans over to ask if I like the show. I do—Faada Freddy and Ndongo, along with their band, are phenomenal performers whom I rarely get to see, as they don't frequent many underground concerts—and I tell him so with a smile.

He looks at me skeptically, eyebrows raised as he asks: *Do you think that this is really hip hop?*

What is *real* hip hop? What is hip hop, really? Underground hip hop that draws on indigenous performance sounds like the internationally circulating recordings I described in Chapter 2—the same ones that early underground rappers so vocally detested. What, if anything, distinguishes them?

At Falsower's house, I take advantage of my visit to record an interview with Don Zap (Fig. 6.2). He tells me about his history with hip hop, listening to US artists like Public Enemy before PBS. He notes that to be "real rappers," they needed to emulate US artists—this is the foundation. "But," he tells me, "after this musical base we have to represent our own sector. We had to put our own touch. And that's what gives us Senegalese rap."

In Rap Galsen, this generic imperative to localization translates to a belief that hip hop realness is musical as well as lyrical. One after another, rappers point out that in the United States, different cities and regions have their own styles. Mostly, they cite G-funk and Dr. Dre, describing them as West Coast adaptations of the original hip hop from the East Coast. Hip hop's spatialized origin myth goes beyond ghetto marginality and socially conscious lyrics to establish the South Bronx as the fount of an unmarked musical style that spreads—to Compton, to Senegal—and is made local, that *must* be made local if it is to remain real hip hop. Localized hip hop becomes, in a way, a redundant term; hip hop is always already localized, not only in its lyrics, but in its very sounds.

FIGURE 6.2 Don Zap at Falsower's house.

If to incorporate indigenous sounds into hip hop—to create something that is identifiably Senegalese—is as much or more a distinctly hip hop practice than it is the localization of a globalized form, then why this question about Daara J, this debate over the "realness" of the music? On the roof in Grand Yoff, Don Zap continued,

> But first you should hear the tempo to know it's rap, but hear little touches that let you know what sector it comes from.
>
> You should have a cultural connotation to show where the music comes from, but we all have the same denominator.

"What are those connotations?" I push, and he obliges with more detail,

> Often, we bring Senegalese and African instruments.
>
> Like with funk; if it's African or Senegalese, there is the tempo that distinguishes it from other genres.
>
> If that disappears, we come back to African music that we already know.
>
> Sometimes it happens that the hip hop disappears.
>
> So you should put that down first and then add color to show where it comes from.
>
> There is African music, but you have to respect the norms to stay part of hip hop.

Here, musical form is revealed to be as important as musical representation. For this is not only about which specific musical elements localize hip hop, but how they do so; not only about what the music evokes for its listeners—cultural rootedness for local audiences, or Africa as a trope of tradition for international ones—but the generic practices through which it becomes hip hop. Hip hop's history of cutting and looping sounds allows for music that is definitively Senegalese and also authentically hip hop in how it is constructed, in its very form.

Yet the indigenous musical elements in hip hop are often re-created in the studio, not digitally sampled. Talking about "Aythia Gnu Dem," Books says, "There are a lot of people who ask if the tama is a sample. It's not a sample. We brought a drummer and he played it. We paid him. And we cut the things we wanted to use and took out what we didn't." I remember Baye Njagne's description of "Joyu Askan Wi," of the korist coming in to play over an already-composed beat. And Kalif of Undershifaay, who said, "You can't just have a drummer come and say, 'Go ahead, play.' Because he's learned a music that is different than ours. So what we do is compose the beat and then call the musician to play accompaniments; this isn't using African rhythms, but it's like a mix." New compositions, these songs exploit hip hop's layered and cyclical form to give the impression of sampling locality and the past.

In January 2017, young rapper Ngaaka Blindé's new song "Tathiouma" was wildly popular among equally young Senegalese audiences. I first heard the song when the video played on television in an apartment where I was hanging out with a group of men, hip hop fans, all at least a decade and a half older than Ngaaka Blindé and his fans. We're riveted on the dark dance cypher, with its flashes of sabar and contemporary dance movements, the *simb* (lion mask), dancing along. Ngaaka Blindé's nasal, drawling lyrics ebb and flow with the triple rise and fall of the percussion-only beat. The hip hop disappears; we come back to an African music that we already know. As the video ends, my companions erupt in appreciation, even as one man hedges—But he's doing mbalax, not hip hop—and agreement echoes around the room.

Toussa told me modestly, in her family home in 2011,

> There's a way of using the drum in the hip hop instrumental that will become an mbalax rhythm, and you shouldn't do that.
>
> I'm not strong in this, but sometimes I hear a song and I hear that it doesn't have a hip hop rhythm.

"At the base it's hip hop," said Lamine Ndao.

> Even if there is traditional music that used other time [signatures], because between hip hop and traditional music the time is different, you have to modify traditional music to make it hip hop, and that takes a certain work and reflection.
>
> Because if it doesn't sound like hip hop, people will hate it.
>
> So it's the way you use the instruments, within a hip hop norm.

These repeated warnings stressed what hip hoppers heard as a fundamental difference between hip hop's simple meter (where the beat is divided in multiples of two) and indigenous music's compound meter (where the beat is divided in multiples of three). This metric binary is itself a bit of a musical invention; although compound meter is not common in US hip hop, 12/8 instrumentals are not unheard of. But, rappers insisted, there are norms to follow. There is a correct, normal time. There is a tempo to respect. And these are different—different from tradition, in its locally limited sonic presence. This is global time that assimilates tradition into itself.

Ngaaka Blindé's song was not mbalax by any stretch of the imagination. But neither, the consensus seemed to say, was it quite hip hop. Rap Galsen's metric binary of musical time means that if something is not hip hop, if it is too indigenized, if non–hip hop time wins out, then it might as well be mbalax. And the problem with mbalax, as we've seen, is its insular locality, expressed not only in its connections to praisesinging and power, but in its very rhythms.

Keyti said,

> I think first, the idea of mbalax is talking directly to Senegalese people because the rhythm is local, not international, so people recognize themselves more in that rhythm.
>
> Let's not forget that hip hop still functions under the European or western pattern of rhythm, while mbalax is 100 percent Senegalese in terms of BPM or bars—the way of counting the bars is different.

Over and over, rappers linked mbalax's local dominance to its global anonymity and attributed both to its rhythms, incomprehensible to a western ear. They noted that, even within Africa, mbalax has not had the same international success as musics like contemporary Nigerian pop (Afrobeats). Alou, of KTD Crew, said,

> Mbalax remains popular because it is the identity of Senegalese people. But we haven't succeeded in exporting it. You only hear mbalax in Senegal. Even if you hear people talk about Youssou N'Dour, who has traveled a lot, and who is known through the whole world, when he goes to Europe or to the United States it's another music that he does, he does acoustic music or something else different. Because mbalax is hard to listen to.

I remember trying desperately to find the downbeat in my sabar drumming class in Los Angeles in 2008. I recall several occasions where I've asked students in a US music department to move with me in time to an mbalax song, only to watch them shift from side to side in unintentional polymeter. And I remember bouncing with Lamine Ndao to the right and to the left, outside a small hip hop show in Dakar in 2011, embodying a shared musical time that unites hip hop around the world.

And this is why it matters that Rap Galsen is localized through specifically hip hop practices. Hip hop time is a sonic expression of the gendered binaries through which Rap Galsen defines itself (see Chapter 5). It is modern, not traditional;

globally resonant, not locally limited; serious, not easy; voiced, not silent. But hip hop time also dissolves these same binaries. Musical layering and hip hop meter assimilate indigenous music into hip hop form—render it *as*, rather than *in*, hip hop—to produce music that is differently, globally local. Tradition is then refigured in and through hip hop time—the time that distances indigenous music from hip hop, the time that distinguishes the local from the global, the time that brings them all back together.

GLOBAL FLOWS

> The beat is only one half of a rap song's rhythm. The other is the flow. When a rapper jumps on a beat, he adds his own rhythm. Sometimes you stay in the pocket of the beat and just let the rhymes land on the square so that the beat and flow become one. But sometimes the flow chops up the beat, breaks the beat into smaller units, forces in multiple syllables and repeated sounds and internal rhymes, or hangs a drunken leg over the last *bap* and keeps going, sneaks out of that bitch.
>
> JAY Z (2011, 12)

On a lazy day in 2012, with no concerts to attend and no interviews scheduled, I take advantage of the fact that the power is on and treat myself to an afternoon of music videos and local TV in my apartment in Dakar. The new hybrid advertisement/music video for the hip hop website Boyjump.sn comes on, and I watch, intrigued, as an image of a djembe with a set of turntables posed on top gives way to clever representations of the website's features—music videos, news, etc. My head tips to the side as, over an unusual 12/8 beat, I see and hear an impressive collection of rappers, from the earliest generations to the newest, including Maas, Xuman, Maxy Krazy, Big D, Books, Nix, ResKp, Simon, FuknKuk, and Big Fa. Sharp snare hits on the 2 and 4 wrest the beat into what is almost hip hop time, but the hand drums' triple feel dominates. I'm glad that no one is there to see the broad grin that spreads across my face, as the rappers' by-now-familiar flows either fall into a predictable lilt—doubling the hand drums' compound rhythms instead of dialoguing with them, veering dangerously close to the speech patterns of women's taasu—or haltingly stumble and slide across the beat.

"I think that the similarity between American rap and Senegalese rap is rap," said Drygun, seated across from me in Galsen Shop, an array of local streetwear behind him.

Because you can't rap over anything other than 4/4.

When you rap, it is over an instrumental, you can do it over whatever you like but you are always going to count 1-2-3-4, 1-2-3-4.

It's always over the measure . . .

Rap, or more generally, hip hop, is universal.

Even Japanese people who do hip hop will always rap over 1-2-3-4.

So, this is a measure.

Rap is 8 bars, 16 bars, 32 bars—whatever you want but always over the measure . . .

So the only difference is the language, other than that rap is universal and you will always rap over a time that is square [*carré*].

Rap is square.

Watching the BoyJump video, I heard and felt this conflict between hip hop and indigenous musical time. The instrumental, even with its added snare hits, was not "square" enough to accommodate a normal hip hop *flow*; that is, the rhythmic patterns and cadences of a rapper's lines, the intricate interweave of lyrical delivery and musical track. Because musical time structures instrumental and verbal performance, which are intimately connected in indigenous genres and in hip hop, the realness of hip hop instrumentals is a crucial prerequisite for the realness of hip hop verbal performance as an aesthetic (as much as representational) practice.[5] And here origin narratives, or contestations of them, once again resurface. Lamine Ndao told me,

The old school will say that hip hop is like taasu.

But how?

No!

This can't be.

I need to say that it can't be.

If you take someone who does taasu and you give him a hip hop beat, he's going to pass to the side . . .

If you listen to taasu you're going to say, "that's taasu that people talk about as being like hip hop?"

They aren't the same.

With taasu, people just talk and talk, maybe without stopping.

With hip hop there are norms, there is a refrain that comes, when the music changes your flow should change, you are going to use certain techniques just to try to have the same feeling as the beat.

I don't know what to say about taasu.

We have already heard that taasu is not like hip hop; male rappers said hip hop was socially conscious, while taasu was easy. Hip hop voiced the street and called for social change, while taasu belonged to a complex of indigenous verbal performance practices that propped up power in the postcolony (see Chapter 4). We remember they said taasu—a women's performance genre that negotiates gendered personhood in the context of accelerated social change—was easy, sexualized, feminine, just like mbalax (see Chapter 5). We hear these binaries (re)sound again in narratives of musical time, as taasu—verbal flow in indigenous time—brings us back, once again, to mbalax. "Taasu isn't rap," said Thiat of Keur Gui, on the balcony of his apartment in Parcelles Assainies. "It's a flow, when you hear that flow you think immediately of mbalax. Rap isn't mbalax. It's a different time than mbalax. Mbalax is cacophony, it's a not a correct, normal time."

Repeating, echoing narratives of flow recall origin myths and reinscribe the gendered inventions of musical time through which hip hop works to sound youth experience in Dakar. But these narratives also mark hip hop time and form as infinitely more universal than the experiences of marginalization they so often mediate; as we have seen, hip hop myths of the ghetto actually inscribe temporal and spatial distance between contemporary African American and Senegalese experience (Chapter 4). As Kalif said,

> When I listen to Lil Wayne, he recounts his life, even though here we have a different reality.
>
> But it's a little similar, what is similar is what is universal, in hip hop music in general, which is to say the rhythm, the technique, the flow; that is universal.
>
> You can go to Japan and they will use the same techniques and rhythms.
>
> In school, you learn poetry and rhythms.
>
> There are flows you find in France, Africa, and the United States.
>
> There are words that are universally hip hop.

By now, we have encountered these words that are universally hip hop in Rap Galsen, from central hip hop tropes—of the underground, the ghetto, and the street—to the African American Vernacular English that inflects rappers' lyrics and conversational English. But Kalif's gesture to hip hop's global flows is effective precisely because it relies on the linguistic dissonance implied in his list of sites: Japan, France, Africa, the United States. In hip hop flow's rendering of referential lyrical content into musical time, how does language function?

In June 2011, I sit with a group of men around a table on the veranda of a guest house outside Banjul, the capital of The Gambia. Yesterday, I met Books, Lamine

FIGURE 6.3 Arriving in The Gambia with (l–r) Lamine Ndao, Profete, Madou, ResKp, Books, and Musa Gambien.

Ndao, Madou, and our friend Musa Gambien (nicknamed for his country of origin) in Medina, at the first call to prayer in the dark morning hours; after stopping on the side of the highway in our chartered "sept-place" station wagon to pick up ResKp and his young protégée, Profete, we had traveled for hours, all of us exhausted from a concert the previous night that had ended only shortly before our dawn departure, none of us able to sleep for the jolting of potholes and the swerving of the car as the driver tried, unsuccessfully, to avoid them. We exchanged the station wagon for a crowded bus at the Gambian border, heading to the ferry that would take us across the river to the capital city. As we walked from the waiting area to the boat, Books chided me for being a bad photographer and not always having my camera out. I'm not a photographer at all—I protested. The ferry was hot; the midday sun burned. Leaning into the shade of the middle cabin of the boat, I asked Lamine in French how to say "stare" in Wolof, and he looked around us at the curious Gambian passengers and laughed (Fig. 6.3).

Around the table at the guest house, the young men are poking fun at various absent Senegalese rappers, imitating signature onstage movements and parodying particular refrains (Fig. 6.4). The conversation turns to rapping in English, and I join in, exaggerating my stilted lyrics—Oh my baby, I think you so sexy, I want you be my baby, mmm baby. Merci! exclaims Lamine, as the other men cackle.

Only a few weeks later, a Sunday lunch in Medina morphs into a trip to the studio with Simon, Books, and brothers Djiby and Bakhaw of Da Brains. As Bakhaw lays down his verse, Books, Djiby, and Simon abandon their work on their own lyrics

FIGURE 6.4 Watching old performances at the guesthouse in The Gambia.

to intervene in the rhythm of his lines. Finally, Simon fixes a grammatical error and admonishes Bakhaw to rap with clear diction, but the same heat. After a brief relapse into their argument about the use of expletives in the song, Djiby records again. For nearly ten minutes, the four of them tweak the end of his last line, going back and forth between "go to your school" and "go to school"—the difference, in Wolof as in English, a single syllable.

For decades, international rappers, generally from class backgrounds that ensured their fluency in French, have harnessed western languages to make their music more marketable and their messages more widely heard. In contrast, Wolof lyrics represent a deliberate inward turn, an attempt to address social ills in a language that those victimized by them understand, a subversion of local communicative norms, an expression of urban identity as it intersects with colonial history (and this is true, we should note, for international rappers as well, who record songs in Wolof when they want to address local audiences). Yet many underground rappers struggle to get by; as they age, they face growing pressure to contribute to their parents' households, and to marry and support their own families. Wolof-language hip hop's locally sounding voice, with its minimal material benefits, does little to alleviate these pressures. So, Djily Bagdad told me, he was starting to work on some tracks in English. People had suggested that maybe others going abroad would bring that music with them. The local market was not good; concert tickets and albums didn't sell. The only money to be had was elsewhere.

Yet even as the linguistic competence required for a skillful flow might seem to limit many artists to indigenous languages and thus local audiences, Dakar's underground rappers positioned the aesthetics of flow as equal to, if not more significant than, lyrical content when it came to international reach. They reminded me that it was thanks to the flow of early US artists that Senegalese youth without a mastery of the English language first appreciated hip hop. Although by the time Almamy and I discussed this in 2011, he boasted an admirable level of English for someone who had never been outside Senegal, this wasn't always the case. He recalled the gravitational pull of hip hop flows, in the early days of Rap Galsen,

> When we didn't understand English, you'd listen to a Redman rapping or Keith Murray, Eric Sermon, you didn't know what they said but their way of rapping, their flow, it was extraordinary, so that you wanted to listen without understanding what they were saying, like it was a well-drawn picture, their way of rapping, their beats, and that let you be able to listen and know who was really good even without knowing what he was saying.

It stands to reason that if Senegalese youth could appreciate US hip hop based on nothing but its beats and flows, and also make value judgments about it, that the opposite should be true for international hip hop audiences and Wolof-language rap. As Almamy continued,

> Now, you make a song, and either it's the flow that interests people, or you make a song and people understand what you say, and they say that you are really good, and you say things that can help people to surmount their obstacles. If you do a song in French, that can let people who understand French know you are capable, if you do it in English it will make people who understand English understand what you are capable of doing. But if you rap in Wolof they won't understand—then it will be the music and the flow that grab them.

Mame Xa told me in one of our barbershop conversations, "Maybe if you are rapping in English the advantage is that you can go to another country outside Senegal. But . . . it's not just the text that's important but the flow. Or maybe the instruments or something else inside the song. It's not obligatory that you rap in English for your rap to get out. And it's not obligatory that you rap in Wolof for people here to like it, either."

By the time I interviewed Bakhaw and Djiby, we'd met countless times at concerts and in studio sessions. I took a taxi to the landmark they'd given, then asked a woman selling vegetables by the side of the road if she knew where their house was. She directed me down an alleyway and to a doorway, across from where that young man was sitting. Upon reaching him, I repeated my question; he gestured toward a house, its door ajar, and I entered, announcing myself—Assalaamaalekum. We set up in the living room and worked our way through my usual questions, finally getting to language (Fig. 6.5). Bakhaw said,

> Our philosophy is to always rap in Wolof. It's true sometimes we do things in English, but we want to sell our Wolof music internationally. You can rap in English like Lil Wayne but you will never shock the American public . . . Music will never change, and I can achieve that level in no matter what language. Now, when you go to Europe they play Ivorian music and everyone gets it. You can rap in French, but you can't go to France and impress people there.

Djiby picked up where his brother had left off. "We love what Jay Z does even though we don't all understand what he says, we love his style. The Senegalese love people without understanding their languages. Why not love rap in Wolof? The Senegalese who can love a song in English can love a song in Wolof. That's it. We are proud."

Wolof lyrics signal hip hop realness, rejecting colonial language in favor of local impact while simultaneously privileging a hip hop aesthetics of rhythmic interplay—that is, flow—that decenters lyrical meaning. Hip hop voice, then, is defined (and is revealed as gendered) through how it speaks—in hip hop time—as much as what it says. Flow—orality rendered in hip hop time— works with hip hop beats to produce a global musical intelligibility, even if the use of Wolof means

FIGURE 6.5 Djiby (left) and Bakhaw (right), Da Brains.

that much of Rap Galsen's representational lyrical content is *un*intelligible out-side of Senegal. The choice between Wolof and French or English is thus based on myriad factors, including audience, class background, and the complicated dynamic between hip hop realness, pride in and responsibility to local origins and communities, and the desire for financial stability that international market success symbolizes. Whether rappers are minimizing global linguistic coherence in favor of aesthetic appeal or eschewing local topical relevance in favor of global languages, language and flow, like hip hop instrumentals, complicate the idea of hip hop voice as political resistance and tie it firmly to questions of markets and consumption.

REIMAGINING COMMERCIAL HIP HOP

> When the processes of imagining the global and fashioning sounds that might enable access to its stages are situated within the context of local struggles, processes of mediation and commodification become analytically inseparable from conceptions of culture and musical experience.
>
> LOUISE MEINTJES (2003, 220)

At the Liberté V bus terminus, the Orange S'Cool Tour concert is in full swing. As Nix leaves the stage, Bideew bou Bess appears to loud applause. The three brothers' rapped verses alternate with soaring falsetto singing grounded in the familiar triple feel of Fula flutes and gently rocking rhythms. In the tent backstage, I'm surprised to see hardcore rappers standing up to clap along, hands high in the air, marking the second and third pulse of every triple division.

Bideew bou Bess gives way to Cannabis, one of Senegal's most popular mainstream hip hop artists in 2011, whose music sounds like the then-current tracks coming out of the United States. Njaaya follows, and I wonder again why the singer's world-infused neosoul is billed on hip hop shows, until I imagine her on a mbalax stage, her black cape and closely shorn hair clashing with the sparkling gowns and flowing wigs of the other singers, her stationary body and explosive vocals strange against their coquettish dances and soft melodies. Da Brains perform their hits, a series of lighthearted, danceable songs, and again I'm surprised to see underground rappers backstage singing along and dancing in place. Things swing back to the hardcore—Alienzik, then Tigrim Bi—and I'm asked to film again as Simon returns to the stage. Gaston ends the concert.

"Because if it doesn't sound like hip hop, people will hate it," said Lamine Ndao, a sentiment that underground rappers repeated again and again. And yet here they are, hands in the air, enthusiastically participating in what I thought was the "commercial" hip hop that they had described as fundamentally at odds with a hardcore ethos.

Inventions of African tradition, invocations of a global hip hop time that structures instrumental beats and verbal flows: the very processes through which Rap Galsen speaks from, to, and of its origins undermine mythical hip hop binaries of authenticity and commercialism and complicate understandings of voice. When I interview Rap'Adio's Keyti in late 2011, he tells me,

> I'm not mad at mbalax—we got to entertain people, we are supposed to be entertainers. But rappers tend to forget that, I should also entertain people.
>
> You would see people like Talib Kweli, Mos Def, Common, even people like Dead Prez, who are revolutionaries, and those are the rappers who are called conscious rappers, but they know they are still entertainers.
>
> When you are making music, you should entertain people.
>
> When you go on stage, you should entertain people.
>
> You just cannot go on stage and try to bring the revolution on stage, because the revolution is not going on stage, it's in the streets.

He talks about how hip hop "opened doors to a new speech, a new way of thinking, a new way of talking, a new way of analyzing what was going on here." He cites the 2000 elections as a turning point, when rappers had effected a major political shift and were left searching for the next thing to do, and how this logically led to a new commercialization. But, he cautions, "there is no one in Senegal who can escape what is going on in this country, because at one point or another what is going on in this country has a huge impact on your life."

"Look at Daara J," he says. "They found [that balance]. They talk about serious things, but they entertain people."

In their struggle to be heard, hip hoppers inevitably shift their positions on commercialism, sometimes within a single conversation. Telling the history of Rap Galsen, underground rappers described commercial music in one way, pitting the melodic sounds of early international rappers against the hardcore sounds and lyrics of groups like Rap'Adio, Waa BMG 44, and Yatfu (remember that this early hardcore hip hop sounded American and rejected singing). Telling the story of US hip hop, rappers juxtaposed the lyrics and sounds of the originating, conscious East Coast with the trivial lyrics and musical aesthetics of the Dirty South; in fact, well into the second decade of the twenty-first century, underground hip hoppers were using "classic" instrumental tracks that sounded like they were lifted from late 1990s East Coast hip hop.

Commercial beats, said Djily Bagdad, are for people who want to rap about money, women, clubs, parties; people talking about social issues use "classic type beats." But then he catches himself, backpedals. "But the beat doesn't matter a lot, it's a matter of lyrics. When you talk about problems with public transportation, people will say you're defending the people, and that's underground." By 2011, understandings of commercial music had changed. The idea of social consciousness became attached to texts more than anything else, while people opened up to the idea that the music of hip hop—its beats and flows—not only could but should attract an audience. Underground music increasingly reflects current trends in US hip hop and/or includes indigenous instruments, without completely abandoning a taste for its classic beats. "There is no commercial music," said Lamine Ndao.[6]

Of course, there have always been artists—Cannabis, and more recently Akhlou Brick and others—whose Wolof-language music imitates the most current trends in US hip hop and enjoys mainstream success with young Senegalese audiences.[7] And for years, the artists who are widely regarded as foundational groups in Senegalese hip hop and whose careers have successfully straddled Senegal, Europe, and the United States have won over local audiences with traditional instruments, even as they seduce a western audience much more interested in something identifiably "African" than in an offshore version of US hip hop.[8] In his room, the picture of his uncle, Rap'Adio's Iba looking over us, Almamy said,

Daara J plays with live traditional instruments.

Awadi has done it—he brings djembe, you know, this doesn't exist in American rap, it's another music outside of hip hop that comes from Africa.

And many African groups that travel internationally do it.

They don't go on stage with guitar, a drum set, but rather, instead of using a guitar they'll use kora, the xalam, instruments that if you hear them, you might say it's the guitar that's playing, while in fact they are African instruments that can make really great songs, like with djembe or sabar, flute, balafon, they use that.

So it's a question of audience . . .

You shouldn't limit yourself to Senegal.

You should seek an international market.

If you bring beats to Europe or the United States that sample Norah Jones, that isn't going to interest people.

They see this every day.

But if you bring a song with kora, they aren't familiar with that, with balafon—they want to discover what's going on, if you bring this kind of song they'll try to discover what it's about.

African tradition, invented in dialogue with world music markets and transatlantic Afrocentric projects, becomes once again the pivot point for rappers who hope to reach local audiences while possibly tapping into the economic potential of international ones. As Djily Bagdad told me, "I have ideas, for future projects with more traditional stuff. Because sometimes internationally they say you are doing the same stuff as America and France. You have to do your own thing! I think we're going to explore that in our next album, one or two tracks to see how people will appreciate it." To incorporate locally and globally recognizable markers of place and difference aurally marks Rap Galsen's Africanity and lays claim to rootedness and historicity. It negotiates between a market-driven need to mark Otherness and earlier rejections of traditional music as a limiting social practice.

It would be misleading, however, to suggest that underground rappers ever unilaterally rejected traditional music, the international hip hop that they sometimes dismiss as inauthentic, or even, dare I say it, mbalax. Rather, they distinguish real hip hop from these other musics because aesthetics and musical practices mean in specific ways that are enmeshed in, and sometimes constitutive of, local and global histories. Practices of hip hop genre allow the underground to claim indigenous and US musical idioms in ways that are potentially economically fruitful without betraying what it means to *be* hip hop.

If hip hop genre allows for the pulling apart of traditional music and speech, it also allows for the pulling apart of lyrical and musical understandings of hip hop authenticity, as rappers renegotiate the opposition between commercial and underground music that guided their engagements with hip hop over decades. This, in turn, creates a new possibility for them to be heard; that is, to have a voice whose agency is tied not only to political and social intervention, but also to hip hop's potential for financial gain in the face of the materiality of everyday struggle.

DIASPORA AS PALIMPSEST MEMORY

And so, as hip hop moved further into the mainstream in the twenty-first century, its aesthetics changed as well. Where earlier international rappers had framed musical localization as an expression of African identity and collective memory, however, the underground portrayed it as an expression of *hip hop* authenticity and memory. In a conscious practice of musical genre, they mobilized hip hop musical norms to incorporate tradition into their musical repertoire not only through but *as* hip hop; but then, when we remember how Awadi described sampling, or how Xuman talked about flow (Chapter 3), we begin to suspect that these narratives may not be so different after all. In both instances, hip hop's global musicality brings tradition into the present in ways that speak to local experience, seek international audiences, and crucially, differ from mbalax's modern tradition. Stories emerge, converge, and diverge again in the cycling of hip hop time, which layers sounds and narratives, but also loops and repeats them.

To produce hip hop, then, is not only to create instrumental beats and verbally music over them; it is also to discursively produce hip hop as a genre, and, in doing so, to produce voice and/as social audibility. As they sample tradition within a global musical idiom, hip hoppers produce musical narratives of the complex interplay of power, performance, and social change that shapes their everyday lives. These musical processes of articulation, layered with the discursive and practical engagements of myth described throughout this book, position hip hoppers within diaspora as a globally articulating locality that comments on postcoloniality from a critical distance.

In hip hop time, history and myth congeal into aural palimpsest memories of diaspora, and origin stories speak to present circulations as much as past ones. To describe these hip hop processes and products as palimpsests is to invoke the dynamic between musical form and memory. Construing the musical form that emerged from deejaying and sampling as a practice of memory may seem questionable when we consider that producers often do not intend for musical samples to communicate representational meaning. Whether intentional or not, however, hip hop practices of layering form a palimpsest of sound—one that is heard and understood differently by the people who produce it and its diversely positioned listeners. Even as many artists reject an aesthetic genealogy between African music and hip hop, others hear in a hip hop track the repetition, groove, and signifying that reproduce a history of diasporic experience and embodied memories of Africa on the other side of the Atlantic.

Likewise, while this book has primarily addressed conscious processes of collective remembering and myth, the possibility of palimpsest to envelop conscious and unconscious remembering at the same time (Shaw 2002), allows for a more nuanced reading of the divergent constructions of diaspora that are at stake in interpretations of hip hop musicality. If, in the early efforts of international rappers, hip hop's aural palimpsest memory reimagined indigenous performance by tracing it through the transatlantic slave trade and the historical development of African American music, for the underground, hip hop palimpsest layers the global postcoloniality of the US inner city and the African metropole to produce a diaspora that is contemporary and experiential. To consider hip hop and memory as palimpsest allows for both of these versions of diaspora to coexist—and to for them to simultaneously challenge and reinscribe marginalization—because palimpsest memories are conscious and unconscious, overlapping and distinct, constituted not only in performance and discourse, but in listening and interpretation, inclusive of what is said and what remains unsaid. To listen to hip hop as an aural palimpsest memory gives us a way past binaries of truth and fiction, myth and history, to hear how they coexist with and coconstitute each other.

People talk about Senegalese hip hop like it began to talk about
politics in 2011, even though it spoke of this since the beginning.
This is a little reductive, you see; when I hear journalists who write
analyses saying that rap today is interested in politics, that's nonsense.
Those people know absolutely nothing.
Since I was a kid, Senegalese rap has only talked about politics, good
governance, corruption, social justice, racism, women's problems,
prostitution, drug addiction, et cetera.
It is very social and political at the same time.

AMADOU FALL BA

REMIX

Consuming Resistance

ON A SUNDAY in 2015, I crouch with my camera in the inner circle of a hip hop cypher in Medina. Along the perimeter, countless boys and young men press against metal barriers that give way on one side to a massive soundboard. In the center of the cypher, rapper Mollah Morgun, formerly of Keur Gui and one of the guest judges today, paces with a microphone as he speaks to those gathered before the first battle begins (Figs. 7.1 and 7.2).

"Real hip hop was born here," he proclaims, gesturing to the buildings around us. "Medina, Fass, Grand Dakar." Without warning, he bursts into the Rap'Adio refrain,

Ñoo ngiy ñëw di get down, Ñoo ngiy ñëw di get down, Xabaaru 1-2 Ground

"*Yes yes y'all*"; without missing a beat, the crowd throws back the classic lyrics. Surprised, I look around again and confirm that not even half of them could have been born when the song came out in 1998. Morgun continues the refrain, calling out neighborhoods as the youth reply,

Medina—*Big Town*
Medina—*Big Town*
Fass—*Big Town*

FIGURE 7.1 Almamy's Sunday Cipher underway in Medina, 2015.

FIGURE 7.2 Mollah Morgun addresses the crowd at the Sunday Cipher.

As quickly as he'd started rapping, he stops and returns to his speech.

A year earlier, Almamy had told me about his newest project. He said they'd been doing weekly ciphers in different neighborhoods, bringing young, unknown talent together to battle, inviting big rappers to battle the up-and-coming winners from their own 'hoods. I told him it sounds great, that I'd love to come check it out. Yeah—he replied—There was another white girl like you who was coming, but all her questions were about Y'en a Marre. He paused, widened his eyes in emphasis, and leaned closer as he said—I just wanted to tell her, there is no Y'en a Marre here. There's just hip hop.

I left Dakar in 2012 in the middle of a contentious presidential election and large-scale youth mobilizations. The Rap Galsen that I encountered when I returned in the years since is one that, for better or worse, had changed immensely and continually. Nothing was ever again quite as it had been, or as it had seemed; some rappers have stepped away, others have dug in their heels and tried to reclaim a place in the post-2012 scene, and still others, new to hip hop, bring novel stylistic and ideological challenges to the established myths. Coming back to this same block in Medina was, in a way, deeply disorienting; here I was, at a site of mythical beginnings—of the hip hop underground, of this book—that was at once familiar and utterly transformed.[1]

Hip hop myths of resistance metasticized in Y'en a Marre; in the movement's wake, internationally cycling narratives rewrote Rap Galsen as a practice of activism and extramusical mobilization, until "resistance," narrowly defined, threatened to overdetermine what it meant to be a hip hopper at all. Take Almamy, for example: although originally an active member of Y'en a Marre, in his post-2012 efforts to advance hip hop in local neighborhoods, he came up against the hip hop scene's seeming inability to disentangle itself from the overwhelming emphasis on concrete political action that marked the preelection period. The other white girl that Almamy described could be any one of the innumerable investigators—students, PhDs, journalists—who flocked to Dakar in search of Y'en a Marre, eager to document mythical hip hop resistance in the flesh. As Almamy's wording uncomfortably reminded me, she was an interchangeable link in an endless cycle of researchers unified not only in our geopolitical and often racial privilege, but also in our predictable patterns of focused data retrieval and disappearance that predated Y'en a Marre.

"This is the most important point I want to talk about," said N-Jah in English.

Most of the time, when they come in Africa they think they can find easy things.

They think that the artists need images to go over there.

It's not our case.

They must respect the talent from Africa . . .

If you need to interview, you should pay a little something to encourage the artist.

Most of the time they come and do interviews and leave.

And I will never do an interview for a journalist if they don't pay me.

Most of the time, my English interests many journalists from the States.

I did many, many interviews and even a film for a label, I don't want to mention the name, they took the whole day, I went to the cemetery and prayed for my mom, I went to the mosque, I went to play basketball –

that's with someone who is a star in Senegal.

If you want to deal with this kind of artist you need to pay.

That's not right.

I was chastened. I had not paid N-Jah for the interview. He said it was okay, that he knew I was helping up-and-coming rappers with photos and music videos. He got me to fill his moped's tank with gas on the way home.

Books, too, described having worked extensively with foreigners on their projects, and then said,

I want to say, everyone should do what they want, but they should respect what they've told people they're going to do.

Because it's been a while since I've done interviews, because there were too many people who came, worked, and when they were done they were done.

There were a lot of projects they said they would do that they never did.

There are people who haven't done anything up until now.

I hope you'll do what you're supposed to.

It's taken me far longer to do what I was supposed to do than I ever imagined it would. As I worked on this manuscript over the last several years, watching Rap Galsen change and my interpretations increasingly reflect a particular moment that now seemed to be in the past, I grew uneasy about the temporal limitations of my fieldwork. Yet, *Yagg Bawoul Dara*, the Wolof saying goes. In 2011, 5kiem Underground's album by that title—their first in a career that began in the mid-1990s—had been out two years. I recognized the phrase as a proverb and asked Djily Bagdad about it. He told me, "It's like, whatever you're doing, even if it's hard in the beginning, keep doing it and you'll achieve it. It's kind of like 'never say never'." When I bring up the book to friends in Dakar, when I comment on how long it's been, I'm told that this is why it will matter, the space, the time, that the things I'm writing about are history now. And yet I, more than anyone, know that this is a partial and fragmented history that perhaps will not stand up under that weight. And that new stories are already being told.

I began this book by suggesting that the stories people tell about hip hop matter, and I've used its chapters to detail how some of these stories have worked over the past several decades in Dakar: to negotiate postcoloniality, reimagine urban space and global emplacement as experiences of diaspora, and make claims to voice in ways that challenge (but also sometimes reinforce) age, political, and gender hierarchies. I have traced these through stylistic shifts—from the Africanized works of foundational groups like Positive Black Soul (PBS), to the hardcore aesthetics of groups like Rap'Adio, to the middle ground of contemporary underground hip hop, which has opened itself to musical signs of Africa and to current US styles. I have linked these stylistic trends to questions of consumption, showing how Rap Galsen's positive early reception in western and local forums shifted when hardcore rappers from the banlieues and quartiers populaires adopted a performance style and posturing that alienated local audiences while failing to interest international ones; underground hip hop's political involvement, however, eventually led to increased local acceptance and global visibility. I have approached these questions through the lens of genre, noting how hip hoppers have deconstructed and reconstructed indigenous performance and hip hop in ways that sometimes challenge and sometimes reinscribe two fundamental and intertwined hip hop myths: one of urban marginality and Blackness, one of indigenous performance, both implicitly and often explicitly tied to assumptions about voice and resistance. I have shown how these myths give meaning to and are made meaningful through the aural palimpsest of hip hop time.

As I bring this particular retelling of Rap Galsen to a close, I resample the book's central questions about memory, genre, and musical meaning to reflect briefly on the sometimes troubling confluence of scholarly and state interest in Senegalese hip hop. Both, I suggest, center on constructions of hip hop genre that fixate on lyrical and extramusical social consciousness. As this book has shown, however, hip hop in Senegal is and has always been understood as a musical practice, among a complex of musical practices that comprise the traditional, indigenous, popular, cosmopolitan, rural, local, global, and diasporic. If narratives are structures of power that are "constitutive as well as interpretive" (Bruner 1997, 269), then what is constituted, and what erased, as these narratives circulate between Senegal and the west?

In 2011, it seemed fitting that my final interview was with Keyti of Rap'Adio; my fieldwork came to a temporary end in an encounter with someone I associated with Rap Galsen's very beginnings. As he spoke at length about traditional music's inability to effect social change, Keyti landed on taasu, saying. "You've got a lot of this taasu for example, which people are saying rap comes from taasu blah blah blah." With the door opened, I cautiously asked what he makes of this connection that people draw between taasu and hip hop. He answered,

My idea is, you know, scholars, I think they need an explanation to everything.

OK, the people who created hip hop, I mean, yeah they got African origins, but if you see the way it was created, most of the things happened by chance.

You know.

So I cannot really be into the idea that yeah, it came from Africa.

So scholars try to find reasons behind this movement.

But I think sometimes art can also come out of nowhere because it's art.

It doesn't need to be explained.

Now, hip hop in general, the idea that is behind hip hop, they could find reasons for that because it's related for some social, political reasons. But the art form itself—

He sighed loudly.

—I don't know.

It's just art.

I think that might be a little difficult, trying to find links between this and that.

And I think even for hip hop, the elements of hip hop, most of them were created or started without any relation to the others.

It's just at one point in history one person with his movement got them together and said, "this is hip hop."

But they were not really related.

What of hip hop's African origins? What of its rise as a complex of cultural practices in the South Bronx? Origin myths, coconstructed in a feedback loop between scholars, journalists, and artists throughout the African diaspora, sustain and perpetuate themselves. But people also refuse them. The day we sat outside his house in the middle of Ramadan in 2011, Djily Bagdad said,

When you're overseas and you hear of Senegal, you hear it's a huge hip hop culture.

But . . . when you get here you don't find what you expected.

And most the time they're not looking for real hip hop, they're looking for some traditional thing, not real hip hop.

Packing up when the interview is finished, I confess to Djily that I, too had been looking for those traditional things when I got here. It's what I had known to expect.

If, when I first arrived in 2007, the story I sought was one of griots, by 2011, that story had become a partially effaced layer in a narrative of hip hop resistance fixated on what seemed, to me and many others, like a moment of social rupture ("That's nonsense," chides Amadou Fall Ba.) It was purely by coincidence that my time researching Rap Galsen coincided with the birth, maturation, and, some might say, afterlife of Y'en a Marre. Although rappers conceived of and implemented the movement, and a theme song was recorded at one point, Y'en a Marre was fundamentally a political movement. It drew heavily on preexisting hip hop–based social networks comprising several generations of young people connected through aesthetic and cultural practices that had, in the past, proven to be culturally efficacious tools of social commentary.[2] After Abdoulaye Wade lost the 2012 election, Y'en a Marre members turned to social action, like hands-on work in flooded neighborhoods, carefully organized, documented, and publicized. For years, and up to the time of this publication, central members of Y'en a Marre have continued to travel outside of Senegal, billed in universities and other forums as the foremost Senegalese rappers and the face of global hip hop activism.

On the ground, however, it was a different story. The lead-up to the 2012 elections was marked by violent clashes between rappers. Some of Y'en a Marre's adherents took issue with artists who asserted—as Senegalese rappers had for over a decade, including during their previous involvement in electoral politics—that their music itself was their weapon.

After Gotal performed at the hip hop soirée at Cafeteria in September 2011, I was grateful to finally head home shortly before dawn. In the taxi, I received a text message from rapper Don Zap, anxious to confirm that I had already left the event. He told me that a fight had broken out between a group of young rappers affiliated with Y'en a Marre and an individual who had criticized the movement. The dissenter was badly beaten, and a police report was filed.

When I returned to Dakar to do my final follow-up work in 2015, I was dismayed, but not surprised, to find how fraught the topic of Y'en a Marre had become.

I abandoned my plan to conduct recorded interviews. I listened and watched. I excised the specific stories of violence that I had planned to include in this book, realizing that to retell even such public events would shame their victims, whom the larger hip hop community had failed to support. I watched online as rappers abroad—Mollah Morgun (formerly of Keur Gui) in Europe, Makhtar le Kagoulard (formerly of Waa BMG 44 and then Rap'Adio) in the United States—lashed out at Y'en a Marre with accusations of corruption and hypocrisy. I observed as Senegalese friends scoffed at images of Y'en a Marre on the television, chortling—Serves them right! What are they doing meddling in another country?—when some of the movement's still active members were arrested in the Democratic Republic of Congo.[3] I heard senior rappers tell me how, tired of the drama and stress, they had washed their hands of hip hop, instead focusing their efforts on clothing lines. On studying the Qu'ran. On reggae. On getting married and starting a family.

In 2015, I walked with Lamine Ndao to Djily Bagdad's house, where we found him standing on the sidewalk. We talked about his recent trip to Germany under the mantle of Y'en a Marre. He looked glum as he confided that it was hard—people see you traveling and imagine you're getting paid all this money when most of the time, all that's funded is airfare and housing.

In part, hip hoppers' discontent with Y'en a Marre stemmed from the uneven opportunities for travel that it created, as well as the movement's unidentified financial underwriters, which raised suspicion that it had been coopted by local and foreign powers. But there was something more. The movement, in its heyday, had seemed like a predictable outgrowth of underground hip hop, one that echoed earlier mobilizations and addressed the daily realities of life in Senegal; not a rupture, at least not to people who had been in it for decades, but a continuation. The further Y'en a Marre moved into the international spotlight, however, the more tenuous that genealogy became; and this brings us back to one of this book's central contentions—that musical meaning is as central to Senegalese hip hop as are its myths of resistance. We know, now, that the underground historically defined hip hop realness in terms of both lyrical consciousness and musical practice. But Y'en a Marre brought the underground to the global stage in ways that had nothing to do with their music, except in the very broad sense that their music was identified as hip hop and thus read through global myths of resistance.

Sitting in the courtyard of Books's house in winter 2015, Lamine Ndao said,

Sometimes there is the attention of westerners who don't cease contacting artists, and I wouldn't say as artists or as rappers but as activists and members of Y'en a Marre.

So I tell myself, in place of exporting your music, you export your movement, which is to say, you are an activist and that's what you export.

And sometimes that allows you also to perform.

But it's not your work as an artist that's allowed you to overcome barriers, go to the west, do shows and all; most the time you are there to do conferences, it's not for festivals and all, it's for conferences, exchanges, and for the exposure you get there for your movement.

So it would be good for westerners to come also to see what you are doing for your own career, because an artist should also be able to export his music and his talent . . .

I think it's the most important.

Because activism has its moment, it was a period.

As they say, when it's about an electoral campaign, there is a shelf life for that.

I remember when Keyti told me that you can't take the revolution onstage, that people have to remember that hip hop is music, and music should entertain. I remember that countless rappers hoped aloud for more from me. Maybe you'll bring our music back and someone will hear it. Maybe you'll know someone organizing a festival. Maybe we will come to the United States and see you there. The underground's long-awaited move to international visibility seemed to come at a price, to reduce hip hop to a soundtrack for resistance. Myth cycles back, loops, repeats.

This cycling of mythical resistance raises important questions about mobility and privilege. As Keyti and Djily reminded me, narratives about Senegalese hip hop circulate through global terrains of power, from my own US government funding as a graduate student, to the general mobility throughout the world (including access to Senegalese hip hop spaces) enjoyed by North Americans and Europeans and rarely mirrored in the realities of the Senegalese rappers we write about. Although over the last several decades, it has become increasingly common for Senegalese, particularly men, to go to Europe and North America to work and send remittances to their families, such travel has grown increasingly difficult, first with the devaluation of the West African franc in 1994 and again with the restrictions on travel that were put in place after September 11, 2001. As I write this in 2018, I imagine that the Trump regime's enthusiasm for "Muslim bans" will sooner or later affect West Africa (*ñaanuma ko Yalla*).

As a Fulbright scholar in Senegal in 2011, I was taken under the wing of the State Department at the US embassy. In my cell phone, I kept the direct number for the US Marines stationed in the city, who I was told should be my first call if I encountered problems. Just before my year of fieldwork ended, I received an email from the embassy requesting that I meet with visiting congressional staffers, who were interested in knowing more about "how the Hip Hop scene here may interface/affect radicalism, or terrorism." Dinner at one of Dakar's fanciest hotels was offered to sweeten the deal. As I stared at the screen, I recalled rappers' repeated accusations of *espionage*, a playful dig at the power dynamics just under the surface of my fully financed year in Senegal, my competence in their languages, my less-than-compelling explanations of what would happen to their words and music when I took them and returned to the United States. I politely declined the meeting, citing my impending departure and the last-minute interviews I needed to conduct.

Rap Galsen's increasingly visible political activism has coincided, not incidentally, I suspect, with increased financial investment from states (the United States, Senegal, and various European nations) and foreign nongovernmental organizations (NGOs).[4] In addition to awarding sizeable grants to cultural centers like Africulturban, the US State Department has targeted Senegal for its recent cultural diplomacy programs. In 2012, it was the cultural attaché from the US embassy in Dakar who wrote reference letters for the Africulturban-affiliated artists who applied to the inaugural year of the State Department's One Beat program, which brought young musicians from around the world to the United States for collaboration and exchange.[5] Two years later, Senegal was a site for the first edition of the State Department's Next Level program (in partnership with the University of North Carolina, Chapel Hill, and the US NGO Meridian), which, following a more traditional pattern of cultural diplomacy, sent US artists around the world to bring hip hop to local youth.

The US government's increased interest and investment in Rap Galsen over the past several years barely hides a predictable anxiety about hip hop resistance in the context of a just sub-Saharan country with a 95 percent Muslim population and shared borders with Mauritania and Mali, two countries with recent histories of violent religious fundamentalism. Senegal is not unique in this regard. Just as jazz diplomacy projected a race-positive image of the United States during the Cold War (von Eschen 2004), since 2005, US diplomatic cultural programs have mobilized hip hop as a soft power tool in the context of Muslim populations, hoping to stem the tide of Islamism's reactionary rise against US foreign intervention (Aidi 2011, 26–28).[6] In choosing US artists to send abroad as cultural diplomats—and in choosing local artists to support—these programs privilege "socially conscious" artists, mobilizing global hip hop myth to their own ends while encouraging artists to see themselves as individuals rather than as agents of the state (Salois 2015, 412–413).

I don't mean to suggest, however, that state involvement is inherently antithetical to hip hop, or that caution about state cooption of resistance justifies an anticommercialism ideology of "selling out" that would deny artists in the Global South access to financial security in the name of hip hop authenticity. On the one hand, I find it important to distinguish between foreign interventions in Rap Galsen, with their attendant agendas, and investment on the part of the Senegalese state (without assuming the latter is necessarily any more transparent). To uncritically read state investment as cooption ignores how Senegalese cultural intermediaries strategically collaborate with the state to advance hip hop culture.[7] And while Senegalese rappers have generally resisted being used by political candidates or factions, they have also consistently demanded state support in the form of television and radio circulation, cultural ministries, and arts legislation; these demands are, in and of themselves, part of hip hop claims to citizenship.

On the other hand, both foreign and national investments have led to steadily improving material conditions in certain sectors of Senegalese hip hop. State and NGO subsidies to hip hop cultural centers provide underserved youth in the banlieues with access to technology and training—not only in hip hop performance but also in technical skills like videography. Young women's participation blossoms in these contexts, often through programs created expressly for that purpose with targeted financial incentives from foreign entities for whom gender equality (defined in their own terms) is a pressing social concern. But the benefits of hip hop-focused cultural interventions extend unevenly, if at all, to most of the rappers I've written about in this book, bypassing them to reach "youth" in the first decades of their lives.

"Music Needs No Visa," reads One Beat's homepage in 2018.[8] I think of the young artists who have traveled abroad through State Department programs, and I remember the rappers, older than me, who spoke of their frustration with paying time and time again to apply for a US visa, only to be denied, their money lost. And I wonder if, in bestowing their unequal gifts, these US programs, like the international enthusiasm for Y'en a Marre, don't perform a kind of violence (Ndaliko 2017, 189) on Rap Galsen as they exploit it to further their own agendas.

On a broader level, Rap Galsen's increased access to quality performance spaces and local media exposure since 2011 signals a remainstreaming of hip hop as a result of political and social engagement and the ways in which these are celebrated on the international stage as a testament to Senegal's renowned peaceful democracy.[9] Nevertheless, in the years since 2012, some artists have abandoned hip hop altogether, tired of conflicts over the uneven benefits of the Y'en a Marre movement, suspicious of its concurrence with increased state involvement in hip hop, and skeptical of its impact; some feel that, in focusing on political figureheads, the movement effected highly visible but ultimately superficial change, while leaving intact the systemic injustices that Rap Galsen has historically critiqued. Others remain, retrenching themselves in local hip hop memory, reminding us that real hip hop is not contingent on political agitation, that its roots are in the daily experiences of life in the marginalized neighborhoods of the city, and that its impact is tied to broader social issues alternately addressed through hip hop's lyrical texts and musical form.

Ultimately, the point is not that hip hop cannot be or is not resistant. Rather, to celebrate resistance as overt political activism elides other, subtler (and often contentious) kinds of agential action whose targets overlap with but also supersede the state: poverty, underdevelopment, age hierarchies, perceived global moral threats, and gender roles and identities. Stories about hip hop and hip hop stories speak to how young people negotiate modernity, how they position themselves in a globally interconnected world, how they navigate the splintered social networks of urban life and constitute new ones. Hip hop voices this formative contradiction: that all too often, the large scale, systemic social change of the past century plays out as stasis in the lives of many young people in Dakar. Rap Galsen, as I hope to have shown in this book, is a sounding, musical narrative of, and counternarrative to, social change—one that cannot be reduced to resistance, whether that resistance is expressed through lyrical content or as sonic imposition on public space. For it is not just what hip hop says, or where hip hop sounds; it is about how it means: musically, through time.

Notes

1. Many attribute the term *Rap Galsen,* in which *Sene-gal* becomes *Gal-sen,* to *verlan.* A form of slang used by French hip hoppers with roots in North and sub-Saharan Africa, verlan functions through inverting the first and last syllables of words. The word verlan itself is a phonetic inversion of the French *l'envers,* translated roughly as "wrong way," "in reverse," "topsy turvy," etc. Yet Wolof, too, has words that are correct regardless of the arrangement of the syllables; for example, the word *also* can be said *tamit* or *itam.*

2. Likewise, drawing on W. E. B. Du Bois, J. Griffith Rollefson (2017) describes double consciousness as the US form of postcoloniality that resonates with postcolonial subjects in Europe (and around the world) (6); speaking more generally, Halifu Osumare (2007) notes the centrality of US hip hop narratives of race to understandings of hip hop in other sites, rendering it a "global signifier for many forms of marginalities" (68).

3. These stories, co-constructed between practitioners and scholars, often draw on inventions of African music that themselves emerge, at least partially, from western representations of Africa as a monolithic fount of diasporic culture. See, for example, Pennycook and Mitchell (2009); Osumare (2012); Ntarangwi (2010). Hip hop artists in East Africa also invoke indigeneity, despite the absence of historical links to African America (Ntarangwi 2009; Pennycook and Mitchell 2009; Samper 2004), while outside Africa, Maori rappers in New Zealand also have linked indigenous oral traditions and hip hop (Pennycook and Mitchell 2009).

4. For more on collective memory, see Carroll (1990); Irwin-Zarecka (1994); Knapp (1989); Kansteiner (2002); Wertsch and Roediger (2008); White (1980).

5. Here, I follow Paul Gilroy in viewing the Black Atlantic not as a geographical formation, but rather one constituted in "structures of feeling, producing, communicating, and remembering" (1993, 3).

6. This turn of phrase intentionally invokes Brent Hayes Edwards' formulation of diaspora as a set of discourses of internationalism that work to forge cultural and political links between African-descended people "through and across difference" (2003, 13).

7. Following on postcolonial critiques of how norms of writing and capitalization reinforce privilege and power, I have chosen not to adhere to conventions of capitalizing "west" and "western" throughout the book.

8. Throughout this book, I use the term indigenous, not to suggest static tradition or some authentic, isolated Africa of the past, but rather, to reference the ideas and practices that my interlocutors understood as belonging to Senegal (see Ake 1988, 19) and which did not exclude hybrid musical and cultural practices.

9. I capitalize "Black" throughout the book as a reference to a sense of shared identity that emerges from an "unknown familial/national past" (Touré 2011, ix) while leaving "white" uncapitalized. As this book argues, Senegalese youth understand Blackness not only as referring to shared skin color but also as a specifically diasporic identity, a way of identifying with and in the African Diaspora.

10. I called many rappers by their stage names, as did their friends and fellow artists, although I regularly addressed some, especially those I had met through Modou in 2008, by their given names, or used their given and stage names interchangeably. While I've used stage names throughout most of the book, Almamy tends to go by his given name as much as his stage name, Nigga Mee (Mee is the last syllable in Almamy), and so I mostly write about him as Almamy, which is how I've always addressed him.

11. In using the term "ethnic," I follow common usage in Dakar, where people commonly use the French word *ethnie* or the Wolof *xeet* to categorize people and cultural practices, while recognizing that ethnicity is a pourous and shifting category, not an essential identity.

12. As historian Mamadou Diouf writes, "Postcolonial urban sociology is dominated by a paradigm in which the rural peasantry is regarded as the fundamental expression of indigenous Africa. As a consequence, the city has long been thought of exclusively in terms of the colonial ethnology of detribalization, rural exodus, and the loss of authentically African traits and values" (1992, 49; see also Sommers 2010). Léopold Sédar Senghor, Senegal's first president, construed rural Africa as the font of authentic Black culture.

13. Alcinda Honwana describes hip hop in diverse African locales as a practice of citizenship that contests a politically corrupt status quo, providing a counterhegemonic space for what she terms the "waithood generation" of African youth liminally trapped between childhood and socially recognized adulthood (2012, 111). For more on African youth and hip hop, see Künzler (2007); Ntarangwi (2010, 1318); Osumare (2012, 84); Saucier (2014).

14. Bourba had prophetically spoken these lines on Sen Kumpë's 2009 album *Freedom*.

15. Joseph Schloss (2000, 18) has similarly critiqued literature on US hip hop for failing to place the genre in a larger musical history.

16. For more on the juxtaposition of oral tradition and voice as a central tenet of modernity, see Weidman (2006).

17. In their rich edited volume, *Hip Hop and Social Change in Africa: Ni Wakati* (2014) Msia Kibona Clark and Mickie Mwanzia Koster advocate a focus on hip hop's mobilization for social change rather than its sounds. I am perhaps less convinced than they that scholarship on hip hop in Africa has, to date, focused in a compelling way on its sounds rather than the "use of hip hop as a vehicle to express the time for change" (2014, x). Instead, I suggest that hip hop's relationship to social change cannot be understood only in terms of "[a] rebellion against the establishment, a protest against current conditions, and participation in

revolutionary change" (ibid.). Indeed, to pay attention to how hip hop sounds may provide a more nuanced and grounded perspective on the exact types of mobilization explored in Clark and Koster's volume.

18. Karin Barber builds on earlier work by Mikhail Bakhtin, Roland Barthes, and Julia Kristeva to demonstrate how *oral* performance is entextualized (Silverstein and Urban 1996), that is, made into something that can be repeated and recreated in other contexts.

19. In this, I differ from Kofi Agawu's designation of African music as text, which, he claims, frees it from "the yoke of ostensibly contextual explanations advocated by ethnographers and ethnomusicologists" (2003, 97).

20. Louise Meintjes describes a parallel example of the intersection of genre making and myth, showing how *mbaqanga* musicians in South Africa "mobilize the past and the imagined in their narratives to serve the present" (2003, 33).

21. Some of the notable work that considers the representational significance of hip hop sound includes that of Justin Adams Burton (2017), Loren Kajikawa (2015), Adam Krims (2000), and Robert Walser (1995) in the US context and Adam Krims (2000), J. Griffith Rollefson (2017), and Noriko Manabe (2013) in contexts outside the United States. Hip hop musicality is not limited to its instrumental tracks; Maxwell Williams, in a forthcoming chapter in the *Oxford Handbook of Hip Hop Studies*, points to the musicality of verbal flow as a way beyond "uncritical inferences about sonic representations of identity based upon subjective and inconsistent readings of specific musical figures." In a different move away from lyrical content and musical analysis, Robin G. Kelley (1997) writes of hip hop's "sonic force," as a source of pleasure in the US context, and P. Khalil Saucier (2014), about African hip hop's phonic materiality as "a site of protest, objection, and antiappropriation" (205).

22. For more on the evolution of hip hop instrumentals, see Katz (2012); Keyes (2001); Krims (2000); Rose (1994); Schloss (2004).

23. See Potter (1995), Rose (1991), and Shusterman (1991) for references to hip hop as postmodern expression.

24. Shaw (2002) coined the phrase "palimpsest memory" (8) to describe how ritual and divination practices in Sierra Leone constitute nondiscursive memories of the transatlantic slave trade.

25. This idea of aural palimpsest memories is distinct from what Martin Daughtry has written about as "acoustic palimpsests" (2013). Daughtry suggests that his metaphor may work best for the *object* of research, but that it does not leave space for the very kinds of practitioner discourses that are central to my project here (27). He also cautions that the textuality of the palimpsest metaphor renders it problematic for thinking about sound (29). In my own project, I'm less concerned about this point—first, because I am writing not about sound but about musical form, which are related but not equivalent; and second, because, following Barber (2007), I understand textuality as a useful framework for considering the relationships between utterances and genres that are not written.

26. What emerged from these interactions was the importance that my research participants placed on my knowing and appreciating hip hop outside of my research project, so that we shared a system of aesthetic values and a knowledge of hip hop history, to which I sometimes contributed things they didn't know, and in which I often learned from them.

27. Writing about grime music in the United Kingdom, Richard Bramwell (2015) asserts the importance of the specificity of global flows, demonstrating how the globalization of

African American music necessarily intersects with a heritage of Caribbean migration that mediates Black working class British youth's relationship to both Africa and African America.

28. Fatou Kandé Senghor's *Wala Bok: Une Histoire Orale du Hip Hop au Sénégal* (2015), while also not comprehensive, assembles a broad sampling of oral histories of Rap Galsen, arranged thematically, and includes accounts from many figures who are not featured in this book.

29. Because the people I worked with are public figures, I have, at their request, used their real (stage) names throughout this text. I have occasionally anonymized artists when to reveal their names might embarrass them or cause conflict within the community.

30. Gender expectations and exoticizing imaginings of foreign women as sexually available influenced how rappers attached me to the men they saw me with or the way that they sometimes interpreted my interest in their own musical endeavors. When Books married in the fall of 2011, I was enthusiastically congratulated by one rapper who assumed it was to me, and consoled by another who assumed I'd been jilted.

31. In this, the book is not unique. Writing about resistance studies, Sherry B. Ortner (1995) has suggested that although ethnographic thinness could result from inadvertently superficial engagement, it in fact often betrays a refusal to ask particular questions about the internal politics of dominated groups. When it comes to hip hop studies, the ease with which local examples are plugged into frameworks of global hip hop resistance both invites and obscures ethnographic thinness.

32. It is striking, for example, to read Rosalind Frederick's article "The Old Man is Dead" (2013) and encounter quotes from her interviews that are almost identical to my own.

33. On the one hand, fluent French is a marker of elite class status and sometimes is negatively associated with the mimicry of whiteness; a favorite pastime in Dakar seems to be closely monitoring television hosts and newscasters and delighting in any small errors they make in French. Books surprised me when he commented one day that my imperfect grammar and Medina-inflected accent were the reason for what he saw as my unusually long interviews, where it was quickly apparent that rappers needn't be self-conscious about their own French when speaking with me. On the other hand, my Wolof evolved immensely over the year that I lived in Senegal; as my ability in Wolof continued to improve in the years following the 2011–2012 period in which I conducted much of this research, I found myself reinterpreting, and sometimes retranslating, Wolof-language interviews with new understanding. When translating from Wolof to English, I have attempted (where appropriate) to maintain the emphasis implied in the particular verb form used, which may be neutral or may emphasize the subject, verb, or object. For the most part, I follow standardized Wolof orthography when writing Wolof words; an exception is when song titles use local spellings (based in French orthography), or when writing the names of people or groups. While many rappers write their names using multiple spellings; I've standardized their names here for consistency throughout the text.

34. The photographs included here illustrate the constructedness of these encounters. While there are some candid shots, most of the photographs that I include take one of two forms; some are stills from interviews, an attempt to remind us of the way that I elicited these narratives, behind a camera, in shots that more experienced artists carefully curated themselves. Others are taken from photo shoots my friends requested, and in which they chose the sites and poses. Such photos outnumber images of performances, which were hard to take with the poor lighting prevalent at most shows in 2011.

35. My uneven efforts to write myself into this book are an attempt to mark what Johannes Fabian (1998) has called "presence"; that is, the simple fact of how my identities,

self-ascribed and externally imposed, and my own beliefs, knowledge, and interests influenced interviews and broader interactions during this project, so that I was a part of the narratives that emerged within a complex of power relations, rather than simply privy to them.

36. Following Lila Abu-Lughod (1993), I foreground the places where practitioner concerns align with those of the scholarly and popular audiences most likely to read this book (16).

37. Fabian has cautioned that evoking myth risks (or even seeks to) "[dissolve] contradiction . . . between the artist's time sequence and academic chronology" (2003, 91).

38. Jacob Climo and Maria Cattell note that memory is intimately implicated in anthropological method; we rely on memories, our own and those of our informants, we consult archives and other records, etc. (2002, 8).

CHAPTER 2

1. This was, coincidentally, around the same time as the first, French-language dissertation on Rap Galsen (Moulard-Kouka 2008).

2. In her work on hip hop in Kenya, Carolyn Mose critiques the indiscriminate imposition of ideologically loaded US hip hop categories of underground and mainstream onto African hip hop (2011) and insists on the specificity of the urban context in analyzing hip hop scenes (2013). Likewise, my aim here is not to reify this "good hip hop/bad hip hop" binary (Rollefson 2017, 7) but rather to consider how it informs practitioner narratives.

3. This narrative appears, for example, in Rose (1994), Keyes (2002), Forman (2002), Perry (2004), and Perkins (1996). P. Khalil Saucier and Tryon P. Woods, on the other hand, have critiqued hip hop scholarship's perpetuation of the myth of hip hop's emergence as a response to deindustrialization and racist economic exploitation for minimizing the state's physical violence against Black communities (2014, 277–278).

4. Murray Forman identifies the increasing turn away from "ghetto" and toward "hood" in the hip hop of the 1990s as a recuperation of urban space against these white fantasies of danger and decay (2002, 84).

5. This can be seen across a wide range of sites, including Cuba (Baker, 2011), Germany (Caglar 1998; Diessel 2001), Palestine (Eqeip 2010), and among immigrant and first-generation people of South Asian (Sharma 2010) and Arab (Maira 2008) descent in the United States, to name only a few.

6. Throughout this book, I retain *banlieues* and *quartiers populaires* rather than use English-language terms that don't precisely map onto Senegalese realities.

7. The French displacement of indigenous populations was neither uncontested nor entirely successful, as some, particularly the Lebou, who lived where the new city was to be constructed, resisted the French incursion onto their land in multiple ways, including market strikes and physical resistance (Bigon 2009).

8. The similarities, however, are surface ones. Social marginalization in the French banlieues in the 1980s and 1990s was classed more than it was raced (although these often go together), and French welfare policies alleviated living conditions far more than was ever the case in the US inner city (Prévos 2001; Silverstein 2012; Wacquant 2008). On the other hand, the demographic shift from working class to primarily immigrants and poor people—who are often one and the same—in the banlieues in the twenty-first century suggests an increasing similarity between demonized urban populations in both countries (Boucher 2009). Whether or not the comparison between the US inner city and the French banlieue holds from a sociological or economic standpoint, however, the language and imagery of the ghetto transmitted

through US hip hop lyrics and videos served as an important resource for early hip hoppers in France (Prévos 2001).

9. As hip hop has grown into mainstream acceptance, its venues have improved; we now see hip hop shows at major theaters like the Sorano and the Grand Theatre.

10. Although Bul Faale is often associated with hip hop because of PBS's song of the same name, it was not explicitly a hip hop movement. For more on the role of hip hop in Bul Faale, see Dimé (2017), Ngom (2011).

11. For a more on Y'en a Marre, see Bryson (2014); Fredericks (2014); Gueye (2013); Savané and Sarr (2012).

12. See Juan Carlos Melendez-Torres, in-progress.

13. This is not to say that nothing has changed. Since I interviewed Amadou in 2011, the Senegalese Ministry of Culture, the US Department of State, and various European nongovernmental organizations have funneled money into Rap Galsen, funding new cultural centers, programs, and exchange programs, although these projects, in their focus on youth outreach and education, rarely benefit established rappers (see Remix). Hip hoppers have also creatively mobilized social media to profit from their social consciousness, as in Xuman and Keyti's monetized YouTube channel, where they broadcast *Journal Rappé*, a French and Wolof reportage on current events in Senegal, Africa, and the world. Yet, broadly speaking, little has been done to change the originating experience of the street from which the underground emerged and with which it has always engaged.

CHAPTER 3

1. Paulla Ebron, for example, describes African American encounters with Gambian music in the United States as "central to our sense of connection with Africa: the griots wondrously connected to our imagined past, creating the fictive kinship ties to our African relatives" (2003, 59).

2. For more on the connections between African orality and African American vernacular expression, see Smitherman's 1977 work on African-American speech; Maultsby's 1990 essay "Africanisms in African American Music"; and Oliver's 1970 and Kubik's 1999 works on the blues. For sources that extend these connections specifically to hip hop, see Banfield (2003, 180; 2009, 67); Campbell (2005); Banks (2010); Dyson (1993, 12, 191, 276); Fernandes (2012); Fernando (1994, 32); Flock (2014); Hadley and Yancy (2011, 5); Makinwa (2012); Alim (2009, 1); Perkinson (2003, 146); Pollard (2004); Smitherman (1997, 4); Toop (1991, 8); and Watkins (2005, 239). For sources that extend the griot connection to deejaying and digital music production, see Banks (2011) and Miller (2004).

3. See Assman (1997) for a discussion of *mnemohistory*, the history of memory, which ignores the synchronic to focus solely on memory.

4. Although the djembe is typically not limited to griots, griots do play it in some contexts, including Burkina Faso and Côte d'Ivoire (Charry, 2000, 114).

5. The use of the term *caste* to describe stratified social systems in West Africa is sometimes debated because of its negative connotations. Although not as extreme as systems of social stratification in other parts of the world, Wolof endogamous social hierarchies continue to influence marriage patterns and interpersonal interactions, and so I've maintained the use of this term here. For more on the position of griots vis-à-vis stratified social systems, see Tang (2012, 52).

6. Increasingly, there are exceptions. In Senegal, some all-female sabar ensembles have formed, with limited success. Sona Jabarteh, a Gambian woman, is an internationally renowned kora player.

7. The phenomenon of the roving griot—who shows up to praise or beg at celebrations despite lacking any connection to the family—is distinct from the explicit patron-client relationship that exists between a noble patron and her family griot, and seems to be a practice that arose fairly recently as a side effect of urbanization and the resultant blurring of lines between socially structuring principles of kinship and caste (Hale 1998, 47; McNee 2000, 34).

8. The Ballet National du Sénégal, for example, emphasized Mande practices, taking its cue from Les Ballets Africaines of Guinea (Kringelbach 2013, 40), one of the first national ballets, which had a major influence on the global practice and perception of "West African" music, particularly djembe drumming and dance (Charry 2000, 193).

9. For more on the woloficization of culture in postcolonial Dakar, see Diop and Diouf (1990); Mclaughlin (2008); Swigart (1994); Sylla (1978, cited in Leymarie, 1999).

10. The sabar ensemble comprises a collection of open- and closed-bottom drums in a range of sizes (see also Tang 2007).

11. While the Muride brotherhood occupies a prominent place in Senegalese Muslim practice, three other brotherhoods have significant followings: the Qadiriyya, originating in Baghdad in the twelfth century; the Tijaniyyah, which originated in Morocco in the eighteenth century and spread to Senegal via Mauritania; and the Layene, a small sect specific to the Lebou people and centered in the community of Yoff on the coast of Dakar (Robinson 2000).

12. Female members of the sect are called Yaye Fall, and they also conduct weekly chanting sessions that go late into the night.

13. For more on the relationship between the Baye Fall and ceddo, see Savishinsky (1994); O'Brien (1971).

14. Since Abdou Diouf's ascension to the presidency in 1981, Senegalese nationalist rhetoric has increasingly incorporated themes and models of relationships (such as an emphasis on hard work and master-disciple bonds) drawn directly from the maraboutic disciplines, in an effort to forge national identity among a population that is by nature factional in its devotion to particular Muslim leaders (Panzacchi 1994).

15. Senghor cited parallels between Marxism and indigenous communalism as the basis of a new "African socialism" that he saw as the ideal model for the newly emerging Senegalese state (Genova 2004, 153).

16. Colonial powers took aspects of African life that had previously been flexible, allowing for continuity and change in response to the needs of the community, and heralded them as timeless, static tradition (Ranger and Hobsbawm 1983). Building on the work of Marilyn Ivy, Amanda Weidman (2006) suggests that the idea of invented tradition "unhelpfully sets up a choice between 'invented' and 'real' or 'authentic' traditions" (9), reinforcing a binary between western and indigenous musical practices and ideas that are in fact produced "in and through the colonial encounter" (ibid.). However, I think it is possible, and at times helpful, to note the inventedness of particular traditions as a *feature* of the very coproduction that Weidman notes.

17. In other African cities, these musics were indigenized much earlier. For example, Thomas Turino (2000) describes how indigenized urban popular music emerged in Zimbabwe as early as the 1930s; Christopher Waterman (1991) locates the development of specific genres of "modernized African" and "Africanized Western" popular music in Lagos in the 1920s and

1930s; and several authors have written about the early indigenization of imported western music in South Africa, including Coplan (1985) and Erlmann (1991).

18. While the introduction of Afro-Cuban music to African audiences is generally attributed to the British HMV label's GV series of recordings (later redistributed by Columbia Records), in Senegal, at least, it was also brought directly by Cuban sailors who interacted with Senegalese workers in Dakar's port (Shain 2002).

19. The phrase *sursaut national* is difficult to translate precisely into English; it suggests an awakening, a new consciousness of self, and in this context, a reclaiming of local cultural values in the face of Senghor's emphasis on *la francophonie*.

20. For more on the adaptation of sabar rhythms, see Benga (2002); Diouf (1992); Mangin (2013); Moulard-Kouka (2008); and Tang (2007).

21. Many major mbalax singers claim griot lineages, including Youssou N'Dour, Thione Seck, Fatou Guewel, and Coumba Gawlo, as well as younger artists like Pape Ndiaye Thiopet, Wally Seck (Thione's son), and Aida Samb. At the same time, mbalax's popularity has increasingly opened music making as a profession to youth from nongriot families (Kringelbach 2013, 55). Foundational mbalax singers Omar Pene, Ismael Lo, Baba Maal, and Ousmane Diallo are among those who are not from griot families, as are the younger artists Adiouza Diallo (daughter of Ousmane) and Viviane (N'dour/Chidid). However, it is important to note that, while griot practices continue to constitute a foundational stylistic resource for mbalax musicians, popular music increasingly provides a space in which people who are *not* of griot lineages can work as professional musicians, although not without resistance from their families (see also Skinner 2015, 68).

22. Senegal created its own copyright office, the Bureau Sénégalais du Droit d'Auteur (BSDA), in the early 1970s, during this same period of increased indigenization and commercialization.

23. In 2011, only a few male artists—including Pape Ndiaye Thiopet—were known for using taasu. After a few women, notably Aby Ngana Diop, released popular (noncomedic) taasu recordings in the 1990s, an increasing number of male mbalax singers began including taasu in their music for comedic effect (McNee 2003, 42).

24. Other albums that involve similar production styles include *Presidents d'Afrique,* another solo album by DJ Awadi, as well as his albums recorded with Duggy-T as PBS; these include *Run Cool* and *Salaam.* Daara J's *Boomerang* and *School of Life* albums also follow this general model.

25. This is the same song that inspired the 2010 World Cup theme that was sung by Colombian international pop star Shakira.

CHAPTER 4

1. See also Rollefson (2017) on the artificial division between content and form in hip hop.

2. A few years later, Mame Xa would abandon hip hop under the encouragement of a devout Muslim family member and move to performing slam poetry instead.

3. Ngoyane is a type of music performed with xalam and calabash.

4. A riti is a Wolof one-stringed fiddle.

5. Wango is a Pulaar dance popularized by the singer Baaba Maal (Ngom 2012, 103).

6. Timothy Mangin notes that mbalax artists also describe their music as tradition (2013, 25–26).

7. This is true not only of mbalax, but also of pop genres based on other ethnic traditions.

8. There is, however, one exception to hip hoppers' aversion to praisesinging. Many rappers regularly praise the marabouts who were central to Islam's development in Senegal, like Cheikh Amadou Bamba and Cheikh Ibra Fall. While many, if not most, rappers profess allegiance to living marabouts, it is rare (but not unheard of) to hear living marabouts praised in hip hop. Many of the rappers I spoke with criticized this practice, citing the financial incentive behind it. For more on the influence of Islam in Rap Galsen, see Moulard-Kouka (2008); Ngom (2011); Niang (2014).

9. Singer Omar Pene, for example, has always explicitly eschewed praisesinging (Josselin 2009). The mbalax group Ceddo's song "Jambaat" was censored on government-owned media during the 2000 elections due to its political critiques, as were earlier groups during President Léopold Senghor's reign (Mangin 2013, 64). Mbalax pioneer Youssou N'Dour's music was central to the Set-Setal ("Clean-Make Clean") movement of the early 1990s, in which youth "[redefined] the space and social logic of public places" through murals and cleanliness initiatives (Diouf 1992, 41; my translation). For more on mbalax and Set-Setal, see Biaya (2002); Havard (2009). Mamadou Diouf notes that, as much as mbalax praises the political, religious, and economic elite, it simultaneously contrasts these, "awkwardly and obliquely, to the heroes of the street—soccer players, artists, deceased or lost friends—all models of the trajectories and daily pain of African youth at the end of the past century" (2008, 361).

10. Djily Bagdad, speaking in English, translated '"Joyu Askan Wi" as "Tears of My People." The literal translation is "the crying of the people."

11. Alcinda Honwana has critiqued the way in which African governments have increased access to education without increasing its quality—in terms of both teaching and learning—or its likelihood to lead to employment (2012, 40–46).

12. Perhaps due in part to a bit of sheepishness after having alternately supported and then opposed Abdoulaye Wade in 2000 and 2007, respectively, rappers in 2011 were carefully resistant to cooption by politicians, refusing to endorse candidates and instead calling in more general terms for change.

13. In an interview with James Spady, DJ Awadi of PBS also commented on the difficulties of carving out a space for hip hop in Dakar's sonic landscape for an earlier generation of rappers (Spady 2006b, 651).

14. Rappers also police other rappers. After the now-deceased rapper Pacotille supported Abdoulaye Wade in the 2007 election, for example, many rappers stopped collaborating with him.

CHAPTER 5

1. See McLeod (1999, 142) for a discussion of realness in US hip hop.

2. It is important to note that domestic space in Senegal, while it may not be public, is not necessarily private either. Especially in the quartiers populaires and the banlieues, houses are left open during the day, and neighbors and vendors enter freely, stopping in the doorway to announce themselves.

3. Senegal's family code, even after being revised in 2000 (a change that was implemented in 2013), has institutionalized male supremacy in marriage; when combined with particularly patriarchal interpretations of Islam, which hold considerable sway in an ostensibly secular country, the result has been a restriction of women's rights to their children, to inheritance,

to divorce, and to choose or reject polygyny. Although civil marriages are registered as polyga-mous or monogamous, most men, even those claiming that they plan to remain monogamous, prefer to leave their options open, believing that Islam grants them the right to four wives, although few acknowledge the limitations placed on this practice in the Qu'ran. Many women have told me that as Muslims, they are not permitted to insist on a monogamous marriage contract, regardless of their preference. Thus, despite ostensible rights granted to women in the legal system, dominant patriarchal interpretations of and modes of teaching Islam (where women learn from male teachers invested in those interpretations) at times effectively negate those rights.

4. Gavin Steingo notes the inapplicability of a division between labor and leisure in the context of township South Africa, where leisure is similarly imposed (2016, 189). While I agree that to call the down-time that results from unemployment "leisure" is problematic, I also want to stress how a gendered analysis can further nuance our understanding of leisure time in urban Africa.

5. Robin G. Kelley notes a similar dynamic at play in the United States, where young women's and girls' access to public space is limited, due to both the familial policing of their bodies and movements and their domestic chores (1997, 54–55).

6. See, for example, Rose (1992, 170); Perry (2004, 156).

7. Francesca Castaldi (2006) argues that the drummers at these events stand in for male members of society (83).

8. Lest we be tempted to read sabar dance as a clear assertion of power, however, the fact that these subversions of gendered social values are confined to a space created for this pur-pose means that women remain constrained by "multiple layers of power . . . at the same time as these layers furnished room for negotiation within them" (Morales-Libove 2005, 120).

9. Likewise, Raquel Z. Rivera (2003) notes that many of the women participating in Nuyorican hip hop are perceived as "loose" by their male peers.

10. There have been several cases where prominent male mbalax singers have been accused of homosexuality due to the perceived effeminacy of their behavior. In 2014, for example, mbalaxman Wally Seck began a trend of men carrying large handbags, color-coordinated to their traditional clothing. Hip hoppers were vocal in the general uproar against the practical style, and men emulating the singer were violently attacked in the streets and labeled as goor-jigeen (literally, "man-woman," used to denote gay men in con-temporary Senegal). The dominant gender paradigms reinscribed in hip hop themselves inform queer male identities and relationships in Dakar, which often adopt modes of reci-procity and dominant-submissive roles that characterize normative heterosexual courtship (Ferguson 2017; Teunis 2001).

11. For example, when a group of young women accused of lesbianism were arrested in 2013, activists pointed to the speculative nature of the charges, noting the unlikelihood of public displays of same-sex affection in the increasingly violently homophobic context of Senegal (Corey-Boulet 2013).

12. Around 2014, under the guidance of a local religious leader, rapper Almamy of 23.3 and his manager were vocal in a formal movement against homosexuality. Lesbians, on the other hand, are rarely mentioned in hip hop, perhaps because their relationships are less threat-ening to normative models of masculinity.

13. In her critique of western feminism, Sidra Lawrence writes that "to assume that a woman's power in the private sphere is less valuable because she does not have power in the public sphere relies upon Western devaluation of the domestic" (2011, 68). Lawrence's critique

can be extended beyond western feminism to western liberalism in general, including its (partial) adaptations in the ideas of voice at play here.

CHAPTER 6

1. Although the use of traditional instruments became increasingly common among the underground in the twenty-first century, as of 2017, it was still rare that more than a few tracks on any given album would incorporate traditional music and instruments.

2. This song appears on Gaston's 2011 album, *Touti Wakh Job lu Beuri*, which has an uncharacteristic number of tracks (four) featuring traditional instruments, compared to the majority of albums I listened to during this period, which had one or two.

3. Whether they produce music or not, rappers actively contribute to the composition of musical tracks. Almamy explained his process one day as we sat in his family home in Medina listening to the new album that he and Falsower had recorded together as the duo 23.3: "Sometimes you write a song and then you want to write a beat for it. You go to the studio, you find the beatmaker, you say I want a beat like—" he sang, a short melody followed by a slow drumbeat for a measure or so—"and after he tries to play this, adds the bass, then it comes along. The second song on the album we did like this—I played it with my mouth and then the guy did it."

4. The music and commentary in this chapter is based almost entirely on the perspectives of male rappers, whose careers have lasted long enough to release substantial bodies of work and to allow for stylistic growth. When I worked with the women of Gotal in 2011–2012, they were just beginning to record as a group and as individuals, and they had less to say about these questions of sampling and musical time.

5. While a technical analysis of flow in Rap Galsen is beyond the scope of this book, Adam Krims (2000), Noriko Manabe (2006), and Maxwell Williams (forthcoming), among others, have further analyzed the rhythmic and musical characteristics of hip hop flow.

6. As hip hop has firmly established itself as something different from mbalax, and as popular music has opened more widely to nongriots with the loosening of societal norms, singing has also crept back into hip hop practice and is now generally accepted as something distinct from praisesinging.

7. At the Orange S'Cool Tour concert at Kennedy Highschool, where Books and Y.Dee were dismayed to share a stage with mbalaxmen, rapper Cannabis performed to a crowd of girls who shrieked as loudly for him as for the mbalaxmen that would perform later, while Books's reception was lukewarm.

8. Noriko Manabe (2013) describes similar anxieties over authenticity and localization among Japanese deejays, who draw on local material in various ways to set themselves apart in the global scene.

REMIX: CONSUMING RESISTANCE

1. In the time between my chance encounter with rapper ResKp on a road trip to The Gambia with Sen Kumpë in June 2011 and my follow-up research trips in 2014 and 2015, our marriage inevitably changed my own position in the hip hop scene. Artists whom I'd known and worked with far longer than I'd known my spouse were suddenly perplexed when I showed up to hip hop events without him. Once again, I found myself negotiating a gendered musical world where my position was defined through my relationships, real

or imagined, to Senegalese men. Like many of my former interlocutors, my response to change has been to drift away, to move on to other things. I visit friends, but otherwise I no longer spend much time in hip hop spaces. While most of the material and all the human connections described in this book, then, predate my marriage I am cognizant of the expectation that female scholars disclose these facets of our personal lives, lest we later be accused of work that is somehow neither rigorous nor ethical in having been, however predictably, carried out by a human being.

2. Journalist and Y'en a Marre founder Fadel Barro has spoken about how the movement mobilized existing hip hop networks to its own ends (Haeringer 2011, cited in Fredericks 2013).

3. See Bryson (2014) for more on Y'en a Marre's continued projects after 2012.

4. Kendra Salois has noted the contradictions inherent in maintaining resistance as a defining characteristic of hip hop, even while using it to bolster US economic and political power. She suggests that to focus on the affective labor of musicians would allow us "to take account of unequal power relations at a systemic level while continuing to see musicians' agency within those relations" (2015, 409–410).

5. Personal communications with embassy and Africulturban staff.

6. Of course, the US scholars and artists involved in these programs view them in a somewhat different light. Describing the State Department's Next Level program, its director, Mark Katz (2017) notes hip hop's power to unite people across cultural difference, and links this explicitly to hip hop origins myths of urban marginality, in a moment of what Chérie Rivers Ndaliko has described as "the admittedly contagious rhetoric of global connectedness through shared artistic expression" (Ndaliko 2017, 188). Even as he acknowledges the problematic power imbalances inherent in cultural diplomacy, however, Katz seems to accept that "the goal of diplomacy is to foster mutual understanding and respect among citizens of different nations" (Katz 2017, 4). While Katz juxtaposes hip hop diplomacy (and cultural diplomacy more broadly) with the State Department's increasing focus on counterterrorism under the Trump administration, my experiences in Senegal, five years prior to Trump's ascent to power, suggest that the difference is one of degree rather than focus.

7. Geoffrey Baker (2005) makes this same argument in regards to Cuban hip hop (372).

8. The quote is drawn from an interview with Kenyan musician and One Beat participant Blinky Bill. https://1beat.org/ Accessed June 1, 2018.

9. As we've come to expect, these commercial changes go hand in hand with aesthetic ones; underground artists experiment more and more with traditional rhythms and instruments, even to the point of violating what as recently as 2012 seemed like rigid metric boundaries between hip hop and traditional music.

Bibliography

Abu-Lughod, Lila. 2008 [1993]. *Writing Women's Worlds: Bedouin Stories*. Berkeley: University of California Press.

Agawu, Kofi. 2003. *Representing African Music: Postcolonial Notes, Queries, Positions*. New York: Routledge.

Aidi, Hishaam. 2011. "Leveraging Hip Hop in US Foreign Policy." *Al Jazeera English*. November 7. http://www.aljazeera.com/indepth/opinion/2011/10/2011103091018299924.html.

Ake, Claude. 1988. "Building on the Indigenous." In *Recovery in Africa: A Challenge for Development Cooperation in the 1990s*, edited by Pierre Frühling. Stockholm: Swedish Ministry of Foreign Affairs, 19–22.

Alim, H. Samy 2011. "Global Ill-Literacies": Hip Hop Cultures, Youth Identities, and the Politics of Literacy." *Review of Research in Education* 35(1): 120–146.

Alim, H. Samy, Awad Ibrahim, and Alastair Pennycook, eds. 2009. *Global Linguistic Flows: Hip Hop Cultures, Youth Identities, and the Politics of Language*. New York: Routledge.

Another Africa. 2010. "A Modern Griot: Youssou N'dour." October 10, 2010. Accessed May 7, 2018, from http://www.anotherafrica.net/music/a-modern-griot-youssou-ndour.

Antoine, Philippe, and Jeanne Nanitelamio. 1991. "More Single Women in African Cities: Pikine, Abidjan, and Brazzaville." *Population: An English Selection* 3: 149–169.

Appert, Catherine M. 2017. "Engendering Musical Ethnography." *Ethnomusicology* 61(3): 446–467.

Appert, Catherine M. 2016a. "On Hybridity in African Popular Music: The Case of Senegalese Hip Hop." *Ethnomusicology* 60(2): 279–299.

Appert, Catherine M. 2016b. "Locating Hip Hop Origins: Popular Music and Tradition in Senegal." *Africa* 86(2): 237–262.

Appert, Catherine M. 2015. "To Make Song Without Singing: Hip Hop and Popular Music in Senegal." *New Literary History* 46(4): 759–774.

Apter, Andrew. 2007. *Beyond Words: Discourse and Critical Agency in Africa*. Chicago: University of Chicago Press.

Assie-Lumumba, N'Dri Thérèse. 1997. "Educating Africa's Girls and Women: A Conceptual and Historical Analysis of Gender Inequality." In *Engendering African Social Sciences*, edited by Ayesha Imam, Amina Mama, and Fatou Sow. Dakar: CODESRIA, 297–316.

Assmann, Jan. 1997. *Moses the Egyptian: The Memory of Egypt in Western Monotheism*. Cambridge, MA: Harvard University Press.

Avery, Kenneth S. 2004. *A Psychology of Early Sufi Samā: Listening and Altered States*. New York: Routledge.

Baker, Geoffrey. 2011. *Buena Vista in the Club: Rap, Reggaetón, and Revolution in Havana*. Durham, NC: Duke University Press.

Baker, Geoffrey. 2005. "Hip Hop, Revolución! Nationalizing Rap in Cuba." *Ethnomusicology* 49(3): 388–402.

Bakhtin, M. M. 1986. *Speech Genres and Other Late Essays*. Translated by Vern W. McGee; edited by Caryl Emerson and Michael Holquist. Austin: University of Texas Press.

Banfield, William C. 2009. *Cultural Codes: Makings of a Black Music Philosophy*. Lanham, MD: Scarecrow Press.

Banfield, William C. 2003. "The Rub: Markets, Morals, and the 'Theologizing' of Music." In *Noise and Spirit: The Religious and Spiritual Sensibilities of Rap Music*, edited by Anthony B. Pinn. New York: New York University Press, 173–183.

Banks, Adam J. 2011. *Digital Griots: African American Rhetoric in a Multimedia Age*. Carbondale: Southern Illinois University Press.

Banks, Daniel. 2010. "From Homer to Hip Hop: Orature and Griots, Ancient and Present." *Classical World* 103(2): 238–245.

Barber, Karin. 2007. *The Anthropology of Texts, Persons, and Publics: Oral and Written Culture in Africa and Beyond*. Cambridge: Cambridge University Press.

Bauman, Richard. 2004. *A World of Others' Words: Cross-Cultural Perspectives on Intertextuality*. Malden, MA: Blackwell Publishing.

Bauman, Richard, and Charles L. Briggs. 1990. "Poetics and Performance as Critical Perspectives on Language and Social Life." *Annual Review of Anthropology* 19: 59–88.

BBC News Africa. 2014. "Africa's Musical Crusaders: New Generations of Griots." October 14. Accessed February 10, 2015, from http://www.bbs.com/news/world-africa-29162685.

Benga, Ndiouga Adrien. 2002. "The Air of the City Makes Free." In *Playing with Identities in Contemporary Music in Africa*, edited by Mai Palmberg and Annemette Kirkegaard. Stockholm: Nordiska Afrikainstitutet, 75–85.

Behrman, Lucy C. 1970. *Muslim Brotherhoods and Politics in Senegal*. Cambridge, MA: Harvard University Press.

Betts, Raymond F. 1971. "Establishment of the Medina in Dakar, Senegal, 1914." *Africa: Journal of the International African Institute* 41(2): 143–152.

Biaya, Tshikala Kayembe. 2001. "Les Plaisirs de la Ville: Masculinité, Sexualité et Féminité à Dakar (1997–2000)." *African Studies Review* 44(2): 71–85.

Bigon, Liora. 2009. *A History of Urban Planning in Two West African Colonial Capitals: Residential Segregation in British Lagos and French Dakar (1850–1930)*. Lewiston, NY: Edwin Mellon Press.

Boucher, Manuel. 2009. "L'éxperience du Ghetto. Stomy, Roger, Abou et leur Clan: Rebelles et Débrouillards." *Déviance et Société* 33(2): 221–248.

Bradley, Adam. 2008. *Book of Rhymes: The Poetics of Hip Hop*. New York: Basic Civitas.

Bramwell, Richard. 2015. *UK Hip-Hop, Grime, and the City: The Aesthetics and Ethics of London's Rap Scene*. New York: Routledge.

Briggs, Charles L. 1988. *Learning How to Ask: A Sociolinguistic Appraisal of the Role of the Interview in Social Science Research*. Cambridge: Cambridge University Press.

Briggs, Charles L., and Richard Bauman. 1992. "Genre, Intertextuality, and Social Power." *Journal of Linguistic Anthropology* 2(2): 130–172.

Brown, Jeffrey. 2004. "Senegalese Singer Youssou N'Dour Speaks About His Music and His Message." *PBS Newshour*. September 10, 2004. http://www.pbs.org/newshour/bb/entertainment-july-dec04-ndour_9-10/. Accessed on November 1, 2015.

Bruner, Edward. 1997. "Ethnography as Narrative." In *Memory, Identity, Community: The Idea of Narrative in the Human Sciences*, edited by Lewis P. Hinchman and Sandra K. Hinchman. Albany: State University of New York Press, 264–280.

Bryson, Devon. 2014. "The Rise of a New Senegalese Cultural Philosophy?" *African Studies Quarterly* 14(3): 33–56.

Buggenhagen, Beth. 2011. "Are Births Just 'Women's Business'? Gift Exchange, Value, and Global Volatility in Muslim Senegal." *American Ethnologist* 38(4): 714–732.

Burton, Justin Adams. 2016. *Posthuman Rap*. New York: Oxford University Press.

Caglar, Ayse S. 1998. "Popular Culture, Marginality, and Institutional Incorporation: German-Turkish Rap and Turkish Pop in Berlin." *Cultural Dynamics* 10(3): 243–261.

Campbell, Kermit Ernest. 2005. *"Gettin' Our Groove On": Rhetoric, Language, and Literacy for the Hip Hop Generation*. Detroit: Wayne State University Press.

Carroll, Noël. 1990. "Interpretation, History, and Narrative." *The Monist* 73(2): 134–166.

Castaldi, Francesca. 2006. *Choreographies of African Identities: Négritude, Dance, and the National Ballet of Senegal*. Urbana: University of Illinois Press.

Charry, Eric. 2000. *Mande Music: Traditional and Modern Music of the Maninka and Mandinka of Western Africa*. Chicago: University of Chicago Press.

Clark, Msia Kibona and Mickie Mwanzia Koster, eds. 2014. *Hip Hop and Social Change in Africa: Ni Wakati*. Lanham, MD: Lexington Books.

Clifford, James. 1986. "Introduction: Partial Truths." In *Writing Culture: The Poetics and Politics of Ethnography*, edited by James Clifford and George E. Marcus. Berkeley: University of California Press, 1–26.

Collins, Peter. 2010. "The Ethnographic Self as Resource." In *The Ethnographic Self as Resource: Writing Memory and Experience into Ethnography*, edited by Peter Collins and Anselma Galinat. New York: Berghahn Books, 228–245.

Coplan, David. 1985. *In Township Tonight: South Africa's Black City Music and Theatre*. Johannesburg: Raven Press.

Corey-Boulet, Robbie. 2013. "Accused Lesbians in Senegal Freed for Lack of Evidence." *Voice of Africa*, November 20. Accessed May 1, 2017, from http://www.voanews.com/a/accused-lesbians-in-Senegal-freed-for-lack-of-evidence/1793998.html.

Crane, Susan A. 1997. "Writing the Individual Back into Collective Memory." *The American Historical Review* 102(5): 1372–1385.

Creevy, Lucy. 1996. "Islam, Women, and the Role of the State in Senegal." *Journal of Religion in Africa*, 26(3): 268–307.

Curtin, Phillip. 1971. "Jihad in West Africa: Early Phases and Inter-Relations in Mauritania and Senegal." *Journal of African History* 12(1): 11–24.

Daughtry, J. Martin. 2013. "Acoustic Palimpsests and the Politics of Listening." *Music and Politics* 7(1): 1–34.

Diaw, Aminata. 1993. "The Democracy of the Literati." In *Senegal: Essays on Statecraft*, edited by Momar Coumba Diop. Dakar: CODESRIA, 291–323.

Diessel, Caroline. 2001. "Bridging East and West on the 'Orient Express': Oriental Hip-Hop in the Turkish Diaspora of Berlin." *Journal of Popular Music Studies*, 13(2): 165–187.

Dimé, Mamadou. 2014. "De *Bul Faale* à *Y'en a Marre*: Continuités et Dissonances dans les Dynamiques de Contestation Sociopolitique et d'Affirmation Citoyenne Chez les Jeunes au Sénégal." *Africa Development* 42(2): 83–105.

Diop, Momar Coumba, and Mamadou Diouf. 1990. *Le Sénégal sous Abdou Diouf*. Paris: Karthala.

Diouf, Mamadou. 2008. "(Re)Imagining an African City: Performing Culture, Arts, and Citizenship in Dakar (Senegal), 1980–2000." In *The Spaces of the Modern City: Imaginaries, Politics, and Everyday Life*, edited by Gyan Prakash and Kevin M. Kruse. Princeton, NJ: Princeton University Press, 346–372.

Diouf, Mamadou. 1996. "Urban Youth and Senegalese Politics: Dakar 1988–1994." *Public Culture* 8: 225–249.

Diouf, Mamadou. 1992. "Fresques Murales et Écriture de l'Histoire: Le Set-Setal à Dakar." *Politique Africaine* 46: 41–57.

Diouf, Omar. 2009. "Makhtar Fall Alias Xuman, Rappeur: 'Il Faut Dire les Chose Comme Elles Sont'." *L'Observateur*, February 7, Accessed March 15, 2015, from http://www.seneweb.com/news/Immigration/makhtar-fall-alias-xuman-rappeur-il-faut-dire-les-choses-comme-elles-sont_n_21019.html.

Duneier, Mitchell, Philip Kasintz, and Alexandra K. Murphy. 2014. "An Invitation to Urban Ethnography." In *The Urban Ethnography Reader*, edited by Mitchell Duneier, Philip Kasintz, and Alexandra K. Murphy. Oxford: Oxford University Press, 1–8.

Durham, Deborah. 2000. "Youth and the Social Imagination in Africa." *Anthropological Quarterly* 73(3): 113–120.

Dyson, Michael Eric. 1993. *Reflecting Black: African-American Cultural Criticism*. Minneapolis: University of Minnesota Press.

Ebron, Paulla. 2002. *Performing Africa*. Princeton, NJ: Princeton University Press.

Edwards, Brent Hayes. 2003. *The Practice of Diaspora: Literature, Translation, and the Rise of Black Internationalism*. Cambridge, MA: Harvard University Press.

Eisenberg, Andrew 2012. "Hip-Hop and Cultural Citizenship on Kenya's 'Swahili Coast'." *Africa* 82(4): 556–578.

Eqeip, Amal. 2010. "Louder than the Blue ID: Palestinian Hip-Hop in Israel." In *Displaced at Home: Ethnicity and Gender Among Palestinians in Israel*, edited by Rhoda Ann Kanaaneh and Isis Nusair. Albany: State University of New York Press, 53–71.

Erlmann, Veit. 1999. *Music, Modernity, and the Global Imagination: South Africa and the West*. New York: Oxford University Press.

Erlmann, Veit. 1991. *African Stars: Studies in Black South African Performance*. Chicago: University of Chicago Press.

Fabian, Johannes. 2003 [1983]. *Time and the Other: How Anthropology Makes Its Object*. New York: Columbia University Press.

Fabian, Johannes. 1998. *Moments of Freedom: Anthropology and Popular Culture*. Charlottesville: University Press of Virginia.

Feld, Steven. 2012. *Jazz Cosmopolitanism in Accra: Five Musical Years in Ghana*. Durham, NC: Duke University Press.

Ferguson, Jason L. 2017. "'From the Heart': Sex, Money, and the Making of a Gay Community in Senegal." *Gender and Society* 31(2): 245–265.

Fernandes, Sujatha. 2012. "The Mixtape of the Revolution." *The New York Times*, January 29. Accessed January 20, 2012, from http://www.nytimes.com/2012/01/30/opinion/the-mixtape-of-the-revolution.html?_r=1.

Fernando, S. H. 1994. *The New Beats: Exploring the Music, Culture, and Attitudes of Hip Hop.* New York: Anchor Books.

Flock, Elizabeth. 2014. "A Female Rapper Busts onto Senegal's Male-Dominated Hip Hop Scene." *The Global Post*, June 22. Accessed February 1, 2015, from http://www.globalpost.com/dispatch/news/regions/africa/senegal/140616/toussa-senerap-GOTAL-rapper-west-african-hip-hop.

Forman, Murray. 2002. *The 'Hood Comes First: Race, Space, and Place in Rap and Hip-Hop.* Middletown, CT: Wesleyan University Press.

Foster, George M., and Robert G. Kemper. 2009. "Anthropological Fieldwork in Cities." In *Urban Life: Readings in Urban Anthropology*, 5th Ed., edited by George Gmelch and Walter P. Zenner. Long Grove, IL: Waveland Press, 5–19.

Fredericks, Rosalind. 2013. "'The Old Man Is Dead': Hip Hop and the Arts of Citizenship of Senegalese Youth." *Antipode* 46(1): 130–148.

Fredericks, Rosalind and Mamadou Diouf. 2014. "Introduction." In *The Arts of Citizenship in African Cities: Infrastructures and Spaces of Belonging*, edited by Mamadou Diouf and Rosalind Fredericks. New York: Palgrave, 1–23.

Geertz, Clifford. 1973. *The Interpretation of Cultures.* New York: Basic Books.

Genova, James E. 2004. *Colonial Ambivalence, Cultural Authenticity, and the Limitations of Mimicry in French-Ruled West Africa, 1914–1956.* New York: Peter Lang.

George, Nelson. 1998. *Hip Hop America.* New York: Penguin Books.

Glover, John. 2001. "'The Mosque is One Thing, the Administration is Another': Murid Marabouts and Wolof Aristocrats in Colonial Senegal." *International Journal of African Historical Studies* 33(2):351–365.

Gueye, Marame. 2013. "Urban Guerilla Poetry: The Movement Y'en a Marre and the Socio-Political Influences of Hip Hop in Senegal." *Journal of Pan-African Studies* 6(3): 22–42.

Gubrium, Jaber F., and James L. Holstein. 1998. "Narrative Practice and the Coherence of Personal Stories." *The Sociological Quarterly* 39(1): 163–187.

Gupta, Akhil, and James Ferguson. 1992. "Beyond 'Culture': Space, Identity, and the Politics of Difference." *Cultural Anthropology* 7(1): 6–23.

Hadley, Susan, and George Yancy, eds. 2001. *Therapeutic Uses of Rap and Hip-Hop.* New York: Routledge.

Hainard, Francois. 2001. *Femmes Dans Les Crises Urbaines—Relations de Genre et Environnements Précaires.* Paris: Karthala.

Hale, Thomas A. 1998. *Griots and Griottes: Masters of Words and Music.* Bloomington: Indiana University Press.

Heath, Deborah. 1994. "The Politics of Appropriateness and Appropriation: Recontextualizing Women's Dance in Urban Senegal." *American Ethnologist* 21(2): 88–103.

Heath, Deborah. 1990. "Spatial Politics and Verbal Performance in Urban Senegal." *Ethnology* 29(3): 209–223.

Havard, Jean-François. 2009. "Tuer les 'Pères des Indépendances'? Comparaison de deux Générations Politiques Post-indépendances au Sénégal et en Côte d'Ivoire." *Revue Internationale de Politique Comparée* 16: 315–331.

Helbig, Adriana. 2014. *Hip Hop Ukraine: Music, Race, and African Migration.* Bloomington: Indiana University Press.

Hobsbawm, Eric, and Terrence Ranger, eds. 1992. *The Invention of Tradition*. Cambridge: Cambridge University Press.

Honwana, Alcinda. 2012. *The Time of Youth: Work, Social Change, and Politics in Africa*. Sterling, VA: Kumarian Press.

Irvine, Judith T. 1973. *Caste and Communication in a Wolof Village*. PhD dissertation, University of Pennsylvania.

Irwin-Zarecka, Iwona. 1994. *Frames of Remembrance: The Dynamics of Collective Memory*. New Brunswick, NJ: Tranaction Publishers.

Jay Z. 2010. *Decoded*. New York: Speigel and Grau.

Josselin, Maire-Laure. 2009. "Le 'Triomphe' d'Omar Pene." *RFImusique*, October 31. Accessed February 10, 2015, from http://www.rfimusique.com/musiquefr/articles/118/article_17803.asp.

Kajikawa, Loren. 2015. *Sounding Race in Rap Songs*. Oakland: University of California Press.

Kansteiner, Wulf. 2002. "Finding Meaning in Memory: A Methodological Critique of Collective Memory Studies." *History and Theory* 41: 179–197.

Katz, Mark. 2012. *Groove Music: The Art and Culture of the Hip Hop DJ*. New York: Oxford University Press.

Katz, Mark. 2017. "The Case for Hip-Hop Diplomacy." *American Music Review* 46(2): 1–5.

Kelley, Robin G. 1997. *Yo Mama's Disfunktional! Fighting the Culture Wars in Urban America*. Boston: Beacon Press.

Keyes, Cheryl L. 2002. *Rap Music and Street Consciousness*. Urbana: University of Illinois Press.

Knapp, Steven. 1989. "Collective Memory and the Actual Past." *Representations* 26: 123–149.

Krims, Adam. 2000. *Rap Music and the Poetics of Identity*. Cambridge: Cambridge University Press.

Kringelbach, Hélène Neveu. 2013. *Dance Circles: Movement, Morality, and Self-Fashioning in Urban Senegal*. New York: Berghahn Press.

Kubik, Gerard. 1999. *Africa and the Blues*. Jackson: University Press of Mississippi.

Kunreuther, Laura Ellen. 2014. *Voicing Subjects: Public Intimacy and Mediation in Kathmandu*. Berkeley: University of California Press.

Künzler, Dietrich. 2007. "The 'Lost Generation': African Hip Hop Movements and the Protest of the Young (Male) Urban." In *Civil Society: Local and Regional Responses to Global Challenges*, edited by Mark Herkenrat. New Brunswick, NJ: Transaction Publishers.

Lawrence, Sidra. 2011. *It's Just this Animal Called Culture: Regulatory Codes and Resistant Action among Dagara Female Musicians*. PhD dissertation, The University of Texas at Austin.

Leymarie, Isabelle. 1999. *Les Griots Wolof du Sénégal*. Paris: Maisonneuve and Larose.

Loum, Tefaye. n.d. "Cinemas Awa, Al Karim, Vox Pikine, Havre de Cinéphiles. *Xibar.net*. Accessed May 7, 2018, from https://www.xibar.net/CINEMAS-AWA-AL-KARIM-VOX-Pikine-havre-de-cinephiles_a40312.html.

Manabe, Noriko. 2013. "Representing Japan: 'National' Style among Japanese Hip-hop DJs." *Popular Music* 32(1): 35–50.

Manabe, Noriko. 2006. "Globalization and Japanese Creativity: Adaptations of Japanese Language to Rap." *Ethnomusicology* 50(1): 1–36.

Maira, Sunaina. 2008. "'We Ain't Missing': Palestinian Hip Hop—A Transnational Youth Movement." *CR: The New Centennial Review* 8(2): 161–192.

Makinwa, Thiat. 2012. "Video: Keyti's Revolutionary Rhymes." *OkayAfrica*, February 23. Accessed April 20, 2012, from http://www.okayafrica.com/2012/02/03/video-keytis-revolutionary- rhymes/.

Mangin, Timothy. 2013. *Mbalax: Cosmopolitanism in Senegalese Urban Popular Music*. PhD dissertation, New York University.

Matlon, Jordanna. 2015. "'Elsewhere': An Essay on Borderland Ethnography in the Informal African City." *Ethnography* 16(2): 145-165.

Matory, J. Lorand. 2006. "The 'New World' Surrounds an Ocean: Theorizing the Live Dialogue between African and African American Cultures." In *Afro-Atlantic Dialogues: Anthropology in the Diaspora*, edited by Kevin Yelvington. Santa Fe: School of American Research Press, 151–192.

Maultsby, Portia. 1990. "Africanisms in African American Music." In *Africanisms in American Culture*, edited by Joseph E. Holloway. Indianapolis: Indiana University Press, 326–355.

Maxwell, Ian. 2003. *Phat Beats, Dope Rhymes: Hip Hop Down Under Comin' Upper*. Middletown, CT: Weslyan University Press.

Maxwell, Ian. 1997. "Hip Hop Aesthetics and the Will to Culture." *Australian Journal of Anthropology*, 8(2): 50–70.

Mbaye, Jenny Fatou. 2011. *Reconsidering Cultural Entrepreneurship: Hip Hop Music Economy and Social Change in Senegal, Francophone West Africa*. PhD dissertation, London School of Economics and Political Science.

McLaughlin, Fiona. 2009. "The Ascent of Wolof as an Urban Vernacular and National Lingua Franca in Senegal." In *Globalization and Language Vitality: Perspectives from Africa*, edited by Cécile B. Vigourous and Salikoko S. Mufwene. London: Continuum, 142–170.

McLaughlin, Fiona. 2000. "'In the Name of God I Will Sing Again, Mawdo Malik the Good': Popular Music and the Senegalese Sufi *Tariqas*." *Journal of Religion in Africa* 30(2): 191–207.

McLeod, Kembrew. 1999. "Authenticity Within Hip-Hop and Other Cultures Threatened with Assimilation." *Journal of Communication* 49(4): 134–150.

McNee, Lisa. 2000. *Selfish Gifts: Senegalese Women's Autobiographical Discourses*. Albany: State University of New York Press.

Meintjes, Louise. 2003. *Sound of Africa: Making Music Zulu in a South African Studio*. Durham, NC: Duke University Press.

Melendez-Torres, Juan Carlos. In progress. "Claiming Creation: Contesting Authorship and the Development Agenda in Senegalese Hip Hop."

Miller, Paul D. 2004. *Rhythm Science*. Cambridge, MA: MIT Press.

Morales-Libove, Jessica. 2005. *Dancing a Fine Line: Gender, Sexuality, and Morality at Women's Tours in Dakar, Senegal*. PhD dissertation, Rutgers, The State University of New Jersey.

Mose, Caroline. 2013. "'Swag' and 'Cred': Representing Hip Hop in an African City." *Journal of Pan African Studies* 6(3): 106–132.

Mose, Caroline. 2011. "Jua Cali-justice: Navigating the 'Mainstream-Underground' Dichotomy in Kenyan Hip-Hop Culture." In *Native Tongues: The African Hip-Hop Reader*, edited by Paul Khalil Saucier. Trenton, NJ: African World Press, 69–104.

Moulard-Kouka, Sophie. 2008. *"Senegal Yeewuleen!" Analyse Anthropologique du Rap a Dakar: Liminarité, Contestation et Culture Populaire*. PhD dissertation, University of Bordeaux, France.

Mudimbe, V. Y. 1988. *The Invention of Africa: Gnosis, Philosophy, and the Order of Knowledge*. Bloomington: Indiana University Press.

Ndaliko, Chérie Rivers. 2017. *Necessary Noise: Music, Film, and Charitable Imperialism in the East of Congo*. New York: Oxford University Press.

Ndiaye, Mariéma. 2011. "Analyse du Processus d'Élaboration du Buget dans une Société de Gestion Immobilière: Cas de la SICAP SA." MA Thesis, Centre Africain d'Études Supérieures en Gestion.

Nelson, David. 2007. "Defining the Urban: The Construction of French-Dominated Colonial Dakar, 1857–1940." *Historical Reflections/Réflexions Historiques* 33(2): 225–255.

Ngom, Fallou. 2012. "Popular Culture in Senegal Music: Blending the Secular and the Religious." In *Performance and African Identities*, edited by Toyin Falola and Tyler Fleming. New York: Routledge, 97–124.

Niang, Abdoulaye. 2014. "Le Rap Prédicateur Islamique au Sénégal: Une Musique 'Missionnaire'." *Volume! La Revue des Musiques Populaires* 10(2): 69–86.

Niang, Abdoulaye. 2006. "Bboys: Hip Hop Culture in Dakar, Sénégal." In *Global Youth? Hybrid Identities, Plural Worlds*, edited by Pam Milan and Carles Feixa. New York: Routledge, 167–185.

Nora, Pierre. 1989. "Between Memory and History: Les Lieux de Mémoire," Translated by Marc Roudebush. *Representations* 26: 7–24.

Ntarangwi, Mwenda. 2010. "African Hip Hop and the Politics of Change in an Era of Rapid Globalization." *History Compass* 8(12): 1316–1327.

O'Brien, D. B. Cruise. 1971. *The Mourides of Senegal: The Political and Economic Organization of an Islamic Brotherhood*. Oxford: Clarendon Press.

Oliver, Paul. 1970. *Savannah Syncopators: African Retentions in the Blues*. Worthing, UK: Littlehampton Book Services.

Omoniyi, Tope. 2009. "'So I Choose to Do am Naija Style': Hip-Hop, Language and Postcolonial Identities." In *Global Linguistic Flows: Hip Hop Cultures, Youth Identities, and the Politics of Language*, edited by H. Samy Alim, Awad Ibrahim, and Alastair Pennycook. New York: Routledge, 173–193.

Ortner, Sherry B. 1995. "Resistance and the Problem of Ethnographic Refusal." *Comparative Studies in Society and History* 37(1): 173–193.

Osumare, Halifu. 2012. *The Hiplife in Ghana: West African Indigenization of Hip Hop*. New York: Palgrave Macmillan.

Osumare, Halifu. 2007. *The Africanist Aesthetic in Global Hip Hop: Power Moves*. New York: Palgrave.

Panzacchi, Cornelia. 1994. "The Livelihoods of Traditional Griots in Modern Senegal." *Africa: Journal of the International African Institute* 64(2): 190–210.

Pareles, Jon. 2014. "Commanding the Stage with Words and Dancing Feet: Youssou N'Dour Performs at the Brooklyn Academy of Music." September 14, 2014, *The New York Times*. Accessed May 7, 2018, from http://www.nytimes.com/2014/09/15/arts/music/youssou-ndour-performs-at-the-brooklyn-academy-of-music.html?_r=0.

Pennycook, Alastair, and Tony Mitchell. 2009. "Hip Hop as Dusty Foot Philosophy: Engaging Locality." In *Global Linguistic Flows: Hip Hop Cultures, Youth Identities, and the Politics of Language*, edited by H. Samy Alim, Awad Ibrahim, and Alastair Pennycook. New York: Routledge, 25–42.

Perkins, William Eric. 1996. "The Rap Attack: An Introduction." In *Droppin' Science: Critical Essays on Rap Music and Hip Hop Culture*, edited by William Eric Perkins. Philadelphia: Temple University Press, 1–45.

Perkinson, James W. 2003. "Rap as Wrap and Rapture: North American Popular Culture and Denial of Death." In *Noise and Spirit: The Religious and Spiritual Sensibilies of Rap Music*, edited by Anthony B. Pinn. New York: New York University Press, 131–153.

Perry, Imani, 2004. *Prophets of the Hood: Politics and Poetics in Hip Hop*. Durham, NC: Duke University Press.

Perry, Marc D. 2008. "Global Black Self-fashionings: Hip Hop as Diasporic Space." *Identities: Global Studies in Culture and Power* 15(6): 635–664.

Piot, Charles. 2001. "Atlantic Aporias: Africa and Gilroy's Black Atlantic." *The South Atlantic Quarterly* 100: 155–170.

Pollard, Lawrence. 2004. "Rap Returns Home to Africa." *BBC News*, September 2, Accessed February 1, 2015, from http://news.bbc.co.uk/2/hi/africa/3622406.stm.

Potter, Russell A. 1995. *Spectacular Vernaculars: Hip Hop and the Politics of Postmodernism.* Albany: State University of New York Press.

Pough, Gwendolyn D. 2004. *Check It While I Wreck It: Black Womanhood, Hip-Hop Culture, and the Public Sphere*. Boston: Northeastern University Press.

Prévos, Andrew. 2001. "Le Business du Rap en France." *The French Review* 74(5): 900–921.

Ranger, Terrence. 1983. "The Invention of Tradition in Colonial Africa." In *The Invention of Tradition*, edited by Eric Hobsbawm and Terrence Ranger. Cambridge: Cambridge University Press, 211–262.

Resnick, Danielle, and James Thurlow, eds. 2015. *African Youth and the Persistence of Marginalization: Employment, Politics, and Prospects for Change*. London: Routledge.

Rivera, Raquel Z. 2003. *New York Ricans from the Hip Hop Zone*. New York: Palgrave Macmillan.

Roberts, Allen, and Mary Roberts. 2003. "Music and Memory Among Senegalese Sufism." In *The Interrelatedness of Music, Religion, and Ritual in African Performance Practice*, edited by Daniel K. Avorgbedor. Lewiston, NY: Edwin Mellon Press, 347–370.

Robinson, David. 2000. *Paths of Accommodation: Muslim Societies and French Colonial Authorities in Senegal and Mauritania, 1880–1920*. Athens: Ohio University Press.

Rollefson, J. Griffith. 2017. *Flip the Script: European Hip Hop and the Politics of Postcoloniality.* Chicago: University of Chicago Press.

Rose, Tricia. 1994. *Black Noise: Rap Music and Black Culture in Contemporary America*. Middletown, CT: Wesleyan University Press.

Rothberg, Michael, Debarati Sanyal, and Max Silverman, eds. 2010. *Noeuds de Mémoire: Multidirectional Memory in Postwar French and Francophone Culture*. New Haven, CT: Yale University Press.

Salois, Kendra. 2015. "Connection and Complicity in the Global South: Hip Hop Musicians and US Cultural Diplomacy." *Journal of Popular Music Studies* 27(4): 408–423.

Samper, David. 2004. '"Africa is Still Our Mama': Kenyan Rappers, Youth Identity, and the Revitalization of Traditional Values." *African Identities* 2 (1): 37–51.

Saucier, Paul Khalil. 2015. *Necessarily Black: Cape Verdean Youth, Hip-Hop Culture, and a Critique of Identity*. East Lansing: Michigan State University Press.

Saucier, P. Khalil, and Tryon P. Woods. 2014. "Hip Hop Studies in Black." *Journal of Popular Music Studies* 26(2–3): 268–294.

Savané, Vieux, and Baye Makebe Sarr. 2012. *Y'en a Marre: Radioscopie d'une Jeunesse Insurgée au Sénégal*. Dakar: L'Harmattan-Senegal.

Savishinsky, Neil J. 1994. "The Baye Faal of Senegambia: Muslim Rastas in the Promised Land?" *Africa: Journal of the International African Institute* 64(2): 211–219.

Schloss, Joseph G. 2004. *Making Beats: The Art of Sample-Based Hip-Hop*. Middletown, CT: Wesleyan University Press.

Scott, David. 1991. "That Event, This Memory: Notes on the Anthropology of African Diasporas in the New World." *Diasporas* 1(3):261–284.

Scott, Joan Wallach. 2017. *Sex and Secularism*. Princeton: Princeton University Press.

Senghor, Fatou Kandé. 2015. *Wala Bok: Une Histoire Orale du Hip Hop au Sénégal*. Dakar-Fann: Éditions Amalion.

Senghor, Léopold Sédar. 1964. *Liberté 1: Negritude et Humanisme*. Paris: Éditions du Seuil.

Shain, Richard M. 2009. "The Re(public) of Salsa: Afro-Cuban Music in Fin-De-Siècle Dakar." *Africa: The Journal of the International African Institute* 79(2): 186–206.

Sharma, Natasha Tamar. 2010. *Hip Hop Desis: South Asian Americans, Blackness, and a Global Race Consciousness*. Durham, NC: Duke University Press.

Shaw, Rosalind. 2002. *Memories of the Slave Trade: Ritual and the Historical Imagination in Sierra Leone*. Chicago: University of Chicago Press.

Shipley, Jesse Weaver. 2013. *Living the Hiplife: Celebrity and Entrepreneurship in Ghanaian Popular Music*. Durham, NC: Duke University Press.

Shusterman, Richard. 1991. "The Fine Art of Rap." *New Literary History* 22(3): 613–632.

Silverstein, Paul A. 2012. "La Patrimoine du Ghetto." In *L'Atlantique Multiraciale*, edited by James Cohen, Andrew Diamond, and Philippe Vervaecke. Paris: Karthala, 93–116.

Silverstein, Michael, and Greg Urban, eds. 1996. *Natural Histories of Discourse*. Chicago: University of Chicago Press.

Simone, AbdouMaliq. 2005. "Urban Circulation and the Everyday Politics of African Urban Youth: The Case of Douala, Cameroon." *International Journal of Urban and Regional Research* 29: 516–532.

Simone, AbdouMaliq. 2001. "On the Worlding of African Cities." *African Studies Review* 44(2): 15–41.

Skinner, Ryan Thomas. 2015. *Bamako Sounds: The Afropolitan Ethics of Malian Music*. Minneapolis: University of Minnesota Press.

Smitherman, Geneva. 1999. *Talkin' That Talk: African American Language and Culture*. New York: Routledge.

Smitherman, Geneva. 1997. "'The Chain Remains the Same': Communicative Practices in the Hip Hop Nation." *Journal of Black Studies* 28(1): 3–25.

Smitherman, Geneva. 1977. *Talkin and Testifyin: The Language of Black America*. Detroit: Wayne University Press.

Snipe, Tracy D. 1998. *Arts and Politics in Senegal: 1960–1996*. Trenton, NJ: Africa World Press.

Sommers, Marc. 2010. "Urban Youth in Africa." *Environment and Urbanization* 22(2): 317–332.

Spady, James G. 2006a. "Interview with Amadou Barry of PBS (Positive Black Soul)." In *The Global Cipha: Hip Hop Culture and Consciousness,* edited by James Spady, H. Samy Alim, and Samir Meghelli. Philadelphia: Black History Museum Press, 639–646.

Spady, James G. 2006b. "Interview with Didier Awadi of PBS (Positive Black Soul)." In *The Global Cipha: Hip Hop Culture and Consciousness,* edited by James Spady, H. Samy Alim, and Samir Meghelli. Philadelphia: Black History Museum Press, 648–655.

Steingo, Gavin. 2017. *Kwaito's Promise: Music and the Aesthetics of Freedom in South Africa*. Chicago: University of Chicago Press.

Stewart, Kathleen. 1996. *A Space on the Side of the Road: Cultural Poetics in an "Other" America*. Princeton: Princeton University Press.

Swigart, Leigh. 1994. "Cultural Creolisation and Language Use in Post-Colonial Africa: The Case of Senegal." *Africa: Journal of the International African Institute* 63(2): 175–189.

Touré. 2011. *Who's Afraid of Post-Blackness? What it Means to Be Black Now*. New York: Free Press.

Tang, Patricia. 2012. "The Rapper as Modern Griot: Reclaiming Ancient Traditions." In *Hip Hop Africa: New African Music in a Globalizing World*, edited by Eric Charry. Indianapolis: Indiana University Press, 79–91.

Tang, Patricia. 2007. *Masters of the Sabar: Wolof Griot Percussionists of Senegal*. Philadelphia: Temple University Press.

Tardio, Andres. 2011. "Q-Tip & Michael Rapaport Continue Feuding About Tribe Called Quest Documentary." *HipHopDx*, June 30, 2011. Accessed May 7, 2018, http://hiphopdx.com/news/id.15784/title.q-tip-michael-rapaport-continue-feuding-about-tribe-called-quest-documentary.

Taylor, Timothy D. 1997. *Global Pop: World Music, World Markets*. New York: Routledge.

Teunis, Niels. 2001. "Same-Sex Sexuality in Africa: A Case Study from Senegal." *Aids and Behavior* 5(2): 173–182.

Toop, David. 1991. *The Rap Attack: African Jive to New York Hip Hop*. Boston: South End Press.

Tsing, Anna. 2000. "The Global Situation." *Cultural Anthropology* 15(3): 327–360.

Turino, Thomas. 2000. *Nationalists, Cosmopolitans, and Popular Music in Zimbabwe*. Chicago: University of Chicago Press.

Van Hoven, Ed. 2000. "The Nation Turbaned? The Construction of Nationalist Muslim Identities in Senegal." *Journal of Religion in Africa* 30(2): 225–248.

Vernière, Marc. 1973. "Campagne, Ville, Bidonville, Banlieue: Migrations Intra-urbaines vers Dagoudane Pikine, Ville Nouvelle de Dakar (Sénégal)." *Cahiers ORSTOM Série Sciences Humaines* 10(2–3): 217–243.

Von Eschen, Penny. 2004. *Satchmo Blows up the World: Jazz Ambassadors Play the Cold War*. Cambridge, MA: Harvard University Press.

Wacquant, Loïc. 2008. *Urban Outcasts: A Comparative Sociology of Advanced Marginality*. Malden, MA: Polity Press.

Walser, Robert. 1995. "Rhythm, Rhyme, and Rhetoric in the Music of Public Enemy." *Ethnomusicology* 39: 193–217.

Waterman, Christopher Alan. 1990. *Jùjú: A Social History and Ethnography of an African Popular Music*. Chicago: University of Chicago Press.

Watkins, S. Craig. 2005. *Hip Hop Matters: Politics, Pop Culture, and the Struggle for the Soul of a Movement*. Boston: Beacon Press.

Weidman, Amanda. 2006. *Singing the Classical, Voicing the Modern: The Postcolonial Politics of Music in South India*. Durham, NC: Duke University Press.

Weiss, Brad. 2009. *Street Dreams and Hip Hop Barbershops: Global Fantasy in Urban Tanzania*. Bloomington: Indiana University Press.

Wertsch, James V., and Henry L. Roediger III. 2008. "Collective Memory: Conceptual Foundations and Theoretical Approaches." *Memory* 16(3): 318–326.

White, Hayden. 1980. "The Value of Narrativity in the Representation of Reality." *Critical Inquiry* 7(1): 5–27.

Williams, Justin A. 2013. *Rhymin' and Stealin': Musical Borrowing in Hip Hop*. Ann Arbor: University of Michigan Press.

Williams, Maxwell. Forthcoming. "From Black Hipsters to Black Hippy: Flow and the Cultural Genealogy of 'Neo-Bohemian' Hip Hop." In *The Oxford Handbook of Hip Hop Studies*, edited by Justin D. Burton and Jason Lee Oakes. New York: Oxford University Press.

Wright, Bonnie L. 1989. "The Power of Articulation." In *Creativity of Power: Cosmology and Action in African Societies*, edited by W. Arens and Ivan Karp. Washington, DC: Smithsonian Institute Press, 39–57.

Wunderlich, Annelise. 2006. "Cuban Hip-hop: Making Space for New Voices of Dissent." In *The Vinyl Ain't Final: Hip Hop and the Globalization of Black Popular Culture*, edited by Dipannita Basu and Sidney Lemelle. London: Pluto Press, 173–175.

Young, Jason. R. 2007. *Rituals of Resistance: African Atlantic Religion in Kongo and the Lowcountry South in the Era of Slavery*. Baton Rouge: Louisiana State University Press.

Zeleza, Paul Tiyambe. 2003a. "The Creation and Consumption of Leisure: Theoretical and Methodological Considerations." In *Leisure Time in Urban Africa*, edited by Paul Tiyambe Zeleza and Cassandra Rachel Veney. Trenton, NJ: Africa World Press, vii–xli.

Zeleza, Paul Tiyambe. 2003b. *Rethinking Africa's Globalization. Volume 1: The Intellectual Challenges.* Trenton, NJ: Africa World Press.

DISCOGRAPHY

5kiem Underground. 2009. "Joyu Askan Wi." *Yagg Bawoul Dara*. Dakar: Jolof4Life/99 Records.

23.3. 2010. "Guem sa Bop." *Sunu Thiono Seen Noflaye*. Dakar: Underkamouf Records.

Books. 2012. "Wakhal Sa Baye." Dakar: Independent release.

Books. 2011. "Fly On." Dakar: Independent release.

Daara J Family. 2010. "Bayi Yoon." *School of Life*. London: Wrasse Records.

Daara J Family. 2010. *School of Life*. London: Wrasse Records.

Daara J Family. 2004. *Boomerang*. London: Wrasse Records.

DJ Awadi. 2010. *Présidents d'Afrique*. Dakar: Studio Sankara.

DJ Awadi. 2008. *Sunugaal*. East Sussex, UK: Mr. Bongo.

Gaston. 2011. "Khikeuma." *Tutti Wakh Job lu Beuri*. Dakar: Def Dara Productions.

Gotal. 2013. "Gotal Connection." Dakar: Independent Release.

Idrissa Diop. 2012. "Fly On." *Voyage (Travel)*. Dakar: Gelongal.

Ngaaka Blindé. 2017. "Tathiouma." *Jeego*. Dakar: Keyzit.

Nix. 2010. "Nio Farr." *Rimes de Vie*. Dakar: Kénène Productions.

Niamu Mbaam. 2010. "Menunu Happy." *Guddi Leer*. Dakar: DEF-XEProductions.

Pee Froiss. 1997. "Lara Biranane." *Affaire bou Graw*. Dakar: KFS Productions.

Positive Black Soul. 2001. *Run Cool*. New York: Wea/Warner.

Positive Black Soul. 1996. "Respect the Nubians." *Salaam*. London: Mango/Island Records.

Positive Black Soul. 1996. "Return of da Djelly." *Salaam*. London: Mango/Island Records.

Rap'Adio. 1998. "Xabaaru 1-2-Ground." *Ku Weet Xam Sa Bop*. Dakar: Fitna Prod.

Rap'Adio. 1998. *Ku Weet Xam sa Bop*. Dakar: Fitna Prod.

ResKp. 2008. "Diar Diar." *Dafa Jot*. Dakar: Optimist Productions.

Sen Kumpë. 2008. "Aythia Gnu Dem." *Freedom*. Dakar: Jolof4Life/99 Records.

Simon. 2009. "Rap Legnou Wax." *Maxama Mer*. Dakar:Jolof4Life/99 Records.

Simon. 2006. "Abdoulaye." *Diggué Boorla*. Dakar: Jolof4Life/99 Records.

Simon. 2006. "Borom Xél." *Diggué Boorla*. Dakar: Jolof4Life/99 Records.

Tigrim Bi. 2010. "Rongognou Guetto."*Gëm Gëm du Faatu*. Dakar: Jolof4Life/99 Records.

INTERVIEWS

Almamy Bathily (23.3). 2011. Personal interview. Medina/Dakar, Senegal. July 20.

Almamy Bathily (23.3). 2008. Personal interview. Sacré Coeur, Senegal. July 18.

Anta (Gotal). Personal interview. Ouakam/Dakar, Senegal. October 7.

Baïdy (Bideew bou Bess). 2011. Personal interview. Parcelles Assainies, Senegal. September 28.

Baye Njagne (5kiem Underground). 2011. Personal interview. Medina/Dakar, Senegal. August 10.

Baye Njagne (5kiem Underground). 2008. Personal interview. Medina, Dakar, Senegal. July 23.

Big Fa. 2011. Personal interview. Ouakam/Dakar, Senegal. September 8.

Books (Sen Kumpë). 2011. Personal interview. Mermoz/Dakar, Senegal. August 19.

Books (Sen Kumpë). 2008. Personal interview. Medina/Dakar, Senegal. July 23.

Bourba Jolof (Sen Kumpë). 2008. Personal interview. Medina/Dakar, Senegal. July 23.

Da Brains. 2011. Personal interview. Liberté V/Dakar, Senegal. September 21.

Djily Bagdad (5kiem Underground). 2011. Personal interview. Medina/Dakar, Senegal. August 8.

Djily Bagdad (5kiem Underground). 2008. Personal interview. Medina/Dakar, Senegal. July 2.

Daara J. 2011. Personal interview. Liberté VI/Dakar, Senegal. September 26.

DJ Awadi. 2011. Personal interview. Amitié III/Dakar, Senegal. September 19.

Don Zap. 2011. Personal interview. Grand Yoff/Dakar, Senegal. August 16.

Drygun (Yatfu). 2011. Personal interview. Dakar, Senegal. October 10.

Gaston. 2011. Personal interview. Parcelles Assainies, Senegal. September 28.

Gotal. 2011. Personal interview. Parcelles Assainies, Senegal. September 3.

Fall Ba, Amadou. 2011. Personal interview. Mermoz/Dakar, Senegal. September 9.

Falsower. 2011. Personal interview. Grand Yoff/Dakar, Senegal. August 11.

Falsower. 2008. Personal interview. Sacré Coeur, Senegal. July 18.

FuknKuk. 2011. Personal interview. Dalifort, Senegal. September 29.

Imam Assane (Zair ak Batine). 2008. Personal interview. Medina/Dakar, Senegal. July 18.

Kalif (Undershifaay). 2011. Personal interview. Yoff, Senegal. August 28.

Keyti. 2011. Personal interview. Dakar, Senegal. October 11.

Kilifa Gary (Zair ak Batine). 2008. Personal interview. Medina/Dakar, Senegal. July 18.

Kronic (Undershifaay). 2011. Personal interview. Yoff, Senegal. August 28.

KTD Crew. 2011. Personal interview. Medina/Dakar, Senegal. September 27.

Lady Sinay. 2008. Personal interview. Medina/Dakar, Senegal. July 26.

Maestro DD (Zair ak Batine). 2008. Personal interview. Medina/Dakar, Senegal. July 18.

Mame Xa. 2011. Personal interview. Sacré Coeur/Dakar, Senegal. August 24.

Mamy (Alif). 2011. Personal interview. Liberté V/Dakar, Senegal. October 4.

Mollah Morgan (Keur Gui). 2008. Personal interview. Dakar, Senegal. August 1.

Mouna. 2011. Personal interview. Dakar, Senegal. October 10.

Ndao, Lamine. 2011. Personal interview. Mermoz/Dakar, Senegal. July 21.

Ndao, Lamine. 2015. Personal interview. Medina/Dakar, Senegal. March 15.

Niamu Mbaam. 2011. Personal interview. Pikine, Senegal. September 22.

Nix. 2011. Personal interview. Dakar, Senegal. August 22.

N-Jah. 2011. Personal interview. Yoff, Senegal. September 19.

Profete. 2011. Personal interview. Grand Dakar, Senegal. August 23.

ResKp. 2011. Personal interview. Mermoz/Dakar, Senegal. October 11.

Simon. 2011. Personal interview. Medina/Dakar, Senegal. August 17.

Simon. 2008. Personal interview. Dakar, Senegal. July 18.

Sorra, Coumbis. 2011. Personal interview. Almadies, Senegal. September 8.

Thiat (Keur Gui). 2011. Personal interview. Parcelles Assainies, Senegal. October 6.

Thiat (Keur Gui). 2008. Personal interview. Dakar, Senegal. August 1.

Toussa. 2011. Personal interview. Guidewaay, Senegal. August 20.

Xuman. 2011. Personal interview. Liberté VI/Dakar, Senegal. September 20.

Y.Dee. 2011. Personal interview. Sipres/Dakar, Senegal. August 8.

Index

CPSIA information can be obtained
at www.ICGtesting.com
Printed in the USA
BVHW042339211022
649761BV00003B/101